GLIDERS OVER HOLLYWOOD

*AIRSHIPS, AIRPLAY,
AND THE ART OF
ROCK PROMOTION*

PAUL RAPPAPORT

'So, you want to work in the music business? How much do you know about it? No one in their right mind could countenance such a career! But if you must, then you need this book. Rapper was there. Not only that, but he remembers most of the detail, which is more than can be said for his subjects, who have a tendency to rewrite history as they would have liked it or justify actions that should have put them in jail. It's about as close as you can get to the action without having that gold Access All Areas pass.'
NICK MASON, PINK FLOYD

For my parents, Walter and Vera Rappaport, who made a wonderful difference in the world, and especially in my sister's and mine. Sharon, Adam, Sam, and my sister Ruth, who have always loved and believed in me. Little Richard, the emancipator—first to uncork the power of rock'n'roll and let it rip. Guitar heroes who are in my fingers—Dick Dale, Chuck Berry, Keith Richards, Michael Bloomfield, Jimi Hendrix, Peter Green, Jeff Beck, Jimmy Page, Eric Clapton, Billy F. Gibbons, and the Three Kings, Albert, Freddie, and B.B. And . . . Les Paul, for the sexiest tone I've ever gotten from an electric guitar.

GLIDERS OVER HOLLYWOOD

AIRSHIPS, AIRPLAY, AND THE ART OF ROCK PROMOTION

PAUL RAPPAPORT

A Jawbone book
First edition 2025
Published in the UK and the USA by
Jawbone Press
Office G1
141–157 Acre Lane
London SW2 5UA
England
www.jawbonepress.com

ISBN 978-1-916829-18-3

Printed by Short Run Press, Exeter

1 2 3 4 5 29 28 27 26 25

PROLOGUE
YOUR BOOTLEG
IS NOT WHAT YOU
THINK IT IS **5**

INTRODUCTION
SETTING THE
STAGE **21**

PART ONE

FEATURING

BRUCE
SPRINGSTEEN

KAREN
CARPENTER

JANIS JOPLIN

JIMI HENDRIX

MILES DAVIS

MIKE
BLOOMFIELD

TONY BENNETT

RANDY
CALIFORNIA

BLUE ÖYSTER
CULT

AEROSMITH

ELTON JOHN

BOZ SCAGGS

BOSTON

IAN HUNTER

PETER TOSH

ELVIS COSTELLO

THE NEW
BARBARIANS

BOOMTOWN RATS

THE MUSIC
INSIDE **28**

SOMEBODY
TO LOVE **38**

FREE RECORDS &
SAVAGE WINOS **45**

ONE OF
THE GANG **57**

SPIRIT OF
CALIFORNIA **67**

AGENTS OF
FORTUNE **80**

A ROLLING STONE
& A MONKEY **88**

CHILI DOGS FOR
BREAKFAST **93**

BIG GREEN LIGHT
IN THE SKY **99**

DON'T FALL OFF
THE PORCH **112**

HEADS DOWN,
FREAK 'EM OUT **119**

TOUGHER THAN
THE REST **131**

YOUR PURSE IS
ON FIRE **137**

I DON'T LIKE
MONDAYS **148**

PART TWO

FEATURING

TOMMY
TUTONE

BILLY JOEL

LOVERBOY

BOB DYLAN

PAUL
MCCARTNEY

PINK FLOYD

THE ROLLING
STONES

CHRIS
WHITLEY

GRATEFUL
DEAD

TOMMY
CONWELL

JUDAS PRIEST

BRUCE
DICKINSON

JOURNEY

ALICE IN
CHAINS

15 THE TWELFTH FLOOR **158**

16 THE EVERYMAN **167**

17 READING THE TEA LEAVES **175**

18 100 PERCENT ROCK'N'ROLL **181**

19 BEASTS IN THE BIBLE **188**

20 MEET THE BEATLE **203**

21 MOMENTARY KAOS **210**

22 STEEL WHEELS & GUITAR LESSONS **235**

23 THE MAGIC TRICK **248**

24 DAMAGE CONTROL **265**

25 50 CHOCOLATE SOUFFLÉS **276**

26 CHANGING OF THE GUARD **283**

27 PREPARE TO LAUNCH **297**

EPILOGUE
THIRTY THREE AND A THIRD **315**

SPECIAL THANKS **316**

YOUR BOOTLEG IS NOT WHAT YOU THINK IT IS

JULY 7, 1978. The Roxy, Los Angeles. The general manager of the LA rock giant KMET-FM has me collared. He's holding my shirt tight against my throat and is starting to bang my head against the club's upstairs wood paneling. He's screaming in my face and using the thud of my head hitting the wall to accent his every word.

'THIS [*bang*] IS [*bang*] THE LAST [*bang*] TIME [*bang*] K-M-E-T [*bang*] WILL EVER [*bang*] DO A LIVE BROADCAST [*bang*] WITH COLUMBIA RECORDS! [*bang bang bang*]'

My head hurts. But in between the banging, I can't help but wonder, *How did I get here?*

• ● •

That was Friday evening. Three days earlier, on Tuesday morning, Bruce Springsteen's manager, Jon Landau, had called me to explain that even though Bruce was about to play a sold-out concert at the LA Forum, he felt that it would be what we called a 'quiet show.' Because the tickets had sold out so fast in advance there wasn't the usual buzz around town, and Jon didn't feel like Bruce and the band had taken Los Angeles by storm.

I explained that LA is a big town, and with so much always going on it's hard to get attention. He asked what I thought about doing a live broadcast of the show on KMET. I told him I thought it would deliver the power punch he was looking for. Then I asked when he wanted to do it.

'This Friday.'

I was shocked. At that time, I was the western regional album-rock promotion man for Columbia Records, well-seasoned with nine years in the music biz under my belt. I had pioneered live concert broadcasts over the FM airwaves and was adept at producing them. But a live broadcast would take two weeks, minimum, to put together. With a myriad of live recordings being done in those days, you had to book a mobile sound truck with a good engineer well in advance to ensure their availability. The radio station had to schedule its own engineers for an off-site day and get their remote equipment together. Most importantly, there was the phone company, Pacific Bell Telephone, who would be in charge of connecting two stereo 15K lines from the venue to the radio station for the best sound quality. Ma Bell was a corporate entity, and it normally took them *forever* to set these things up.

I didn't know if we could pull off *Live At The Roxy* in time, but I was tight with a gal from the phone company, so I figured I had a fighting chance. I told Jon to give me a minute to check on a few things. I quickly called Wally Heider Studios to see if their mobile truck was available, and asked for the great Biff Dawes to be the engineer. Luckily, both were free. I called Jon right back but told him that if we were going to do this, he needed to let me know right away. He said he'd speak to Bruce.

Bruce Springsteen is a very cerebral guy. He thinks a lot—about lyrics, shows, his career . . . you name it. It can take him a little while to make up his mind. Back then, if you asked him a question about a possible interview or promotional idea, he'd often say, 'I gotta think about that for a little bit.' The next day, if you asked the same question, he might reply, 'I gotta think about that one for a little bit longer.' In Bruce Speak, that meant, *Forget it—it's not gonna happen.* You learned to drop the subject and move on to the next idea.

I suppose that's what Jon was dealing with now, because I didn't get the *GO* call until about 4pm that afternoon. That meant producing what would usually be a two-week project in just three days. Cue adrenaline rush. Holy shit!

Live broadcasts over the FM format were a huge part of building Bruce's career. As good as his records were, there was nothing like the experience of seeing and hearing him live in concert. That's still true to this day.

Along with a handful of other Columbia Records execs, I had been on a mission to break Bruce since I first heard *Greetings From Asbury Park, NJ* and saw his early live performances. By 1978, Bruce was a rock'n'roll phenomenon—the Elvis Presley of our time. In some ways, he was larger than that, because the messages in his songs resonated deeply within us. Like Bob Dylan, Bruce was a poet who spoke for us. He put our innermost feelings into words in a way that made us feel understood and complete. Songs like 'Badlands' had us pumping our fists in the air. *Yeah! That's what I'm talking about!* And when I say *on a mission*, I mean a mission like the one The Blues Brothers were on. *A mission from God.*

I was at a planning meeting in a large New York hotel suite, which all of Columbia's regional promotion people had been flown in to attend. The head of album rock, Mike Pillot, and I were trying to get additional funding for more Bruce live broadcasts. The VP of promotion, Bob Sherwood, said he had budgets to worry about. Wound tight and exasperated from trying to make the case, I resorted to jumping up and down on the couch and screaming back at him.

'This is rock'n'roll history! I don't care where you get the money from! Fucking steal it!'

In those days, passion was rewarded. Sherwood could see the momentum that was building for Bruce. He gave us the money.

Of course, the other important part of *Bruce Live At The Roxy* is the radio station the show would be broadcast on: KMET-FM. The Mighty Met. 'A little bit of heaven, ninety-four point seven, KMET, tweedle-dee.' (And, for those of you who lived in Southern California and remember those heady days, 'A whoo-ya to ya!') The planets aligned when the greatest superstar FM disc jockeys in Southern California all found themselves working together under the same roof: B. Mitchell Reed, Jeff Gonzer, Richard Kimball, Steven Clean, Bob Coburn, Mary Turner, Jim Ladd, Cynthia Fox, Ace Young, Paraquat Kelley, and Barry Hansen (aka Dr. Demento), to name just a few.

In the late 70s, rock music was at an all-time high. The KMET format allowed the jocks to be irreverent and rebellious, to speak their minds, and they all had wonderful individual personalities. They each touched our hearts in their own way, and KMET became a beacon for the baby boomer generation and the music we all shared. Led by the talented program director Ms. Sam Bellamy, the station at its peak boasted a seven percent share of the market, sometimes beating the all-powerful Top 40 stations in town. To put this into perspective, the usual market share for a healthy rock station in Southern California was around a three; four was huge, and seven was totally off the charts. For a precious few years, KMET *owned* Los Angeles.

When you plug the greatest rock'n'roll star into the largest rock'n'roll amplifier, sparks fly, leading to an explosion felt by an entire city. The marriage of Bruce's live performance with KMET's powerful airwaves was the perfect storm—and it blew the fucking lid off Los Angeles. But the behind-the-scenes story is an incredibly wild ride that very few people knew about at the time or even know about now—not even Bruce and Jon realized how insane everything was backstage as we mounted that now celebrated broadcast.

· ● ·

As soon as I got the green light from Jon, I immediately called Sam and asked to have an emergency meeting with her and the general manager at KMET first thing on Wednesday. At the meeting I asked for Mary Turner to be the host of the show. Mary had been an early supporter of Bruce, and they'd bonded after a wonderful interview she did with him. I also pointed out that none of us had ever pulled a live broadcast together in just three days, and I begged them to make sure that everything was double-checked ahead of time, and that their crew arrived early on the day of the broadcast.

Jon put the tickets on sale first thing Thursday morning. One might think that's the easy part, but nothing would be easy on this adventure. A thousand kids lined up at the Roxy. The box office opened for a short period, then closed again, at which point a near riot occurred. At the time, the Roxy had about 450 seats. No one had thought to count the line and let the back half know that there weren't going to be enough tickets for them.

We had assumed that when KMET announced the live broadcast, it would help stem the tide of ticket requests, since those who couldn't get into the show could still listen and experience it live over the radio. Nothing doing. Within an hour, I got a panicked call from Sam.

'Rap, I have two hundred kids in my lobby at the radio station looking for tickets! They are becoming very unruly and shouting that we and the record company took a lot of seats for ourselves, celebrities . . . I need you and Jon Landau to go on the air with Ace Young and explain that didn't happen—and soon.'

Then I got a call from downstairs. We had a bunch of kids in *our* lobby, too, demanding the record company give back their tickets to the people. The truth was, I had taken only ten tickets to cover the label, knowing that most of them should go to fans. As for radio personnel, they'd all be working backstage anyway, so they didn't need tickets. It was just bad optics: because the line that day had been so huge, it appeared that not that many tickets had been sold to the public before the club abruptly closed the ticket window and declared the show a sellout. Now there were kids everywhere, clamoring for tickets, and the hysteria was Beatles-esque.

This show was, in fact, the one that spurred promoters in the future to hand out numbers to kids in line for potential sellout events so that they'd know they were assured a ticket, while those past that number were dismissed rather than having to wait forever, only to be disappointed. But that was the future. Right now, I had to call Jon and explain the situation.

Jon did not want to go on the KMET airwaves, but I explained that the story was going to need some weight from Bruce's camp, not just me representing the record company. So, we called in together to talk to Ace, the station's newsman. I remember it being a little painful because Ace was trying to be his proper reporter self, digging deep into the story, and Jon and I were just trying to diffuse the powder keg. In the end, it all got sorted out, and I was on to my next drama, which was all the other artists, managers, and celebrities looking for tickets. I spent the rest of that day, and the next, fending off requests in the nicest way possible, not wanting to offend anybody. I think I caved and gave one pair of tickets to Linda Ronstadt, but hey, it's Linda Ronstadt . . .

I had the painter Tom Christopher design some bright red commemorative T-shirts that read *Bruce Springsteen—E Street Band—*

Roxy July 7, 1978, rendered in the Roxy's art deco style. Amazingly, he produced them overnight. We would leave one on each seat for the fans to find as they entered the club.

For two and a half days straight, my phone was ringing off the hook, from the time I entered the office to the time I left. I had a trusty checklist with me at all times, and I was continually going over every single item, large or small, not wanting to miss a beat.

On the day of the show, I came down to the club early, hoping to see the sound truck arrive by noon and someone from Ma Bell connecting the 15K lines—and, of course, hoping to greet some KMET personnel. No one showed. In those days before cell phones, all you could do was wait, hope, and smoke cigarettes. I had quit smoking in 1973, but I had one that afternoon.

Finally, at 3pm, there was some action—and all at once. Biff Dawes and the Wally Heider sound truck showed up; the phone company guy arrived and was shown upstairs to the phone box to connect the lines. My buddy Gus Krueger, the engineer for KMET, showed up too, and all of this made me feel a bit better. Even so, with an 8pm show, we were cutting it close. It takes a long time to set up amps and drums, mic them properly, and then tweak everything to get a great recording. Not to mention the adventures the phone company could take you on.

Not long after that, Bruce's producer and engineer, Jimmy Iovine, showed up with the rest of the Springsteen crew. Landau introduced him as Jimmy 'Shoes' Iovine. He was a very cool guy, and my biggest memory of him was when he turned around to enter the sound truck. Sticking high out of the right back pocket of his jeans was a very large pink hairbrush.

Man, I thought, *this guy has a set of balls.*

The KMET general manager's secretary showed up around 5pm holding a clipboard and asking me for a backstage pass. I only had so many of them, and I told her that with all due respect, we had all the essential people covered, and no GM's assistant or clipboard was needed for any other live broadcast I'd ever done. Then two of the GM's family members showed up, and I was asked for more passes. I asked why they were here, and the secretary told me they'd come to 'guard the equipment.' Yeah, right.

Before long, the rest of the KMET crew was here—music director Jack Snyder, renowned disc jockeys Bob Coburn and Jeff Gonzer, and the legendary Jim Ladd. They were all friends, which gave me a sigh of relief. Then the GM himself arrived. I want to be kind here, but there is no way to describe his behavior other than boozy and belligerent. He was wearing a suit decked out with Metromedia Broadcasting badges all over it like a military general, as if somehow, they would make a difference to someone. He demanded to know why there was no backstage pass waiting for him. I tried to explain that the woman with a clipboard took one, then his family members, and so on, and that I'd only been given a limited amount of them. The rest I had given to his KMET crew, who each had a specific job for the broadcast. He continued ranting in a very loud voice, so I asked him to wait just a minute. I ran upstairs and begged Landau for another pass. Jon looked at me sideways.

'I know, I know,' I said.

The GM came upstairs to the dressing room area where we were setting up a broadcast booth in the hallway overlooking the stage. Having done many live broadcasts before, we all knew what had to be done, and we were well into it. All of a sudden, the GM started barking orders. He reached into a black bag he was carrying and began to hand out walkie-talkies. I tried to explain that we didn't need them—'It's a very small space up here, and even if we need someone from the truck, we just yell down to the parking lot below through that open window over there.' He brushed passed me like he didn't even hear me and insisted his people use the walkie-talkies.

Jack, Bob, Jim, and Gus looked at me, rolling their eyes and shaking their heads in embarrassment. It started to become comical. One of them would be at the end of the short hallway, literally looking at the other and talking over a walkie-talkie. Then Mary showed up, eyes gleaming with excitement. The GM came back downstairs and handed her a script he had written.

Nobody writes scripts for live broadcasts. Perhaps the host has a few notes with them as reminders, but that's it. It's all done off the cuff—describing the scene, the anticipation, and so on. This script started out with something like this:

'First he rocked them in New Jersey! Then he rocked them in New

York! Then he rocked them at the Forum here in LA! And tonight, he's gonna rock you from the Roxy!'

Mary chuckled and said, 'Don't worry, I've got this covered.' It was going to be an especially big night for her. She had been there from the beginning, believing in Bruce and turning all of Los Angeles onto his music. Now she would get to present a piece of rock'n'roll history. But the GM wouldn't let it go.

'I wrote this,' he said, 'and you're gonna read it! And everything else on here too,' he added, referring to more poorly written jargon, and quite the opposite of hip.

There was no way the Lauren Bacall of Rock'n'Roll, as I used to call her, was going to belittle herself reading this stuff on the air, much less in front of one of the greatest rock stars of all time—and a friend of hers, too.

'There is nothing in my contract that says I need to read this *shit* on the air!' Mary fought back. 'I'm not doing it.'

'Really?' the GM replied. 'Fine, you're not the host anymore. I'll have Coburn do it.'

In the half-hour since this guy showed up, he was tossing hand grenades everywhere he treaded. The upstairs area was now in disarray as his crew began performing duties that he demanded were necessary, instead of the stuff we all knew had to be accomplished. And very quickly, I might add, as we were getting close to show time. I was watching, little by little, as everything I'd worked so hard for began to go down in flames. Then I looked over and saw something I never thought I'd ever see in my life. My good friend Mary Turner was crying.

Mary Turner was one tough gal—not the crying type—and to see her in this state shook me. I hugged her and tried to console her, but I could see she was crushed and embarrassed, not only for herself but for the station she was so proud of. She and Bruce were bound tight in the rock'n'roll narrative, and this was supposed to be his night; in a special way, their night together. She apologized to me for all the chaos, but I told her not to worry—I knew what was up and there were enough of us there who knew what to do to fix it. I felt awful, but I needed to run back upstairs and get hold of this thing.

Backstage, I was greeted by Jack.

'Rap, we've got a problem. We only have one line connected. The phone guy is still here working on it, but I'm not sure when he'll figure it out.'

'What does that mean?' I asked. 'We'll only hear the broadcast out of one speaker on one side?'

'No, it will come out of both speakers, but it will sound mono.'

'Oh,' I said, letting out a big breath. 'Well, that's not the worst thing that could happen. Listen to Bruce's records—they're all smooshed up like mono sound anyway.'

Jack chuckled. We both needed a bit of levity. I'd always appreciated the Bruce Springsteen power punch sound, which to me emulated the in-your-face sonics you got from great rock'n'roll mono singles like Gary US Bonds' 'A Quarter To Three.'

'I'll go ask Bruce for some extra time.'

With one line down, last-minute plug-ins, and everyone running around the hallway panicked and talking on walkie-talkies, my buddy Gus thought I needed some calming down. He pushed me into the men's bathroom, brought out a vial of coke, and had me do a couple of quick hits (to calm me down?!). I must admit, I did feel a bit better walking out of the men's room, but only for a moment, as I was immediately greeted by the GM, who was furious at all the confusion and uncertainty which, of course, he had created. He decided to blame me—perhaps not remembering the part where I begged everyone to show up early. This guy was pretty big, drunk, and pretty much out of his mind. He was getting madder by the second, and his face was getting redder and redder.

He finally collared me, holding my shirt tight against my throat with his right hand, and started banging my head against the hallway's dark wood paneling, yelling about how this would be the last time the station would ever do a live broadcast with us.

Dude, I'm thinking, *you have no idea how right you are!* But I had to remain calm and professional, even as my head was repeatedly being whacked against the wall.

Then the GM turned and looked at Bob Coburn.

'Okay, *you're* now the host of the show. Go back to the station and do it from there.'

Coburn was shocked, as we all were.

'What? I need to do it from here, where the event is happening. Besides, I want to see the show!'

'Go back to the station, NOW!' the GM yelled. 'And here's the script.'

Bob was mortified, but at the time didn't carry the weight Mary did, so he acquiesced.

I pulled myself together and started for the dressing room. I needed to talk to Bruce and buy some time. I couldn't let one of his biggest nights be marred in any way, but after three days and nights of no sleep and all the insanity that was taking place, I was pretty much on the fritz. I gave my head a shake to refocus, but all that did was restart the big headache from my recent head-banging experience.

Totally faking it, I sauntered into the dressing room and asked, in the most nonchalant manner, 'Hey, Boss, you don't care if the show starts exactly on time, at eight o'clock sharp, right?'

'Nah, whenever you're ready, just let us know.'

'Thanks.'

I ran out and right over to Jack.

'I just bought us fifteen minutes—now let's go tell Ma Bell to get that line up!'

Jack Snyder was and is one very cool and calm dude.

'I'll handle it,' he smiled.

Just then, the GM threw another fit. 'I've had it!' he exclaimed. 'I'm done!' He took his headset and walkie-talkie, threw them on the floor, and stormed out of the club. Everyone turned and looked at each other—it was like a hurricane had passed. For the first time since he'd arrived, there was a sense of calm in the air—it almost felt balmy by comparison. Jim Ladd came up to me, put his hand on my shoulder, and said, 'Don't worry Rap, we've got this.'

It was the first time all evening that I'd felt reassured.

'The line's up!' Jack screamed. 'Let's go!'

Now everyone's adrenaline was pumping big time. Bruce and the band were announced, and the crowd went crazy. But instead of going right into a song, Bruce decided to first speak to everyone in the audience and those listening on the radio, first to thank them and then to the ticketing misunderstanding.

'Hey, hey . . . gimme some lights up here. How you doin'? All right. I'd like to say a few things first. First, I'd like to thank yous for comin' down—I'd like to thank LA for treatin' us the way they have. It's been fantastic the last few days in town.

'I know there was a lot of people that waited a long time in line outside, and there was a lot that didn't get in for one reason or another. And I want to apologize to 'em and say that I'm very sorry—if I could, I would have liked to invite the whole town. So, for the folks that didn't get in and had a hard time out on the street, I'd like to say I'm sorry, it was my fault, and I wasn't trying to turn this into no private party, 'cos I don't play no parties anymore, except my own. So gimme a little slap-back on this microphone! *ONE!* We're gonna do some rock'n'roll for ya!'

The band exploded into Buddy Holly's version of 'Rave On.' The audience exploded out of their seats. And it only got more exciting from there. It's one of the all-time greatest rock'n'roll shows you'll ever hear, filled with Bruce's charm and some of his best fun stories. The Roxy was alive like I'd never seen it before—it was pure magic between artist and fans. The walls were vibrating.

I needed to take a breath. I went outside to get some air with the thought of listening to the broadcast on my car radio for a few minutes to check out the sound. The scene I came upon as I left the club is one I'll never forget.

First off, there had to be at least two hundred kids outside the Roxy Theater with their ears pressed against the walls, listening in. But the most overwhelming event was the one taking place right in front of me on the Sunset Strip. There was the usual Friday night traffic jam as the regulars cruised up and down Sunset Boulevard. But tonight, *everyone* was listening to the live broadcast! It was a summer night, and all the cars had their windows rolled down. You could hear Bruce and The E Street Band pumping out of every single car speaker echoing up and down the Strip. When the traffic came to a standstill, some kids even got out of their cars and danced in the street. I was witnessing a night that no one in Los Angeles was ever soon going to forget—rock'n'roll history, for sure.

When I went back into the club, it was total pandemonium. Band and audience had melded into one singular rock'n'roll machine. The place was hot with sweat, fans moving and grooving themselves into a euphoric state.

Finally, the band took a fifteen-minute break. I went upstairs and caught a glimpse of something I probably wasn't supposed to see. Just before they closed the dressing room door, Bruce sat down on a couch, took his shirt off, leaned over a giant metal tub, and one of the roadies took a bucket of ice-cold water and doused him with it. I watched a big cloud of steam rise off his back. You wanna talk about the hardest-working man in show business? Bruce Springsteen looked like a boxer halfway through a fifteen-round heavyweight fight.

When Bruce and the band came back for the second set, he riled up the crowd.

'All I wanna know is, are you out there?!'

The crowd cheered, and then Bruce uttered those famous words: 'Well then, bootleggers out there in radioland, roll your tapes!'

I loved it, the crowd loved it, and probably the only people not thrilled about it were the Columbia Records sales force. I had fought bootleg phobia during the first Springsteen broadcast on KWST-FM in 1975. The sales guys didn't want it because they felt that if fans got hold of a bootleg, they'd eschew buying any official album release. I had to make the point over and over again that anyone who was a big enough fan to buy a bootleg was also the kind of fan who could not do without owning any of Bruce's official albums. How did I know? Because I was a huge music fan myself, and I bought and enjoyed bootlegs of Bob Dylan, The Byrds, and The Rolling Stones. But I always needed to own the real thing as well. For fans, bootlegs are just extra extensions of the artists they love so much.

I knew who the bootleggers were, and I always considered the fact that they chose certain acts to bootleg as *a good thing*—it proved an artist's overwhelming popularity and genuine drawing power. 'Yes,' I would tell the concerned label personnel, 'there will definitely be a bootleg. And I can tell you who's gonna make it, and when it's gonna come out. But the bootlegs will only serve to heighten the artist's awareness, help spread the word—and believe it or not, will lead to selling more official records.' They only half believed me, but they had to admit that live broadcasts really did help the momentum of most any artist's trajectory. And now, here we were live at the Roxy Theatre, proving the point once again.

The second half of the show completely blew the roof off the place. Bruce told a story in the middle of his heartwarming 'Growin' Up' about how his parents had tried to dissuade him from *the music thing* and get him back into college, and how his dad referred to his electric guitar not as a Fender guitar, not a Gibson, but always as 'that *goddamned* guitar!'

The end of the show featured 'Rosalita' into 'Independence Day' into 'Born To Run' into 'Because The Night' into 'Raise Your Hand.' The second encore was one of Bruce's favorites, 'Twist And Shout.'

The show had lasted over three hours and the crowd was delirious. The folks that were lucky enough to be there still talk about it to this day.

· ● ·

After the show ended, I was totally exhausted. All my anxiety from the last three sleepless days and nights abruptly came to a halt. I had nothing left. I was totally tapped out, physically and emotionally. It was about 3am when the dust cleared and I went across the hall to the Roxy's private bar and collapsed into a big comfy chair. I was all alone, staring out the front window at a deserted Sunset Boulevard.

I was feeling very good inside. I didn't need anyone to thank me. I knew I'd played an important role in something very special. I felt fulfilled. Then Bruce walked in.

I was so tired I couldn't get up out of the chair. I knew I should, but I was so spent I didn't even care. I just looked up and smiled.

'Hi, how ya doin'?'

Bruce could see I was toast, so he crouched down to talk to me.

'Rap, all these people have been coming up to me, telling me what you did to put this together and how hard you worked. You have no idea how hard *I am* working to make this thing happen, and I can't thank you enough.'

He took my left hand in his and kissed it. Other than my father, I'd never been kissed by another man—certainly not by a budding superstar.

But the beauty of it was that the gesture was just from one guy to another, looking eye to eye, both knowing they were in it for the long haul, both knowing what it was going to take to accomplish the mission, and both knowing that with each other's particular talents, they'd just completed a most important part of that mission.

Bruce went back into the club and I was left with my own thoughts. Suddenly, it dawned on me that my job wasn't entirely done. KMET was going to want to repeat the broadcast from the tape they had made, and I was going to be making cassettes from that tape to give to Jon, Bruce, the Columbia Records execs, and some fans around town. For sure there was going to be a bootleg, and those guys were probably going to create the boot from one of the cassette copies that would be floating around.

There was one big problem. Bob Coburn had read all that crap from the GM's original script during the live broadcast. Not only had he read the dopey introduction, but the GM had him break up the flow of the concert by cutting in, every few songs, to read some more nonsense or to max out the station's call letters. Usually, when we did a live broadcast, all of that stuff was put aside; the show went on uninterrupted, with the accent on the music and performance. But not this time. No, this time, for some godforsaken reason, a crazy man had shown up and put a spanner in the works.

I needed to get hold of Gus—or Goose, as we called him—and fast. Lucky for me, he was still at the club.

'Goose, I need a *really big* favor. You and I have to go over to the station now and edit that tape before the show runs again and copies are made. There's gonna be all that extra shit on there from Coburn that your GM insisted he say. We need to make the show as seamless as possible, and we need to help Bob Coburn sound as good as he can as well for the rebroadcast. Bob wasn't allowed to do this in his normal, classy style, so I know he can't be a happy camper either.'

'Yeah, I get it,' said Gus. 'Why don't we just go home, get some sleep, and you come over this afternoon and we do it then.'

'Because there is no way I'm going to be able to sleep until this is done. I can't give the show like it is to Jon, Bruce, or anyone. It was so exciting live that you guys probably got away with it, but upon repeated listens, it's gonna suck. Everyone and anyone who hears this show again needs to hear the show that you and I are about to produce. The one they *think* they heard.'

'Rap, it's 4am.'

'Yep, I told you it was a big favor.'

Gus let out a long sigh. 'Okay. Let's go.'

We went back to the station and pulled out the big reel of tape. Gus also pulled out his vial again. Thank God he had it, because after what I'd been through the last three days, coffee, no matter how strong, wasn't going to cut it. We took a couple of big hits and went from being totally spent to instantly awake and focused. As it turned out, we were going to need this last bit of rocket fuel.

The voiceovers were longer and worse than we'd thought. Gus and I worked on that tape for two hours straight, editing out every last piece of extra Bob Coburn speak that we could. The music was running pretty seamlessly now. Gus Krueger was quite an artist when it came to editing. Then we came to one place in particular where Coburn was reading a part of the script that I just couldn't handle. The problem was, he was speaking over one of Max's drum beats.

'FUCK!'

I was really pissed.

'I can take care of that,' Gus said, 'and you'll never know.'

'Gus, for you to do that, you'll need to edit out one or two of Max's drumbeats, but make it seamless. It has to make musical sense, like he didn't miss a beat—it's impossible.'

'I can do it, trust me.'

We looked down at all the small pieces of tape that we'd edited, now lying all over the floor.

'Gus, this is the master. If you fuck it up, everyone will know someone edited this thing.'

'Rap, I swear I can do it. I've done it before.'

I'd seen the great work he'd done over the last two hours. I believed in him. I took a big breath.

'Okay, let's do it.'

We took the last two hits left in the vial.

Refocused, Gus rocked the tape back and forth, listening to its every sound.

'Right here,' he said.

I held my breath. He sliced through the tape with a razor blade. He reached up, got a piece of white editing tape, and put it across. We played the tape back. Coburn's voiceover was gone. Max's drums were seamless. Gus Krueger was a magician.

We hugged. I couldn't thank him enough. The master reel had so much white editing tape running through it that it looked like a zebra. But I knew it sounded great. Finally, my job was done. We left the building at 6am. I went home, fell on the bed with my clothes on, and didn't wake up until late that afternoon.

For those who heard the re-broadcast on KMET, got hold of any of the cassettes made, or for anyone who owns the original bootleg of that show, this is the version you heard. The original, thank God, was cut up, and all the unpleasant parts lay in little pieces on the engineering room floor of the Mighty Met, disappeared forever.

The next time I saw Bob Coburn, he gave me a wink and a smile. All was as it should be in the land of rock'n'roll. And as time passed, the Roxy broadcast has become widely regarded as Bruce Springsteen's finest.

• ● •

That was just one episode in the rock'n'roll adventure of a lifetime. Somehow, luck and destiny conspired, and I found myself in the middle of many of my rock heroes' lives working for Columbia Records for more than thirty-three years. Indeed, I helped many of them break through and others have their music heard by a much wider audience. I formed wonderful relationships with artists like Bruce, Bob Dylan, Billy Joel, Elvis Costello, The Rolling Stones, Pink Floyd, and more. Each project I worked on arrived with a unique set of challenges, and those challenges required truly imaginative solutions. They all led to fun and extraordinary escapades. Some of these adventures may seem unbelievable, but this is not a book based on a true story—it *is* the true story, and everything you're about to read really happened.

SETTING THE STAGE

IT'S GETTING CLOSE to midnight, and I'm wired out of my mind. It's not from drugs, which I left behind so long ago. I just got back from a rockin' band rehearsal. Our keyboard player decided we should try to cover 'Kid Charlemagne' by Steely Dan. This musical masterpiece is very sophisticated, top-of-the-line stuff, full of chords like C7#9, F6/9, and Bb13. Fuck, I've never even heard of thirteenth chord! But that's because I'm a power-chord rock guy.

Be that as it may, the band is so good that before we knew it, we were off and flying. The other guitar player and I just let loose and found ourselves in the stratosphere of inspired guitar solos.

Bono says, 'It's still an extraordinary thing to behold the sound of a rock'n'roll band in full flight.' Keith Richards concurs, reiterating how musicians live for those magic moments when each band member is in sync, cooking along to reach a euphoric state that rivals sex. When the music takes me over, I just explode inside. Like the crescendo of a big fireworks display, sky lit up with multicolored sparkles. My body starts to move, and I find myself in a combination of Chuck Berry's duck walk and Keith Richard's slouch. That's what rock'n'roll music does for me, and I suspect you as well. Where else can you find such a feeling? I'm in heaven as the drums beat and the amps blare. I'm so high it takes me a couple of hours to chill and come back to earth. Hopefully I'll finally get to sleep around 1am.

I played in bands throughout high school and college. In fact, I was in a renowned pioneering LA punk band when I first learned that Columbia Records was looking for a part-time college rep at UCLA to promote their new music. For a while, I considered making music my life's work. I played in a hip jam session at a small Santa Monica restaurant that started at 8pm and finished when the sun came up. The feeling of playing into the wee hours with local greats like conga master Big Black while the rest of the world slept was enchanting. We were in our own dimension. The notes flying out of those sessions were transcendent. But alas I knew deep inside I would never survive life on the road. The idea of a steady paycheck appealed to the Capricorn-grounded part of me, and I thought the other part—the big imagination and being a bit of a show-off—might serve me well.

• ● •

An astonishing musical renaissance took place in the 1960s and early 70s. It seemed like every genre of music had been growing for years, waiting for this moment to blow wide open. Whether it was country music, with its roots in the Appalachian Mountains, jazz percolating in New Orleans, R&B, folk, pop, rock, or blues, it all seemed to arrive as one big explosion. When the British Invasion began, with The Beatles and The Rolling Stones leading the charge, all hell broke loose. The world would be blessed with some of the best and most creative talent in the history of recorded music.

The music being made had great importance to us. Songs by these artists were not just pop ditties, they reflected our lives and the culture of the day. And the culture of the day was riveting. Massive social change was sweeping the country. Revolutions abounded—civil rights, women's rights, the war in Vietnam. Old taboos were shed, making way for new ideas on how to live and celebrate life. With the internet and social media years away, the music acted as a tribal telegraph to a baby-boomer generation of young idealists eager to bust out and change the world. Songs like Bob Dylan's 'Blowin' In The Wind,' Marvin Gaye's 'What's Going On,' The Rolling Stones' 'Street Fighting Man,' and CSNY's 'Ohio' helped shape our lives.

The music had such a profound impact on us that it became like a religion. Not only could we visualize ourselves in it, but it had the power to transform us—the power to heal us. Music was no longer just a luxury meant to entertain it was a necessity. Indeed, many of our discussions centered around the new stereo equipment we were buying to better hear these artists' messages in the finest sound fidelity we could afford.

New record stores sprung up all over America and became the churches and temples for this new religion where we found the music that inspired and drove our lives. This music became so popular that it arrived by the pallet at Tower Records—a new concept of supermarket record store. The demand was so great, so immediate, that when new hit releases arrived at Tower, the managers left the tall stacks of albums on the wooden skids as fans streamed into the store, grabbing them off faster than the clerks could sort them into bins.

The record business that I entered in 1969 was just beginning to find its new self. With this explosion of new music, a fair amount of label personnel—made up mostly of men who had been working in the business since the 1950s—struggled to understand the new culture and the music itself. Although they were happy to be riding this new wave of talent and excitement, the higher-ups realized they needed the next generation of record executives—the people who came from, and were living in, this music. Hence, college representative programs were established by some of the major labels in order not only to have young street teams promoting their wares but also to discover and shape a new generation of record executives for the future.

Nowhere was there a larger staff and total commitment to the college rep program than Columbia Records. I would arrive at the label from a blue-collar background, having grown up in the small town of Bellflower, California, beginning as a college rep at UCLA and eventually rising to become a Senior VP in New York City. My mission became not only promoting and marketing this music I believed in but doing it in ways that were fun and that put big smiles on fans' faces.

• ● •

There were few rules in the music business during the 1970s and 80s. Money was rolling in like crazy, and with so many new artists on the scene, the competing record companies were having trouble just keeping pace. At Columbia, aside from established artists like Bob Dylan, Simon & Garfunkel, Santana, and Janis Joplin, all of a sudden there was a burst of great new talent as albums began to appear from Billy Joel, Bruce Springsteen, Blue Öyster Cult, Aerosmith, Journey, Loggins & Messina, and more. Over time, these unknowns would become superstar acts, each selling millions of records.

Characters abounded, and not just the artists. Managers, attorneys, promoters, disc jockeys, and record company personnel all had individual looks and mannerisms. People were applauded for their unique and creative character traits. Indeed, they were celebrated. The music industry personnel were just as big a show as the artists themselves.

And just like in the movie *Guys & Dolls*, everyone had a nickname. Instead of Sky Masterson, we had the famous Chicago FM disc jockey Sky Daniels. Instead of Big Julie, we had legendary promotion man Heavy Lenny. Redbeard was a well-known music director at a big Dallas rock station, and, yes, he had a long red beard. Pioneering FM Rock programmer Norm Winer created the on-air alter ego Old Saxophone Joe, and there was a rambunctious young man from WMMS-FM in Cleveland, coined Kid Leo, who's worthy of his own book.

I love nicknames, and I've been making them up for people for as long as I can remember. One of the guys at Columbia, Rich Tardanico, I christened the T-Bird. Warren Williams was known as W.W. ('Dubya, Dubya'); Greg Phifer was Phife Doggy; Larry Reymann was Ramos, as in Gin Fizz; Ron Oberman was Obi-Wan; Gail Bruesewitz was Brueser. On any given day, Eva Pfaff could be Christmas Eva, Eva Destruction, or Evie Ray Vaughan; Linda Kirishjian was Linda Pinda, or Mr. Christian from *Mutiny On The Bounty*; Jim McKeon was Mac, or Macker; and I was Rap, or Rapper.

We lived in a party atmosphere. It's not that we didn't take our work seriously, we enjoyed celebrating.

We've just gone Top 10 with our new band, let's have a toast!

Wow, we're #5 with a bullet—let's go for drinks after work!

We hit #1! P-A-R-T-Y!

We had so many parties we didn't have the time or manpower to produce them all ourselves. Believe it or not, a side business emerged of people who exclusively planned parties for record companies.

Everyone was flush with cash, and expense accounts had no ceilings. Let me repeat: expense accounts had no ceilings. Work started at 10am, we didn't have to wear a tie, we went to clubs and concerts as part of our job, and we got all our records for free. If we stayed out late at a club hanging with an artist or band, we could come into the office at noon, and no one cared. In fact, it was expected, as everyone knew we had been out all night. It was not uncommon to hear an assistant answer the phone, 'Yeah, Rap was out late last night with Ronnie Wood. He'll be in around noon.' No one cared. So long as the work got done, it didn't matter. Working for a record company wasn't a job so much as it was a lifestyle.

We witnessed the debut of major artists like Elton John, Billy Joel, Bruce Springsteen, Genesis, and David Bowie performing in the small clubs and theaters that popped up everywhere to support all this new music. We saw rock'n'roll history in the making, and shortly after that, we would become an integral part of writing that history. Yes, some of it could be described as sex, drugs, and rock'n'roll, but it was so much more than that.

It was a world like no other. A world where imagination knew no bounds and there was plenty of money to make our visions and dreams come true. A world and a business that we made up as we went along. A world where no one seemed to grow up, just a bunch of big kids posing as mature adults, somehow put in charge of what would become one of the biggest industries on the planet—the record business.

• ● •

I once had the great pleasure to meet Brian Wilson at a television show some friends produced during the early 2000s. I grew up in Southern California, part of the 60s surf scene, and I was a huge fan of The Beach Boys and especially Brian. I loved the surf and hot rod songs, but the more intimate songs like 'In My Room' reached into my soul. Brian showed young men like me that it was okay to be sensitive and have feelings.

When I entered the studio, Brian was at the piano, rehearsing his classic song 'Surfin' USA' with his backup singers. I walked up and waited to introduce myself. Right in the middle of the song, he looked up at me as if he'd known me forever, eyes twinkling, and shouted, 'Isn't this a great song?' Not great because he wrote it, but as an expression of his love for a song that just happened to be written by him.

That's the way I feel about this book. It's a celebration of the love I have for these special times and the people who meant so much to me. It has been calling out to me to be written for years. When that calling finally became a roar, I knew it was time to bear down.

I wrote this book to capture the magical times, so that people wouldn't forget but also to show the many behind-the-scenes folks whose lives were so colorful they brought a warmth and laughter to the world. I have a special dream that perhaps one day we might get back to making art the priority in our music business. Art lifts our souls in the same wonderful, inexplicable way as love. That's why we light up when hearing our favorite songs.

If you want to know what it felt like to be there, to experience the whole scene first hand, to get the inside track on how it really all went down, these stories are for you. I welcome you to follow me down the rabbit hole to a magical place that will bring you laughter and reveal the inner workings of the music biz that you may have often wondered about. It's a ringside seat to the circus and comes with an All Access Backstage Pass.

Keep rockin',

Rap~

PART ONE

FEATURING

BRUCE SPRINGSTEEN

KAREN CARPENTER

JANIS JOPLIN

JIMI HENDRIX

MILES DAVIS

MIKE BLOOMFIELD

TONY BENNETT

RANDY CALIFORNIA

BLUE ÖYSTER CULT

AEROSMITH

ELTON JOHN

BOZ SCAGGS

BOSTON

IAN HUNTER

PETER TOSH

ELVIS COSTELLO

THE NEW BARBARIANS

THE BOOMTOWN RATS

THE MUSIC INSIDE

MY MOM, VERA, once told me that when I was a baby, she would put me in a cardboard box so I couldn't escape while she did her chores. She played classical music to keep me amused. She said the music kept me entertained for long periods. I loved it.

My first memory of music's big impact is from when I was very young. I was visiting a friend who had a record player and a few yellow vinyl 45s. The song that really got to me was Harry McClintock's 'Big Rock Candy Mountain,' the story of a hobo's paradise. It painted vivid scenes in my head of a place where '*hens lay soft-boiled eggs*,' where there were '*cigarette trees*' and '*lemonade springs*.' My favorite part, which appealed to my inner rebel, was when McClintock sang about jails made out of tin, where '*you can walk right out again, as soon as you are in*.'

I listened to that record over and over and over again, each time letting myself disappear deeper and deeper into this wonderful magical world. Listening repeatedly to a song became a habit of mine that continues to this day. Once a song gets into my head, you can find me in my car with the volume cranked to the max, bouncing in my seat, mouthing the words and flailing hand gestures to accentuate all. It's a wonder I haven't caused any accidents. The music more than likely will be from the treasure trove of rock that I grew up with: The Rolling Stones' 'Rip This Joint,' The Kinks' 'Life On The Road,' Fleetwood Mac's 'Go Your Own Way' featuring Lindsey Buckingham's fabulous guitar solo, Tom Petty's 'Runnin' Down A Dream' with Mike Campbell's blistering solo at the end, or anything ZZ Top—'A-haw, haw, haw, haw!' I have been known to push the repeat button five or six times in a row.

You may find all of this funny from a guy who was born in 1948, but the truth is, on any given day, I feel like I'm somewhere between eleven and thirty-five. I don't know if it was the record business that kept me young or my perpetual youth that kept me in the record business. Either way, that's how I feel.

The reason I point to those exceptional guitar solos and highlight ZZ Top, featuring the great Billy Gibbons, is because I love the guitar so much. It has been a faithful companion to me for my whole life, and I've worked very hard to become a good player myself.

Most guitarists of my generation cite Elvis Presley as the catalyst that got them interested in playing the instrument. The first time I saw guitars that spoke to me, I was seven years old. On Sunday mornings, when my parents slept in, I would turn on the TV to amuse myself. But in 1955 in Los Angeles, there wasn't much to watch at that time. I would tune into the Cal Worthington Dodge *Country Music Time* show, which was exciting because it was broadcast live from Cal's enormous car lot. Every Sunday you could see up-and-coming country acts playing live on a stage on the lot. Cal, wearing his trademark white Stetson, introduced all the artists, and he'd showcase an array of different cars between acts in all different colors with big white prices painted on their windshields. Then he'd offer a warm, downhome smile and say, 'Hope you're enjoying our show, now come on down to Worthington Dodge for a great deal!'

As I watched the performers, I was immediately entranced by the guitars they played. Their curvy shapes appealed to me, and each artist had a different type that seemed to fit their persona. Some guitars were large, some a bit smaller; some had thin necks, others quite wide; all of them were fashioned from different kinds of beautiful wood—mahogany, ash, maple, walnut, spruce. Most striking to me was that each guitar seemed to have its own soul. When the player hit the strings, a unique voice would ring out helping to bring the singer's songs to life. The songs had messages in them, and there was always anticipation and excitement in the air as we waited to see what each performer would sing about. An artist with a guitar slung over their shoulder became a larger-than-life entity carrying a particular kind of gravitas. Later in life, I would come to understand the importance of the message that Woody Guthrie had placed on his guitar, 'This machine kills fascists.' But even at the young age of seven, I could see that the guitar was a living thing—and that through it, one could express their feelings in a myriad of ways.

The attraction was so strong that I told my parents I needed to learn how to play the guitar. They called the local music store, and a woman showed up at our house to, supposedly, point us in the right direction. She told us that learning to play the traditional Spanish-style guitar, as she called it, would hurt my fingers, so she suggested I begin with a lap-steel (a smaller version of a country pedal-steel guitar). My parents believed her, and I was too young to know any better.

I began learning a few country things. It wasn't what I had wanted, but one of the players I often saw on *Country Music Time* was a guy with curly hair named Red Rhodes. He played pedal steel too, and I thought he was cool. Perhaps some of that cool could rub off on me. Also, the instrument was electric, and when I plugged it into my 1955 Fender Champ amplifier (which I still own), I was jazzed.

Hawaiian music is another genre where lap steel is heard prominently. I wasn't into that at all, but one year later, at a recital, a girl my age showed up doing the hula wearing a grass skirt that rested on her hips well below her bare midriff. As I was playing, she began to sway back and forth, right in front of me. Between her legs moving in and out of the grass skirt and me catching a glimpse of more skin beneath her belly button than I'd ever seen before, I was getting hypnotized. I began feeling a little wiggly-wobbly. I knew I liked what I was seeing, but at eight years old I had no idea why. All I knew was that Hawaiian music all of a sudden sounded better and better!

The girl and I became good friends and pen-pals. It was puppy love all the way until, a year later, my mom made me break off the relationship because the girl wasn't Jewish, and she worried I might marry out of the faith.

'Hey, Ma, I'm only nine years old!'

• ● •

As a kid, I always had a big imagination, and I followed my own beat. When I was in grade school, while other kids were playing baseball, I was in my homemade laboratory, which took up a whole side of my bedroom. I had all kinds of fancy beakers and flasks with glass tubes running this way and that. Back then, chemistry sets mostly gave instructions on how to distill water and make different inks and perfumes. But being enamored with the race for space, I quickly struck out on my own, learning how to build rockets and make rocket fuel. I perfected the fuel, which could send a rocket so high it went out of sight. The trouble was that it landed with such force that the nose of the rocket broke every time it hit the ground.

Taking a lesson from the people at NASA, who were retrieving their astronauts from splashdowns in the ocean, I thought, *Wow, I could do that. The neighbors behind us have a pool! All I have to do is figure out the rocket's launch trajectory from our front yard so that it lands behind the backyard fence squarely into that pool . . .*

Through trial and error, I began to perform a series of missions that all went fairly well at the beginning. Finally, the rocket was landing in the pool without a scratch. Now, all I had to do was calm down their huge Siberian Husky when I jumped over the fence to retrieve the rocket. When it landed, there was always some residual fuel that would fizz around in the water for a while, but I figured it'd be long gone by the time they went for a swim.

Then, one day, the woman who lived there was home when I fired off the rocket. I had barely gotten it out of the pool when she started screaming at me from behind her glass sliding doors and chasing me back over the fence. I bolted into the house as she ran around the block and started banging like crazy on our front door.

Mom looked at me as if to ask, *What's going on?*

I looked up at her sheepishly, gesturing *I don't know.*

Mom opened the door, and the neighbor was breathing fire.

'Do you know your son is firing off rockets and having them land in our pool?! There's rocket fuel bubbling in our pool water! What kind of kid are you raising?' Non-stop, frothing at the mouth, insane screaming that seemed to go on and on and on until my mom finally calmed her down. While the neighbor was screaming, my mom shot me a glance that looked like lightning bolts were coming out of her eyes.

Finally, the woman left in a huff. My mom closed the door and looked at me sternly.

'Paul, really? What the hell were you thinking?' She gave me a good talking to, then winked and asked, 'So . . . how'd you figure *that* out?'

• ● •

My mom led a very exciting life. She was a tomboy who'd grown up in a family of seven brothers and sisters in Baltimore, Maryland. When her older brothers were harassed by the bullies in the neighborhood, she was the one who came out of the house and beat the hell out of all of them. They soon learned that when Vera came out, you better start runnin' . . .

Mom's father, Grandpa Sam, had a bar in Baltimore called the 2 O'clock Club. Working there at a young age, Mom was no stranger to knife fights and gun brawls. She was also friends with the legendary stripper Blaze Starr, who performed there along with a host of other ladies. Mom made friends with all of them.

One of Mom's brothers, Alvin, became a professional magician. I loved visiting him, his wife, and their two sets of twins (a magic trick in and of itself) in Miami. Watching Uncle Alvin perform, I was continually amazed to see doves appear from flaming pans, large steel rings melt through one another only to somehow link together, and loads of different colored silks materialize out of thin air. I got hooked on magic at a very young age— years later, I would be fortunate enough to study under one of the world's greatest magicians and eventually become a professional myself.

Mom was big on health and exercise. She was in great shape right up to the end at the age of ninety-six. At the age of eighty, on a family trip to Costa Rica, she set the record for the oldest person ever to travel by zip line! And she really knew how to have fun. She didn't drink much, but one day when she and my dad were in Las Vegas and she'd had one too many, she sauntered up to Frank Sinatra and blurted out, 'Mr. Sinatra, you can park your shoes under my bed any time!' I'm not sure what Dad thought about that, but it's a true story.

'Paul,' she once told me, 'if you don't break the rules sometimes, you won't have any fun.'

My dad, Walter, was from Brooklyn. He had a big barrel chest and a booming voice to match. He was a major presence and a major character. I took great pleasure in introducing my friends to my father. They'd meet, and he instantly began holding court, explaining how he'd straighten out the world or about life in general. In that buoyant voice, you'd often hear, 'Let me tell you how it is . . . you gotta take the good with the bad, the bitter with the sweet.' And another fave, 'Sometimes you just have to let the idiots be idiots.'

Dad had been in the Navy during World War II. He was an electrician's mate on an attack troop transport ship, the USS *Callaway*. He would tell us about some of the horrific parts of the war, like the time a Japanese kamikaze airplane dove into the middle of the ship and nearly tore it in half. But mostly he'd tell us funny stories. Even though he landed in seven major invasions, he had some lighthearted times in the war as well.

The captain of the ship once called him to his quarters to fix the refrigerator, which no one else had been able to repair. When the captain left, my dad took a look and couldn't figure out the problem either. But having seen an identical unit in one of the storage rooms below deck, he threw the existing refrigerator overboard and replaced it with the new one. The captain thought my dad was a genius and rewarded him with the keys to the food locker.

As an electrician, Dad figured out how to make a hot plate. He could make a homesick sailor a hamburger, give him an ice-cold beer, and serve ice cream for dessert right in the middle of the Pacific Ocean. Dad got so good at making hot plates he started selling them to everyone on the ship. There were so many in use that one evening the ship's electric circuits overloaded and the lights started to dim. Dad and the hotplates were found out. Busted, he had to chip paint off the side of the ship for two weeks.

Walter and Vera got married when the war ended. They made a great team. When I was two years old, they put me in the back seat of their 1950 Ford and drove from Baltimore, where I was born, to Los Angeles, seeking the California dream. They settled in the small town of Bellflower. As soon as they arrived, my dad donned a Stetson, a leather vest, cowboy boots, and a belt with a very large buckle. He was enamored with the West and referred to himself as a cowboy from Brooklyn. He looked like the actor Lorne Greene, who played Ben Cartwright on the TV series *Bonanza*.

My father had a number of hero qualities. When he was young, his dad, Grandpa Arthur, had shared a jewelry business with a few other men. Arthur gave Dad some valuable jewels in a small bag to deliver to another jeweler. As he was leaving, one of the other men spotted him and shot a nervous look at another colleague.

'Hey! What's this?' he asked.

'It's okay,' the other fellow replied. 'It's Rappaport's son.'

That story stuck with me. I never had a master plan for my life, but I knew that whatever I did, I wanted to be that guy—someone who people could trust.

When my sister Ruth was born in 1957, she completed the picture of a very happy family. On Sundays, Dad would take us on long adventurous trips to experience our varied surroundings. We might go down to the harbor, where we could tour famous warships like the *Mighty Mo*, or explore the inside of a submarine. On occasion, he would wake us up early and announce that we were all going out to breakfast . . . in Palm Springs! A mere two-hour drive away. Our dad loved to drive. Sometimes we'd go out to the beautiful rock formations in the Sierra Pelona Mountains, Vasquez Rocks, where I'd do charcoal sketches of the craggy peaks. Ruth and I climbed around to see where the cowboy bandits once hid. Movie companies used the same spot as a film location for Westerns, and they'd constructed a large set of a fort that we played on. Mom made strawberry shortcakes and announced that if we wanted any, we had to climb the largest outcropping of rocks to its highest peak, where she'd be serving.

On Sunday evenings we had dinner out. Nothing fancy: our big treat was going to either McDonald's (brand new at the time) or the local Moffett's Chicken Pie Shoppe.

Our parents always encouraged us and supported every endeavor. When I wanted something that mattered to me a lot, like an electric guitar and an amp, my dad would offer to split the cost with me. They are an important reason behind my success and my sister Ruth's as a cherished educator in San Diego.

Ruth and I attended Downey High. The school produced two popular music groups, The Carpenters and The Blasters. It was also home to Paul Bigsby, known as the father of the modern solid body electric guitar. A lot of cool guitar stuff happened in and around Downey. Leo Fender set up shop not too far from there, and the seminal surf instrumental 'Pipeline' was recorded by The Chantays at Wenzel's Music Town, a local record store with a small recording studio in the back.

One of my high-school classmates was Karen Carpenter. She was one of the sweetest people I ever met. She was a drummer in the high school band and was taught to play a proper drum kit by Frankie Chavez, a tall, handsome Hispanic student. Back then, guys congregated within their own tribes. Each had their own dress code. There were the surfers (that's me) with their bushy hairdos, light blue pants, madras shirts, and Converse tennis shoes; the greasers, usually Hispanic, with slicked-back pompadours, khaki pants, and shiny black shoes; and the Spray Boys with even larger pompadours, plastered to the max with hairspray, wearing overly tight jeans and boots. The rest of the kids dressed in a variety of normal nondescript outfits. Most of the girls back then sported impressive beehive hairdos or flips.

The interesting thing about Karen and Frankie was that they were both outliers in their way. Frankie dressed like his tribe but distanced himself from the rest. And it was especially strange to see a girl play drums back then. Karen didn't seem to care. She was a proud person, clearly pioneering her own path and a path for women in music to come. Frankie went on to have a professional career too, while Karen went on to be a superstar.

Karen sat in front of me in French class and knew I'd always need a helping hand in tests. She would slide over to her right so I could sneak a glimpse at her answers—what a pal. The teacher got suspicious and moved me further up toward the front of the class, but that worked out fine because a really cute blonde now sat to my right. It may not have been the greatest thing for my studies, though.

One night, after an open house at the school, my dad came home and reported that my French teacher, Mr. Maurice, had told him, '*Zee problem weeth your son eez not zee French, it eez zees very cute little girl who seets next to him, here.*' Busted.

We all knew Karen had a band, but she never talked about it. All we knew was that our music teacher, a great guy named Mr. Gifford, was helping her out in some way. When we graduated high school, all of us who played in psychedelic rock bands were shocked that it was Karen who got the record deal, partly because we'd never heard her sing. When we heard her voice on the radio, we discovered a whole other Karen we'd never known.

• ● •

My high school band was called The Jades. It was made up of local guys from Bellflower and Downey: Mike George, Ron McCarrell, Frank Shargo, Ed Myers, and me. (Both Frank and Ron would join me in the years to come in working for CBS Records.) After becoming enamored with the folk movement, I'd finally taught myself how to play a proper acoustic guitar at age fourteen before switching to electric two years later. The Jades began as a surf band but quickly went 'mod,' emulating the British musicians of the time and playing lots of Stones covers. We were actually very good— always at the top of any battle of the bands we'd play in. We also boasted the first strobe light in Downey, California! During our encore, I would put down my Rickenbacker six-string and come up front to sing 'Gimme Some Lovin'' by Steve Winwood and The Spencer Davis Group. I had a tambourine with a hole in the side. I'd stick my finger through the hole and spin the thing high in the air over my head. The strobe light would reflect off the jangles of the tambourine, making tons of little twirling lights go around the room like the disco balls of the future. Foreshadowing the large rock stage productions to come, it was pretty cool-looking, and the crowd loved it.

All the neighborhood kids would come to watch us practice at our home in Bellflower, where it turns out my sister (who loves to manage me) could have been a real manager. Unbeknown to me, she was charging these kids a nickel apiece to get in! I guess we influenced a few of them. One very cool kid who lived across the street, Chris Pierce, visited often and later wound up becoming a professional drummer. Another, Donald MacDonald, became a professional bass player and formed a band with two more kids from around the block. I never realized it, but Donald told me we were like rock stars to them, to the point of seeming unapproachable. Pretty funny.

We used to wear our band clothes and drive into Hollywood to hang out, look cool, and see shows. Once we journeyed out to see Janis Joplin and Big Brother & The Holding Company at a club called the Kaleidoscope. That particular club held shows during the afternoon so that kids under twenty-one could attend. I told the guys we should go around back to the alley because that's where a lot of acts hung out before their show. Sure enough, there was Janis, getting drunk with her band, swigging from a bottle of Southern Comfort. She turned and looked at us with the biggest smile, and it was genuine, not just the booze talking.

'Look at you boys! Look at you *cute* boys! Are y'all in a band or somethin'?'

We were all kind of shy and embarrassed, shrugging our shoulders and staring at the ground.

'Yeah Janis, we sure do like you a lot, and we wanted to come and see you guys in person.'

'Oh, isn't that sweet. You want a hit of this?'

'Sure!'

The next thing you know, we're all sharing hits off Janis's bottle of Southern Comfort. When she hit the stage, she was soused, but it didn't matter. She gave an amazing performance. Late in the show, when she sang 'Ball And Chain,' it rattled us to our core. Janis was the first famous rock performer any of us had ever met, and we never forgot her kindness. And Southern Comfort became the official drink of The Jades.

SOMEBODY TO LOVE

I FIRST MET SHARON, my high school sweetheart and later my wife, at Camp Ramah, a Jewish summer camp in Ojai, California, in 1965. They offered a weeklong retreat for teens who were members of United Synagogue Youth (USY). Sharon had the surfer girl look—long, straight, light brown hair that cascaded down to her waist, and beautiful blue eyes. Perfect.

The Jades played a fair number of teenage dances back then. It was especially fun to play when my girlfriend was in the audience. Sharon tells me that when we'd get back to her house, she'd be ready to make out, but the first thing I would do is take out my Rickenbacker from the case, wipe it down, and put a little polish on it. It's what one usually does after a long gig to take care of a guitar. She understood, she says, she just didn't appreciate the guitar being taken care of before her!

Sharon and I became a hot item. I drove an hour from my home in Bellflower to hers in Van Nuys on a Saturday evening to take her to a movie or dance. Then I'd drive home late at night, get up early Sunday morning, and drive all the way back to take her to the beach. She tanned, I surfed. Aside from the band, surfing began to play a very big role in my life.

As a young teenager, I was seduced by the explosion of the Southern California surf scene. I had seen the movie *Gidget Goes Hawaiian*, and now I thought, *Let me get this straight, you get to ride waves like that and when you arrive back on the beach cute girls are waiting for you in bikinis? I'm in!*

After a late night and a lot of paddling on a Sunday morning at Malibu or Ventura County Line, by the afternoon I was pretty beat. But I'd try to hang around Sharon's house long enough to hear the words from her mom that I looked so forward to each week, 'Paul, would you like to stay for dinner?' That meant more time with Sharon, who I was now hopelessly in love with, and also more of her mother's fine home cooking. Her duck with cherry sauce became my all-time favorite.

I was happy that Sharon's folks had taken a liking to me. They could see I was a good guy, even if at the time my prospects weren't much more than a surfer who played in a band. Eventually, the dinner invitation would become, 'Paul, won't you stay for dinner? I'm making your favorite, duck with cherry sauce!'

• ● •

Sharon's favorite group at the time was the American sunshine pop band The Association. I thought they were very lightweight, and I teased her about them incessantly. 'Cherish' was one of their big hits—ugh, gag me with a spoon. Those British bad boys The Rolling Stones were my guys, and their music loomed large for all of us. If you grew up in LA during the 60s and listened to the Top 40 station KHJ, you might remember how, right before 'Humble Harve' Miller played a Stones song, he would give it some fanfare—you'd hear a deep, powerful voice drenched in heavy echo that announced, 'STONEZZZZZ!'

Another Top 40 station in town, KRLA, was a bit hipper and played deeper tracks from the British Invasion bands during the evening. My favorite DJ was Dave Hull, 'The Hullabalooer.' He would take homework questions from school-age listeners who were stumped and read them over the air. Then knowledgeable kids from around town would call in with the answers. Dave Hull's assistance with our homework was both brilliant radio and a total blast. One night he played a popular Stones song called 'Everybody Needs Somebody To Love.' But the version he played was longer than the one on KHJ, and it sounded much better. It was deeper and richer, the beat more in the pocket, and Jagger's vocals more seductive. I was such a huge fan that I had to have *that* version. But why were there two? I didn't understand it at the time, but I would come to learn that some British artists released different records in Europe and the States. I went to my local record store to investigate.

'Yes,' said the man behind the counter. 'In the States, these are called *imports*. The version of the song you're looking for is on an English album called *The Rolling Stones No. 2*. I can order it for you, but it will cost you eight dollars and take a couple months to get here.'

Back then, eight dollars was an enormous amount of money to a seventeen-year-old blue-collar kid. Even the three bucks for a domestic album was a total luxury for me. I already owned The Stones *12 X 5*, which featured 'Around And Around,' 'Time Is On My Side,' and 'It's All Over Now,' and *The Rolling Stones, Now!*, which contained the aforementioned less stellar version of 'Everybody Needs Somebody To Love.' But I *had to have* the killer import version of that song. So, I ordered it.

Sharon also became a Stones fan, and 'Everybody Needs Somebody To Love' was our song. My *Rolling Stones No. 2* came by boat, and it took a whole summer to arrive. When it finally got here, I immediately drove to Sharon's, where she promptly put it on her portable record player, and we danced to our song. It was very sweet.

In the summer of 1966, Sharon and I saw The Rolling Stones live the first time, at the Hollywood Bowl. She was seventeen and I was eighteen. The band hit the stage, and Mick Jagger leaped high into the air, holding a tambourine over his head. He landed precisely on the downbeat of Bo Diddley's renowned rhythm as the band launched into 'Not Fade Away.' The audience exploded with screams and cheers. We were jumping up and down and singing along, just like you see in the classic video clips of the band.

Fast-forward twenty years and I am seated on a couch next to Mick Jagger at Columbia Records' headquarters in New York, explaining our promotion and marketing plans for his upcoming album. The two most amazing things about this encounter are one, that I know what I'm talking about, and two, that he's listening to me. If you'd told eighteen-year-old me that this might happen one day, well, you get the idea . . .

• ● •

Sharon and I had been inseparable in high school, but I had met her at a very young age, and just before college she was beginning to wonder what it would be like to date other people. She told me she still wanted to see me, but she didn't want to go steady anymore. I couldn't handle the idea of her seeing other guys, so I told her it wouldn't work for me, and we broke up. I was heartbroken, and it took me a very long time to finally get over her and move forward.

Sharon and I wound up attending different colleges. She went to Long Beach State University, I went to UCLA, and we didn't see each other— save for one awkward lunch—for five years.

I didn't know you could fall for more than one girl in a lifetime, but it turns out you can, and it can be a completely different kind of love. I met Gari (short for Garilynn) during my first year at college when I returned to Camp Ramah, this time as a counselor. It's funny how things can change so fast. Instead of the acoustic guitars that we used to bring up to camp, when these kids got off the bus, they were carrying electric guitars, amps, keyboards, and black lights to create a psychedelic ambiance in their bunks. Anticipating something like this, I had brought along my Rickenbacker, just in case any of these kids wanted to jam. Turns out they did.

Gari had a hip 60s look but a very individual style. Her golden-brown hair was cut very short, like Twiggy's, but that's where the similarity ended. Gari had a gleam in her soft brown eyes, a warm smile, and a beautiful figure.

Our musical tastes were quite similar, and we saw a lot of concerts together—Cream, the Stones, and Jimi Hendrix, just to name a few. We loved going to USY dances, too, and our favorite band was a local group out of Westchester called The Roosters. I couldn't wait for them to pull out the twelve-string Rickenbacker and do their version of one of my all-time favorites, 'Look Through Any Window' by The Hollies.

The Rolling Stones concert we attended, on Saturday, November 8, 1969, was memorable because they played two shows in one night at the Forum, and they were extremely late getting started. The shows were meant to be at 7 and 11pm. We had tickets for the second show, so I told Gari's parents that it was going to be a late night. But the first show didn't start until around 9pm, and we waited outside the arena for what seemed like an eternity before the first crowd exited. To make matters worse, there were three opening acts, Terry Reid, B.B. King, and Ike & Tina Turner.

I only remember seeing B.B. King and Ike & Tina before The Stones finally came on, because for Terry Reid's set I was on a payphone in the lobby, explaining what had happened to Gari's mom and dad and telling them I had no idea when we would return home. I tried to assure them that I had not absconded with their daughter and asked them to *please*, *please* let us stay to see the main attraction, no matter how late they went on.

I think the second show started at midnight, and the Stones went on at about 3:30am. All I know is that by the time Gari and I left the Forum, the sun was coming up. It was a legendary show, but her folks did not hide their unhappiness when I finally returned her home the next morning. They did trust me, though, and we were allowed to continue our concert adventures together.

The Jimi Hendrix concert we saw a year earlier, at the Hollywood Bowl, is without a doubt the greatest rock performance I've ever seen in my life. Interestingly, when Hendrix walked out onstage with Mitch Mitchell and Noel Redding, they had the house lights up and there was very little fanfare. Approaching the microphone, Hendrix greeted the crowd casually with a big smile and said something like this:

'Hi everyone, we're gonna start with 'Are You Experienced,' go into 'Voodoo Child,' 'Red House,' jam a bit, and then get into 'Foxy Lady' and 'Fire,' if that's okay with everyone.'

Huh? The intro was so lackluster, I wondered if it was really them. I was expecting the Hollywood Bowl to go dark, some heavy voice in an echo chamber to wind us up, and then an explosion of music and a psychedelic light show. It was just the opposite. For a moment, I felt deflated. But as soon as the music started, it was like a giant electric shock had stunned the audience.

Hendrix instantly transformed himself from an average person into a Rock God, tossing thunderbolts into the crowd, dripping with charisma and a magical aura that seemed to surround him. He appeared to melt into the guitar, and vice versa, the two becoming one organism, twisting, turning, and gyrating in the most sensual and sexual mannerisms. It was like he was making love to the instrument, its feedback blaring like an orgasm. The music that came flying off the stage, with Mitch Mitchell on drums and Noel Redding on bass, was incandescent. No one had ever seen or heard anything like it. No fancy lights were needed. We wouldn't have even noticed if they were there. This was beyond a performance—the Jimi Hendrix Experience was a *happening*.

Hendrix was like a shaman hypnotizing his followers. We were all spellbound. The music got so wild that many audience members began to walk down the aisles toward the stage, as if Hendrix was somehow beckoning them to come closer. All of a sudden, thirty kids jumped into the fountain at the front of the stage and started dancing in the water. Someone at the Hollywood Bowl must have figured that the best way to get the kids out was to turn on the fountain, so they did—and then sixty more kids jumped in! By the end of the concert, Gari and I were at the edge of that fountain, getting splashed by soaked, dancing kids as we swayed to the music, our minds blown.

Hendrix took a moment to address the crowd. 'Hey, be careful not to splash any water up here. There's lots of wires and electrical stuff. That could be dangerous.' Then he and the guys went right on playing.

Emulating the Jimi Hendrix look, I wore white bellbottoms with a blue scarf tied around one leg and a new pair of white bucks (suede shoes). I'd been careful the whole evening to make sure no one stepped on my shoes, but now my treasured white bucks were being trashed by the water and the crowd stepping all over them. And yet, I could have cared less. The Jimi Hendrix Experience was just that—a mind-blowing, mind-expanding adventure. Gari and I and the rest of the crowd had been teleported to a whole other place.

Just when I thought we had reached the pinnacle of euphoria, Hendrix laid down his white Fender Stratocaster, poured lighter fluid all over it, and lit a match. Flames immediately shot up into the air. He got down on his knees and coaxed the fire with his hands to rise ever higher. It must have reached eight feet or more, smoke billowing as the feedback blared relentlessly through the Marshall amps behind him. The band continued to play furiously. That's when the crowd totally lost it—over and out!—minds and bodies exploding from within just like the original Big Bang when the universe was created.

At that moment, things started to get way out of control, but the venue's security staff were powerless to do anything about it. The crowd had taken over the Hollywood Bowl. Now everyone was leaving their seats, moving as close to the stage as possible, grooving with the music. It got so intense that I pulled Gari out of the fray to the right-side aisle, fearing we'd both get hurt in the melee. We watched what was left of the show from there, then left the concert speechless, entranced. Hendrix was clearly on another planet, and he'd just taken all of us on a ride there with him.

In the years since, I've seen hundreds and hundreds of shows by all the greats—Bob Dylan, The Rolling Stones, The Who, Cream, Pink Floyd, Bruce Springsteen, you name it—but I've never seen anything close to what I experienced that evening. There's Jimi Hendrix, then there's a space, then there's everybody else. The same goes for his records. Listen to *Are You Experienced*, *Axis: Bold As Love*, and *Electric Ladyland*, preferably with headphones—nothing comes close.

Gari wound up moving to Santa Barbara to attend college, and the long-distance relationship didn't work out. It seemed like our timing was off somehow. The long, arduous phone calls were getting incredibly expensive and wearing us both out. In the end, she was the one to break it off, and I found myself back on the grieving end of a relationship. It didn't hurt any less than my breakup with Sharon, but one of life's great lessons is that the second one isn't nearly as bad as the first. Having been through one, you know you will make it out alive.

I took my broken heart out to a jetty at one of my favorite surf spots and sat on the end, watching the waves come in. At least I looked cool, sitting there wearing a striking white heavy-knit turtleneck sweater and smoking cigarettes. And the brooding, brokenhearted, tortured soul part played well in the creative artistic lifestyle I was leading. Cue 'Walk Away Renee' by The Left Banke.

FREE RECORDS &
SAVAGE WINOS

I CREDIT MY MOM with me getting into UCLA. I left high school with a B+ average—not high enough for me to be able to consider a major university—and was all set to go to Cal State Northridge. But she told me UCLA was not just looking for A+ eggheads but also for well-rounded, interesting people. She encouraged me to write about all my extracurricular activities in the essay section of the application form. I was totally shocked when I received my acceptance letter. Mom had been right.

I immediately joined the AEPi fraternity and was elected to be RF chairman ('Rat Fink' or 'Rat Fucker') of my pledge class. My job was to come up with plots to harass the brothers of the house, and my claim to fame was building an impenetrable stainless-steel ice chest that held two giant Cadillac horns and a car battery. After attaching a secret switch that only worked one way (once you turned it on, there was no way to shut it off), the thing was welded shut and chained to the third-floor landing of the house at 3am. When we flipped that switch and those horns went off, the blast was so excruciatingly loud that it woke up not just everyone in the fraternity house but the entire neighborhood! People were running out of their apartments and the other frat houses in their pajamas, screaming at the top of their lungs.

'TURN THAT FUCKING THING OFF!'

The university police came. Finally, the president of the fraternity, Harold Moskowitz, beat the chest to death with a sledgehammer. What a night.

Loud music and rebellion were a big part of my college experience. I marched in protest movements against the Vietnam War, in support of the Chicago 8, and for civil rights. And building the reputation of AEPi's ultimate RF Chairman led me to a host of other pranks.

I was beginning to learn blues guitar, and I had a stack of amps in my fraternity bedroom. One of them was a Fender Dual Showman that boasted two fifteen-inch speakers. The sound was very loud and VERY BIG.

Every so often, early in the morning, I would place the large amp on the roof ledge outside my second-floor window, which faced Dykstra Hall, the large dorm across the street. I had a microphone and a record player hooked up to the amp, which allowed me to 'serenade' the dormies. My record of choice was 'Muleskinner Blues' by The Fendermen, a wonderfully loud and obnoxious piece of music with lots of howling.

'GOOD MORNING, CAPTAIN! GOOD MORNING TO YOU . . . HA, HA . . . HA, HA, HA, HA!'

I would put my microphone through a reverb unit, adding some great echo on my voice, and yell into the amp at the top of my lungs.

'Good Morning, Dykstra Hall! Time To wake up!'

Then I'd play the record at concert volume. It blared across Gayley Avenue, shaking the birds out of their trees. Again, the university police showed up, but by then I'd have hidden all the gear in separate pieces in other brothers' rooms. The cops would bust into my space and find me sitting and reading one of my philosophy books. I would stare at them casually, as if nothing had happened.

'What's up?'

'Didn't you hear that loud music?'

'Nope.'

It drove 'em nuts.

Every so often, I could also be seen sneaking into the school canteen, selecting Moby Grape's 'Omaha' on the jukebox, turning the thing up to ten, and running out again. Talk about loud—I would hear '*Listen my friends . . .*' halfway across campus as the canteen folks tried to figure out where the volume knob was. For anyone who cares to know, it's a very tiny switch at the bottom in the back of the thing. Not easily found—probably to dissuade people such as myself from messing with it.

• • •

For my first two years at UCLA, I did okay, getting mostly Bs and Cs in my classes. My junior year was when I discovered philosophy, and I found it utterly fascinating. At the time, the existentialists were in vogue—Sartre, Camus, Bishop Berkeley. Their ideas were incredibly stimulating, and they fit right in with the mind-expansion consciousness of the day. I got straight As, except in logic, which I barely passed with a D. I later felt that almost failing that class helped prepare me for the record business, which ran so much on whims and ego that logic never seemed to get in the way.

My love for drawing came in handy, too, and I became a successful cartoonist for the student newspaper, the *Daily Bruin*. I excelled in social sarcasm about the counterculture and other happenings on campus. Later, when I became a college rep for Columbia Records, my cartoon characters would appear in the ads I did for the label.

Most importantly, I joined a fabled punk band called Mogan David & His Winos, formed by a very talented writer, Harold Bronson, who contributed music articles to the *Daily Bruin* and would later write for *Rolling Stone*, the *Los Angeles Times*, and more. He would also go on to become the co-creator and co-owner of the Rhino Records label.

We called ourselves a Jewish punk rock band long before the word 'punk' was adopted by the music industry. We were one of the first bands to record, manufacture, and release our own album, *Savage Young Winos*, which was a send-up of rock in general. The cover is the spitting image of the *Savage Young Beatles* album with Pete Best on drums, and we made it a fold-out in imitation of The Who's *Live At Leeds*, replete with paper inserts that included my UCLA Music 1 final with a big 'F' circled across the top. (Yes, though I'd learned how to play guitar by ear, I was terrible at the math that plays into music theory, and I flunked Music 1.)

With little to no money, we had to be creative. Our drummer, my good friend Al Albert, worked in a recording studio during the day, and we'd sneak in at night to make our record. And not being able to afford proper typesetting, we hand-typed all of the liner notes in prepared columns that would later be photographed. By now, I had started working part-time at Columbia—more on that later—so we snuck into the offices after hours and used the copy machine to reproduce our inserts. We made a thousand albums with nine inserts each—nine thousand inserts in total. We spent many hours in the copy room.

That album has gone on to become a kind of cult classic. A recent auction on eBay had thirty-nine bidders, with the winning bid at $133.50. The original Beatles album we emulated sells for $65. Go figure.

The Winos did some pretty cool stuff. The band did a cover of *Mad Magazine*'s 'Nose Job,' which made it into the all-time Top 50 novelty songs chart on Dr. Demento's radio show. On 'The Berkowitz Blues'—written for Stan Berkowitz, the entertainment editor for the *Daily Bruin*—instead of playing a pentatonic blues scale on the guitar, I played the lead solo on a typewriter. You get the same blues feel—slow, fast, staccato—but instead of notes, you hear *click, click, click, click . . . space . . . click-click*! Frank Zappa would be proud.

A special moment for us was a live performance in the backyard of Shelly Heber, one of the gals who did the charts for *Billboard* magazine, for a group of friends and hip Hollywood types. We got a great recording out of it, albeit on cassette. I managed to lay down a blistering solo on our version of 'Communication Breakdown.' A highlight for the band was a review by Harvey Kubernik of the *Hollywood Press*, who wrote that our version of the song 'makes like a Tijuana taxi next to the Zep's own donkey of a rendering, if their BBC-Live bootleg is any indication.'

• ● •

My life would change forever with a single phone call during my junior year at UCLA. I was still in the AEPi fraternity but no longer living in the house. One sunny day, a fraternity brother spied me sitting on the steps of the student union and handed me a small piece of paper with a phone number on it. Columbia Records was looking for a college representative—someone to work part-time, bringing the label's music to the college radio station, getting reviews for new albums in the *Daily Bruin*, putting up displays in Westwood Village record stores, and advocating for concerts on campus.

'We figure that's you,' he said.

I had played some of the dances for the fraternity with pickup bands—and I'd kept the brothers up late at night, listening to me practice—so I guess it wasn't too hard to figure out who to give that phone number to. But though I was well versed in who played in what bands, I knew absolutely nothing about the music business—or how any business was conducted, for that matter. I was also skeptical about working for a big corporation, coming from the hippie point of view of working communally instead of competitively in a capitalistic society.

I remember like it was yesterday the initial conversation I had with Bob Moering, who would become my first boss at Columbia Records. I was a bit full of myself, but luckily, he saw past that.

'Hi, my name is Paul Rappaport, and I was given this number to call you about a part-time job at Columbia.'

'Yes, that's right, son. We're looking for someone who is very much involved in the new music that's being made these days.'

'Well, that could be me. I'm heavy into Bob Dylan, Janis Joplin, The Rolling Stones, Jeff Beck, Jimi Hendrix, and everyone else. I'm also a serious blues guitar player.' (Actually, I was still just learning, but I wanted him to know what a big role music played in my life.)

'Well, you sound just right for the job, son, and guess what? You will get to work with all the stars.'

Bob must have thought that fame was the big calling card, but not for me.

'Fuck the stars, man,' I told him. 'I'm not interested in all that glitz—just a serious musician and a lover of music, wondering how all this would work out.'

I can't believe I said that to him. Being ill-mannered is not my way, but I guess it just came tumbling out because I was desperate to keep the music thing pure while trying to wrap my head around working for The Man. Even though Columbia Records was selling art, it was still a corporation, and my radical liberal self was wondering if I wanted to cross that line.

'How much time will it take a week? I'm also a philosophy major, and I'm serious about my education.'

Bob seemed perturbed, as if wondering why he was having to talk someone *into* working for a record company. But he was patient with me, and he continued, telling me the various things that I would be expected to do and what I'd get in return.

'You get $15.00 a week, you get all the records you want for free . . . you get a stereo, you get—'

'What?!' I immediately interrupted. 'Did you just say I get all my records for free?'

'Yes, and you get a stereo and a camera . . .'

'You can keep the camera—are you saying I get *all my records for free*? I mean, like, Columbia is a big label—you guys have Bob Dylan, The Byrds, Janis Joplin . . . hell, you guys have Miles Davis!'

'Yes, that's right son, and all the other label personnel in town share their records with each other as well.'

'Are you kidding me? I'm in! I'm your man! *Definitely!* Where are you located? I'm coming over right now.'

'No, son,' he chuckled. 'Don't come now, I'm very busy. Come a week from today, next Wednesday.'

'Are you sure? You have to *promise me* you will not give this job to anyone else until you meet me.'

Free records. Hundreds of them, if not thousands. My imagination hit slot-machine tilt. My hippie ideals were beginning to vanish as I rationalized my way through this thought process. If working for a record company meant you could get all your records for free, even though it was a big corporation, it couldn't be all that bad, right?

'Don't worry,' Moering assured me. 'Just come next Wednesday at 10am. Here's my address.'

• ● •

Back in 1969, I was driving a bright yellow 1967 fastback Mustang with mag wheels. It had a 390 engine, and I'd been a bit of a street racer until I got stopped by a cop doing 110 miles an hour on the San Diego freeway, racing a GTO. I know someone was watching over me that day, as the cop let me off the hook as long as I promised I'd never race again—street justice, the way it ought to be. As much as I wanted to speed my way to Columbia Records that day, I kept my promise and just smiled and waved to the couple of guys in hot cars who wanted to get it on.

I walked into the lobby of 6430 Sunset Boulevard, which was simply a floor of elevators at the foot of a fourteen-story building with black tinted windows. It looked pretty hip—like something important was inside. I wound up waiting for the elevator next to a guy who was quite small in stature but looked exactly like Eric Burdon from The Animals.

'Hey, are you Eric Burdon?' I asked.

'Yeah.'

'Wow. Cool. Nice to meet ya.'

He looked so much bigger on TV, but even so: this was a portent of a great day.

The Columbia Records office took up half a floor overlooking Sunset Boulevard. It had pretty conservative décor, as far as the desks and chairs were concerned, but there were cool posters on the walls of all the label's recording artists. As I peered past some of the offices doors I could see gold records on display, which gave the place the feel of the real deal. The secretaries were all dressed in fashionable 60s garb and looked hipper than the men, so I could see why Columbia might be looking for someone like me. Most of these guys seemed to be from the 50s, whereas I was part of the new music scene.

Bob was a jovial guy, conservatively dressed, and just a tad plump with a boyish face. He seemed to get a kick out of the way I looked, with my huge Afro (or Jewfro), mustache, and goatee. As we sat and talked, I felt he could see that I was a good guy, had my head screwed on straight, and would be reliable. He had fun telling me some of his old war stories about being in the Navy, and the antics they would pull on the new recruits when they were out at sea. Bob had been a rebel and a prankster in his own way, and I immediately related to him. He talked about how the seasoned sailors would trick the new recruits by telling them to stay up all night and watch for the 'mail buoy,' kidding them that that was how ships got their mail in the middle of the Pacific Ocean, or ask them to run down below decks and bring up the 'saltwater' soap.

After some laughs, Bob suggested we begin right away. He told me that Columbia had a new band, Santana. Their first album was soon to be released and they were booked to play the Santa Monica Civic Auditorium. He instructed me to bring advance pressings of the album to KLA, the

UCLA radio station, and to the *Daily Bruin*. He also wanted to put some 'spots' on the radio to help get the word out.

Ha, I thought to myself. *'Spots' on a radio—just like the saltwater soap. You won't fool me with that one, Moering.*

A call came in that Bob said was private, and he asked if I could leave the office for a few minutes. I walked out and closed the door behind me. As I continued down the hall, I saw a young-looking, handsome guy sitting behind a desk in one of the offices to my right. He looked like the spitting image of Michael Clarke from The Byrds, with the same kind of long, light brown Beatles haircut. He wore a thick white turtleneck sweater and brown suede jacket—classic 60s attire. He was easily the hippest-looking guy on the floor. He motioned for me to come into his office.

'You must be the new college rep, right? Hi, my name is Richard. I just got the job to be the new local promotion manager for Epic Records,' he said, referring to Columbia's sister label. He motioned again to me, this time to close the door. Then he pointed to his desk, where I saw a small mirror and four long lines of white powder.

'Do you know what this is?' he asked.

'Cocaine?' I answered tentatively. I knew a lot about marijuana, but I'd never seen cocaine before.

'Yep. Wanna try some?'

'Sure,' I said, trying to sound nonchalant, but secretly a little apprehensive.

'Here,' he said, handing me a rolled-up dollar bill in the shape of a straw. 'You need to snort one line into each nostril.'

I did. It burned a tad, but other than that, I didn't feel a thing.

By now, Moering was calling me back into his office, so I thanked Richard very much and walked back down the hall, thinking to myself, *Okay, what's the big deal about coke*. I sat down in front of Bob, and all of a sudden, my head exploded. The stuff had taken a minute or two to kick in, but now I was rushing like I was on speed. At first, it felt like a Dexi (which I'd take now and then to stay up all night to study). But now I felt like I was in a dragster shot out of a canon going from zero to two hundred miles an hour. I also felt euphoric and exhilarated—like the king of the world. But I was going so fast that my mind was having trouble keeping things straight.

What an idiot, I thought. *I just got here, and I'm trying to make a good impression. What the hell was I thinking?*

I took some deep breaths, asked for some water, and tried to get it together. Then I asked for a pad and pen and for Bob to repeat everything he wanted me to do so that I would not forget anything important.

Two seminal things happened that day. The first was that I learned to make a detailed list of everything I needed to do for any project so that nothing could ever be missed. It's one of the most valuable tools I've kept with me my whole life. Whether it's a small promotion or a major television special, I imagine the event from beginning to end and make a list of *everything* we need, right down to the smallest details. Then I just go down the checklist, one by one. That way, you can't miss—it's the path to total perfection.

The second thing was, I had acquired a taste for cocaine. First day on the job—welcome to the record business!

• ● •

I went back to the office the next week, and Bob seemed very happy as I went down my checklist of accomplishments.

'What about the spots?' he asked.

'Ha, ha, Bob, you thought you were gonna get me on that one, right? Spots on the radio, ha, ha. Just like the mail buoy and the saltwater soap.'

'You mean you *didn't* put Santana spots on the radio?'

Uh-oh. It seemed like there really was a thing called spots.

'*Commercial advertisement spots*, Paul—for TV and radio. We call them *spots* for short.'

Bob looked a bit disgusted, and I felt a bit foolish. We both realized that even though I knew a lot about the music, I had a lot to learn about the business. Another seminal lesson: whatever you do, *never* assume anything. If you're not sure, ask.

Aside from that little glitch, though, my first year as a Columbia college rep was great. I quickly began to see how the record business worked, and I also got to meet two of my biggest musical heroes, Miles Davis and Michael Bloomfield.

I met Miles when his 1970 septet played UCLA's Royce Hall. I went backstage to introduce myself as the Columbia rep and ask if he needed anything. I was a little scared about doing so, as Miles had a bad reputation for blowing off white folks. I had once dated a girl whose father told me he tried to buy Miles a drink as he came off the stand one night after a club performance.

'Miles,' he began, 'you're my all-time favorite artist in the world. Can I buy you a drink?'

'Get away from me, white boy!' Miles replied nastily.

'Gee whiz, Miles, why do you want to have a chip on your shoulder?'

'It's not a chip, it's a Redwood.'

Thankfully, this time was different. Maybe it was because I looked cool with my Afro and goatee; maybe it was because I had a genuine nature. Whatever the case, when I walked slowly into his dressing room, he looked up as if to say, 'It's okay, come on in.'

Miles looked busy, flitting from one side of the room to the other, viewing music charts, the stage plot. His mind was preoccupied, and I could tell there was a big work ethic at play. He was preparing for his performance, and his attention to detail was impressive.

I wanted to ask him a question or two about music, but he seemed so busy I didn't want to distract him. So, I simply introduced myself as the UCLA Columbia Records college rep and asked if I could get him some water or anything he might need. I cringed a bit inside, not knowing what to expect, but he gave me a big smile that made my month.

'No, I'm cool,' he said in his distinguished raspy voice. I wished him a great show, he thanked me, and I walked out of the dressing room on cloud nine. My meeting with Miles had been brief, but I'd seen how a professional musician goes about his business, and I could tell my friends forever that I'd met the master, he'd been nice to me, and that he was very cool indeed. Miles's performance that night was one of the greatest shows I've ever seen in my life.

Meanwhile, as I've mentioned already, I was trying to learn blues guitar the way I was hearing it on record, with the notes somehow magically sustaining, screaming through the amps in a very big and bold way. So, I was very excited when Columbia's Electric Flag showed up to play a noontime concert at UCLA's Ackerman Union Grand Ballroom. I'd been a huge fan of the band's guitarist, Michael Bloomfield, ever since I was turned on to the early Paul Butterfield albums.

The keyboard player, Barry Goldberg, was late, so Bloomfield stepped up to the microphone to make an announcement—and ask for help.

'Hey our keyboard guy is late, can anyone out there, play keys?'

Yep, those were the days—everything was much simpler and relaxed. A couple of guys raised their hands and were ushered backstage.

Upon hearing his own voice through the PA system, Bloomfield added, 'Hey, this PA sounds really shitty! Isn't this UCLA? Don't you guys have a lot of money?' He was notorious for always telling it like it was, without a filter (not to mention the opposite—telling tall tales).

Goldberg finally showed up, and the band began to play. I was up close, my eyes fixed on Bloomfield. I wanted to learn his hidden secrets. He was playing a 1959 Les Paul, and at the time I had no idea what that meant or how important it was to getting the sound he was achieving. He was also plugged into a pair of Fender Twin Reverb amplifiers using a Y jack, with other assorted smaller boutique amps added for flavor—there must have been five amps in all. It was loud, but he had incredible tone and a wonderful feel for the music.

Bloomfield had a style where he'd kind of bend over with his body and gently cradle the guitar in his hands, lifting it up slightly, cradling it like a baby, all the while coaxing the most amazing notes and phrases from the instrument. He could make you feel sadness, self-righteousness, and even exhilarated, just in the way he bent the notes and altered the volume.

When the show was over, I went backstage to meet him. He was dressed in a blue work shirt, faded blue jeans, and brown loafers with no socks. As with Miles, I introduced myself as the Columbia college rep, then asked him the thing I'd been dying to know.

'Hey, man, how do you get that long sustain on those notes?'

'It's all in the fingers, man,' he replied. 'All in the fingers.'

I thought at the time he was just playing 'rock star' on me, so I thanked him and left. Then, when I got back to my room at the frat, I tried to emulate what I'd seen him do. I turned all my amps up to max volume, plugged in my Rickenbacker, and hit some notes while gently wiggling my finger up and down. Lo and behold, it was the vibrato of wiggling your finger that made the notes sustain. (A good dose of volume didn't hurt, either.)

Holy shit! It was a lightbulb revelation. Bloomfield hadn't been egoing out on me—he was trying to teach me something. I ran out of the fraternity house and back to campus, trying to make it to the ballroom in time to see him again. All the way across campus, I was yelling at the top of my lungs, 'It's in the fingers, it's in the fingers!'

Of course, by the time I got back to the ballroom, sweaty and winded, Bloomfield was long gone, but I had learned a huge secret. Later on, I would learn what a Les Paul was, and how important that particular guitar was to the sound of the blues—and to rock music as well. My best friend, Jades bassist Frank Shargo, gave me his Gibson Melody Maker to continue my quest. It wasn't quite a Les Paul, but it gave some great sustain, and I began to sound much more like the bluesmen I was listening to.

ONE OF THE GANG

IN THE SUMMER OF 1970, Columbia Records' LA branch hired me for a full-time position, even though I still had one year left in school. I had done all that was asked of me as a college rep and more, and now I would continue with those duties while also working in the mail room.

By now, I had discovered that Bob Moering and his sidekick, Terry Powell, were the hottest promotion men in town. Bob was in charge of album promotion and serviced all the different radio formats. He would bring at least three or four albums apiece to stations like KMPC-FM, which played easy listening—show tunes, jazz, pop, and light rock—and to the country, jazz, and classical stations, as well as the new FM underground formats like KMET-FM and KPPC-FM, which played countercultural rock music. He interacted with these stations' music directors (MDs) and program directors (PDs), giving them helpful information about how an album was recorded and inside insights about the artists who made the music. The MDs picked the songs to play; the PDs guided the choices and were also in charge of the air talent and overall sound of the station.

Terry, affectionately known as TP, was small in stature but loomed large in personality. 'The beauty is on duty!' he would announce as he entered a room. Indeed, he was a good-looking guy. He brought 45rpm singles to Top 40 AM stations like KHJ, KFWB, and KRLA and also to some of the formats Bob worked, as the release of singles often preceded an album. Terry would apprise the MDs and PDs of how these songs were moving up the charts at other similar radio stations around the country to prove why a record deserved to be added to their playlists.

Bob and Terry had become celebrities within the industry. They even had a billboard on the Sunset Strip. Yep, you would be driving down Sunset Boulevard, looking up at huge images of the major recording stars and their new album releases, and there, right in the middle of Neil Diamond and Barbara Streisand, would be Bob and TP, smiling down at you, holding a bunch of Columbia albums and singles, with a big headline that read 'The Innovators.'

Bob and Terry took me under their wings and taught me the business. I distinctly remember Terry telling me, 'Work hard, keep your nose clean, and you'll come out smelling like a rose.' Traveling with them to learn the job, I noticed how excited they got when discussing an artist and their recordings with the radio folks. Beyond just bringing the music to these stations, it was their job to influence these programmers to add *their* records before a competitor's. With so many record companies releasing so many albums and singles each week, it was more competitive out there than I ever knew.

Alongside doing the job, I could see that endearing oneself to these people might give you a leg up on getting your records added ahead of everyone else. Terry was a natural comedian. He used to pal around with Epic Records' promotion man, Mike Atkinson, who was known around town as 'Dr. A.' Mike was about the same height as Terry, and they were like the dynamic duo when it came to visiting the Top 40 stations in town. These stations' MDs would see record label promotion men and women on Mondays and decide what they were adding to their playlists on Tuesdays. Mike and Terry, both having larger-than-life personalities, would go into the MDs' offices, play the current records they were working, and then tell jokes or do skits like a stand-up comedy act. Everyone loved them.

The music business is a very social business—a business of relationships and favors. Even more so back in the 70s and 80s. On any given night after work, you could find most of LA's promotion men and women hanging out at the local restaurant/bar called Martoni's, buying dinner and drinks for the scores of disc jockeys, musicians, writers, and other music business types that would frequent the place. One of Bob's regular guests was Johnny Magnus, the legendary 'Prince Of Darkness' who did the evening shift on KMPC and played a fair amount of jazz. Magnus had become so popular that in the early 1960s, Quincy Jones wrote a song about him, 'Nasty Magnus,' which Count Basie recorded. Magnus and I would eventually become buddies.

What a scene. The place was always packed, everybody knew everybody, and there was even a famous waiter who called himself 'Crazy Lenny.' Lenny was gay and very proud of it. He pushed his colorful personality to the limits, swishing and swaggering about, and would perform sensual antics like sticking his tongue deep into a shot glass and rolling it around as if it were in another place. You get the idea. He was always super kind, especially to any of us new kids just entering the business. He made us feel like we belonged. Lenny hosted a private room that you could request for special occasions when you were entertaining someone heavy—think Frank Sinatra. He also used to carry some very powerful illegal booze in small bottles hidden in his pockets—over one hundred percent proof. I remember he once pulled me out in the back alley and said, 'Try this.' The label read *Hot Bananas*. All I know is, after one shot I was having trouble remembering my name.

Besides Martoni's, I was lucky enough to experience some of Hollywood's famous haunts that were synonymous with Tinseltown's golden age. The original Brown Derby restaurant, which looked like a giant derby hat, was still there and was a hang for all the Hollywood film stars and movie people who had their caricatures hung all over the walls. It was quite hip to say, 'Meet me at the Derby for lunch.'

Perino's also catered to the Hollywood elite—Bette Davis had a booth permanently reserved there. Those booths were what it was all about: they were elegantly designed couches with high backs tufted in plush dark maroon velvet that wrapped around the patrons like half a clam shell. Drinks were served in dark Prussian blue glasses. The whole place was a work of art—the food, the drinks, the décor. Everything was a feast for the senses, and all of it signified glamour and sophistication.

We went to Chasen's for their famous chili, and to Villa Capri, a quaint Italian restaurant hidden near the Hollywood Hills that only the in-crowd knew about. Movie stars like James Dean, Marilyn Monroe, and Jimmy Durante would go there, and word was it was also a hangout for the mob. Frank Sinatra, who recorded at Capitol Records just a few blocks away, often used the restaurant as his personal clubhouse, goofing around and singing at the piano bar with pals like Sammy Davis Jr., Nat King Cole, and Lauren Bacall.

Once, when Sharon and I were having dinner there, we saw Sinatra at the bar, motionless, staring down at a shot of whiskey. He was big then—overweight—and dressed in all black. Everyone was keeping their distance, including the bartender. Sinatra never picked up the glass. I kept glancing over while we were eating, but he never budged an inch—he just kept staring at that glass like it was some kind of crystal ball that might offer him an answer. Whatever was going on, it was pretty heavy. Eventually, I looked up again and he was gone—vanished.

Besides wining and dining the radio folks at all these fancy restaurants, we also took them all to see our new artists at the local clubs like the Whisky A Go-Go, the Troubadour, and the Ash Grove. We gave them front-row seats at the Hollywood Bowl and the Greek Theater to see superstar artists like Neil Diamond, Johnny Mathis, and Chicago. But far beyond trying to butter someone up with perks in hopes they would choose to play a Columbia record over the competition, we became good friends with many of these people. I found that if you genuinely cared about them, their jobs, their radio stations, and even their families, a true bond could be established that went a long way when a business decision had to be made. Yes, there was due diligence being done to prove that the records were worthy of airplay, but in the end, the truth is that people play records for people, and a people person could go far in the job of promotion.

• ● •

One of the most important events during this part of my life was my first meeting with Tony Bennett. I certainly wouldn't have guessed it beforehand, me thinking of myself as a rock guy and all, but I was amazed to discover that he was one of the coolest people on the planet.

I was doing well in my job but still questioning how I might fit into the business side of the music industry. Most of the people I'd met in the business were great fun, but they came from another era. It was the *atmosphere* of the entertainment business that excited them most, along with all the perks that went with it. But for me, and others of my generation, it was the music that mattered most. It spoke our truth, characterized our lives, and we were attached to it in an unprecedented way.

I felt out of place. Parts of the music business seemed so disingenuous that I wondered if I even wanted to be in it at all. I loved the music so much, but the business? I had the hippie mentality of being cool and genuine. Could the people I was dealing with relate to me? Could I be successful in the record business with my style and who I was as a person? I was still coming to grips with working for The Man and trying to figure out how to fit in—or if I was even meant to fit in.

This struggle went on for quite a while, until I went to a party late one evening in February of 1971, thrown by Columbia in a swanky hotel at one of Hollywood's famous haunts to celebrate the release of Tony Bennett's new album, *Love Story*. Many of the young movers and shakers who would eventually play big roles in the music industry were present. There also appeared to be a fair number of hangers-on who may or may not have had important enough jobs to warrant them being there. But the biggest thing I noticed about the event was everyone seemed to be there solely for the party. They were not necessarily interested in Tony's new album. The whole thing seemed to lack any real connection with the artist or his music.

Feeling disheartened and frustrated by this, I decided to talk with Tony about it. I waited for the party to end, and when everyone had left, I introduced myself to him. All of my pent-up feelings came tumbling out of my mouth, seemingly without a filter.

'Hi, Tony, my name is Paul Rappaport, and right now I'm the college rep for Columbia at UCLA. I need to ask you some questions, if I could. This whole party seemed so fake to me, so *Hollywood*. I think you've made a really cool album, but I don't think many of these people have even heard it. It's like they just came for the party, taking advantage, eating your food and drinking your booze.' I knew that though Columbia had thrown the party, it would be written down as a marketing expense and charged back against Tony's royalties.

'I'm new to all this,' I continued, 'and I love music so much, but I don't know if my style can fit in—sometimes it seems like so much bullshit to me, and I can't be that.'

Tony was still in his ascot-and-pipe phase, and he looked very dapper indeed. I was expecting him to have a very sophisticated vocabulary to match. Instead, he looked down and said, 'You know, Paul, sometimes it can get pretty fucked up.'

I was in shock. *Oh my God, this guy is so cool.* Tony went on to point out that parts of the business were fabulous, but that yes, some of it was total bullshit. And, after recording and performing for over twenty years, he had seen it all.

'Let me tell you a story,' he said. 'I had built a great career, but one day the music began to change around me. I found my style out of step with what was considered *popular music*. I thought I should change my style to keep up, so I went to see my friend, the great Duke Ellington, for advice. This is what he told me. *Tony, you are a great artist with a gift, a voice with a particular sound and style like no other. You will always have this gift, but if you change, you are going to lose yourself. You are like a great apple. Don't try and change yourself into an orange—you won't be able to do it, and it won't work for you. And you are the greatest Tony Bennett apple we've got! In this business, moods and styles change, but you shouldn't. Things cycle around—just continue to do what you do, and the world will eventually turn back your way. You will be seen and heard again, as you deserve.*'

Tony then turned his attention back to me.

'Paul, you seem like a great guy with a strong passion for music, which is the most important thing in this business. So, I will give you the same advice Duke gave me. Just be who you are, and you will learn to do the business part your way. You do not have to become like other people you see to be successful. In time, you will be seen and appreciated for who you are, and you'll do great.'

I thanked him and left the party feeling like a giant load had been lifted off my shoulders. Little did we both know at the time how incredibly well Duke's advice would play out. Not only did Tony continue to do well in the 70s and 80s, but his appearance on the MTV Awards in 1993 with Red Hot Chili Peppers and his subsequent MTV *Unplugged* album turned on a whole new young fan base to his artistry, catapulting his career into the stratosphere. And I would continue to work my way up the ranks at the LA branch of Columbia Records—and beyond.

Tony was one of our all-time great music treasures, and also one of the most special people I ever had the pleasure to work with. His life would intersect with mine at a most paramount time, just as it was meant to. With his wise guidance, I was able to refocus and put myself on a course that would lead me on the adventure of a lifetime.

• ● •

When I graduated from UCLA, the only uncertainty surrounding my career at Columbia was my draft status. The Vietnam War had taken many lives and Nixon needed more troops. The infamous lottery was announced over the radio, and when they randomly picked birthdates out of a hat, my number came up third. The only thing I'd ever won before that was a big blow-up balloon in the shape of a salami when I entered a local supermarket art contest as a kid. Now I'd won a guaranteed trip to Vietnam. I wasn't sure what it meant after they picked my number—would they come to my house the next day, abduct me, and take me right to the induction center?

Even though I was totally against war in general, I was anxious that I couldn't claim to a judge that I was a consciousness objector. I had told my parents that I knew I was capable of fighting for my country if the chips were down. But there was no way I was going to be used as cannon fodder for the insanity that Vietnam had turned into, especially not for fucking Richard Nixon. Still, I felt bad because my father was a Navy vet who had landed in those seven major invasions in the Pacific fighting for our country. I felt conflicted but also very clear in my resolve. I was going to do whatever it took to avoid the draft.

The people at Columbia Records' Los Angeles branch office had genuinely taken a liking to me, and the feelings were mutual. Bob Moering told me that there was a political storm coming and he was going to leave to work for Warner Bros instead. That would leave his job open, and he told me I should go for it. I told him I wasn't sure about that because, as a musician, I felt I should try to get into the more creative side of the business, like producing records, or at least being an A&R man. Bob gave me a most valuable piece of advice.

'Paul, just get in. Get in however you can, and then down the line you can move laterally however you want, but the hardest thing to do is to get into this business. Columbia is a wonderful company. You'll do great here—take my job.'

Bill Shaler was the new LA branch manager, and he told me that he'd personally hold Bob's job open for me through the summer until we could see if I could avoid the draft. That was huge. The only thing I'll say about it here is that the last day of a grueling few months working with a draft attorney found me in Fairbanks, Alaska, being interrogated by an army psychiatrist—just as out-there, insane, and funny as Arlo Guthrie in the movie *Alice's Restaurant*. But that story is for another time.

I have always felt guilty about not going to Vietnam. As Bruce Springsteen said so eloquently in his Broadway show, not because I felt that it was my duty, but because I never knew who went in my place—but I know someone did.

As for moving forward in any meaningful way with the Winos, I told Harold Bronson I'd been offered a good position at Columbia. I've always loved playing in bands, but Columbia offered security. I began my first prominent job for the label in the fall of 1971 as the album promotion man for LA and the surrounding areas, which included San Diego and Phoenix. I promoted every radio format except R&B, for which there was a separate department.

I hired Harold, who was a year behind me in school, to take my place as the college rep at UCLA. After graduation, however, he found it difficult to land a job in the record company establishment. He was known as a bit of a rebel at a time when the labels were looking for people who would just toe the line. Seeing me now well ensconced at Columbia, he said, 'Okay, if you're gonna do this, I'm gonna go work with Richard Foos at the Rhino Record store in Westwood. He wants to start a label.'

It's fascinating how things can turn out in life, especially if you are lucky enough to find your way—what you are meant to do while you're here on this planet. Harold wasn't meant to work for the establishment, he was meant to create *his own* establishment. He and Richard went on to build one of the most creative and successful record labels ever, and they both became multimillionaires. I would go on to have a great career at Columbia and do quite well for myself too. More importantly, not living life on the road gave us better opportunities to have successful marriages and raise some great kids.

When the Ramones hit big, Harold called me. 'See, this would have been us.' And there's a good chance we could have been. We'll never know for sure, but neither of us are complaining.

• ● •

I did my job just as Bob had taught it to me, but one day, when I was greeted at a big local jazz station with 'Deliveries in the back,' I realized jeans and T-shirts weren't going to cut it anymore. I went out and sprung for some proper clothes. At the time, that meant velour bellbottom pants, paisley shirts, and two-tone platform shoes.

My favorite places to hang out were the FM rock stations: KPPC in Pasadena, KMET in Los Angeles, and KNAC in Long Beach. In the beginning, they were known as underground radio stations because, unlike the Top 40 pop stations, they played all of the new, under-the-radar artists—Pink Floyd, The Who, The Kinks, The Move, Traffic, Jimi Hendrix. Unlike the big Top 40 stations, these new stations had very small budgets; KPPC even started out in the basement of a church, which may have contributed to the original 'underground' moniker. One of the greatest things about these stations was the fidelity you got when you listened to the FM frequency. Unlike AM radio, when you listened to FM you could hear the full round warm tones of all the instruments. And these stations broadcast in stereo, too.

I fit right in with these folks. We were cut from the same cloth. We all looked the same, and the music was *our* music. Even though we did different jobs, we were all on the same mission, to promote this new and exciting music to the world.

I enjoyed listening to the programmers and disc jockeys talk about their visions on how to make great radio, and their aspirations in life. I made many friends and developed long-standing relationships, some of which I still have to this day.

I distinctly remember the first time I did something beyond the norm—the first time I had to think on my feet and make something happen. We had a band called Flash Cadillac & The Continental Kids. They dressed like—and played songs from—the 1950s. They were getting known through their appearance in the movie *American Graffiti* and via some local popular TV shows. But although they were a high-energy live act, the fact that they played 50s covers meant their debut album didn't command quite the same respect as other artists who were building careers on their original material.

Even so, radio stations were somewhat interested, and I had set up an interview at KMET with program director Richard Kimball. The band were due to come to my office, and from there I was going to drive them to the station. Just as they were getting out of the elevators, Richard called and canceled the interview—something had come up, and he felt he no longer wanted to interview them. It wasn't going to be just postponed, it wasn't going to happen, ever.

I felt awful. It was my responsibility to promote and create opportunities for the band, and I didn't want to let them down. I quickly picked up the phone and called the music director of KPPC, who I had become friends with.

'Hey, Peter!' I began, pumping myself to sound as excited as possible. 'You'll never guess who just walked out of the elevator and is heading my way. Flash Cadillac & The Continental Kids! Shit, I can't even believe they're here. Do you want me to see if I can corral them and talk them into driving out to KPPC for an interview?'

My excitement became contagious—now he became excited.

'Wow, do you think you can?'

'Let me see. I'll call you right back.'

The band and their assistant manager strolled into my office. I calmly explained that something had come up at KMET but that I'd switched the interview to KPPC, which I told them was a much hipper station anyway. They loved it.

Off we went, and the folks at KPPC treated them like stars.

Wow, I thought to myself. *I just made something happen out of nothing. I might actually be good at this promotion stuff.*

SPIRIT OF CALIFORNIA

I WAS STILL PRETTY NEW to my job when Randy California, the talented guitarist and writer for the band Spirit, walked into my office holding some big boxes of multitrack tapes. Randy and I had become buddies some years earlier, when I saw Spirit perform at the Kaleidoscope. He and drummer Ed Cassidy (his stepdad) would hang out at the bar in the back of the club while they were waiting for their set, and they were quite approachable. I became a big fan of the band, and sometimes they'd invite me up to their house in Topanga Canyon to watch them practice.

I remember one night at the Topanga house, getting high with the guys on some very powerful marijuana and then, when leaving, having to drive my Mustang in reverse down their very long and narrow driveway, which had a sheer cliff on one side. One false move and you were a goner. It was especially scary while stoned. It seemed to take me forever to inch my way along so slowly in the pitch-black darkness, but I finally made it down to the main road. My heart was still racing as I drove home.

Why the hell did these stoners pick this house to live in? I thought. *With such a ridiculously long skinny driveway and perilous drop?* No one ever perished, so I guess it all worked out.

Spirit were one of the most progressive bands of the day, and Randy was one of the early innovators of creating unique electric guitar sounds. He'd plug his guitar into a small black box that sat on a table next to him. The box was a mystery to everyone. Along with his great songwriting ('I've Got A Line On You,' 'Nature's Way'), he constantly blew minds with the sounds that came out of that magic box.

Randy was highly influenced by Jimi Hendrix, the king of unique electric guitar sounds. They were friends, too, and they'd jammed together quite a bit when Randy played with Jimi in his band Jimmy James & The

Blue Flames. Hendrix used to love to come over to Randy's house because Randy's mom's spaghetti and meatballs was his favorite meal. It's kind of funny to think of him in his outlandish colorful clothing and all his psychedelic glory, sitting down to eat something so basic.

When Hendrix got the offer to go to London, where he formed the Experience, he initially invited Randy to go with him, but Randy's mom thought he was too young and it would be too much for him. I often wonder what would have happened if he'd gone, and how it would have changed rock history.

When he walked into my office that day, Randy was dressed in his usual cool hippie garb, looking very much like Hendrix himself. He dropped the heavy tape boxes down on my desk.

'Here, I'm turning in our record.'

'Randy, I know we're friends and all, but you guys are signed to Epic, and you have to deliver these masters to their A&R department, which is just across the hall.'

'No way, man, they scare me. I'm giving them to you because you're cool.'

At that time, for some of the recording artists who came from the counterculture, the accent was solely on creativity. Their priorities were just making music and living a free life, and they only dealt with the capitalistic 'other world' when they absolutely needed to. They had agents and managers to take care of that stuff. In Ron Wood's autobiography, he talks about himself and other rock notables just driving around in a van, looking for places to play—they could care less about the money during those early years.

No artist I ever met was more of a hippie than Randy California. A beautiful human being, an artist's artist, and one who cared only about making the music. Giving your band's master tapes to someone just because they're cool might sound funny, but it made sense at the time. Randy was turning his creation over to someone from the tribe, someone who could be trusted. His innocence was lovely to behold, even if he seemed a bit naïve.

I assured Randy that the Epic folks were, in fact, very nice people, and that's where the tapes needed to go. But he insisted on leaving them with me. Finally, I took him by the hand and brought him over to Epic. On the way, we had the most remarkable conversation.

I noticed he had a thin high-E electric guitar string looped through his right earlobe like a pirate earring. I asked why he was wearing it.

'I always break an E string at every show,' he said, 'and believe it or not, I can whip this thing out and re-string my guitar faster than any roadie.'

Randy also loved baseball and played for the Topanga Canyon baseball team. He told me that now the record was finished, he was thinking about taking the summer off to play baseball.

'Randy,' I said, 'Epic is going to put this out and want you guys to do a big tour to support the release. What about your priorities?'

His eyes lit up.

'Yeah, Paul, exactly . . . it's baseball season!'

These were the most innocent of times. It wouldn't last forever.

· ● ·

After I started working at Columbia, I would see Sharon's father, Herb Moore, now and then, because he owned the cleaning business where I took my clothes to be laundered. One day, he informed me that Sharon had broken up with her college boyfriend.

'Okay,' I said. Sharon and I hadn't seen each other in so long that I didn't think much of it.

'You should give her a call,' he said.

'Okay,' I answered nonchalantly. I didn't think much past that, either.

I was getting ready to leave with my newly cleaned clothes when he handed me the phone. It was the old black dial type.

'You should call her *now*,' he suggested. 'She's at home.'

I'm not sure what Sharon's parents thought about her former boyfriend, but I knew that they had fond memories of me from our high school days. Either way, when Mr. Moore puts a phone in front of your face and *suggests* that you call his daughter, the words 'no thanks' are not an option.

Truth is, I was kind of curious, so I dialed the number, which I had never forgotten.

'Hi, do you remember me?'

Sharon laughed and knew it was me straight off. I told her what her father had done, and she laughed again. I asked if she wanted to get together, just to say hi. She said yes, and I told her I'd get back to her. A day or two later, I called and asked if she'd like to see the new Lenny Bruce play in Hollywood. She sounded enthusiastic.

As soon as I saw her, all those feelings I'd had for her in high school came rushing back, but this time it was different because we were adults, unhampered by teenage angst. I thought it was the same for her, but I couldn't quite tell because Sharon often plays things pretty close to the vest. A couple of dates later, though, it was apparent that we were both falling back in love, and that we thought the same way about politics and life in general. I asked her if she wanted to be my girlfriend, and she smiled. The surfer girl had morphed into a hippie in patched jeans, her long light-brown hair as beautiful as ever.

Always desperate to remain hip, my biggest fears were getting married, having a dog, and moving to the Valley. I married Sharon. She had a dog. And, after a brief stint living in my apartment in Hollywood, we moved to the Valley. Everything worked out fine.

• ● •

Now that I had a full-time job at Columbia, I could order anything I wanted from CBS Records' deep, rich catalogue of albums (encompassing Columbia, Epic, and other associated labels). I decided to see if the 'get all your records for free' thing really worked. I am a huge rock fan, but I also love jazz, so when I got hold of one of the pink 'gratis order' forms, I listed every single Miles David album on Columbia. There were thirty-six of them at the time.

Ha, I thought, *they're gonna take one look at this and throw it right out.*

I forgot all about the form, and then one day I came back to my apartment at the foot of Laurel Canyon to find a bunch of cardboard boxes in front of my door. I figured they were probably for the guy downstairs at first, but then I saw the label printed on them: 'Phonograph Records.'

Oh my God, really?

I brought the boxes inside and excitedly ripped them open. There they were, as pretty as you please, all thirty-six Miles Davis albums! I couldn't believe it. I sat in the middle of my living room and surrounded myself with these new treasures, marveling at some of the greatest album cover art ever created.

By the time I married Sharon in 1973, I had amassed over ten thousand records. I had no furniture in my apartment, save for a single bed, a small rocking chair, and the stereo Columbia had given me when I was a college rep. But record albums, I had tons of those, and they were scattered everywhere—some on makeshift shelves in my living room, more running down the hallway into my bedroom, and others in the spare room.

Of course, no one can listen to ten thousand albums, and when we finally moved from that apartment—by which time Sharon had also decided it would also be a wonderful idea if we had a kitchen table and chairs—I began to give away a bunch to friends and family. I have been divesting myself of vinyl ever since, but there are still about three thousand records in our downstairs basement, many of them classics with memorable covers. It's time for a new sound system. There is nothing like listening to music with the fidelity of a vinyl record. We used to call it 'black magic,' and it is.

• ● •

The Los Angeles branch office was renowned for being in Hollywood, the epicenter of entertainment, with so much music being made and recorded there, but it also felt like a family. We all looked out for each other; we all felt like we were playing on the same team. In fact, at the time, CBS Records took on the moniker 'The Family Of Music.'

Some of the guys would throw parties at their homes, and the whole branch would be invited: assistants, display and inventory folks, the people from the mailroom, and so on. Everyone brought their wives or significant others too. In those days, most of the people in the business were there because they loved music. Once the party got started and everybody got loose on alcohol and whatever else, a lot of the guys could be found standing in a formation at the head of the living room, perhaps in front of the fireplace, playing percussion instruments along with whatever record was blasting at the time. These were business people, but they were music people first and foremost. Music was in their blood, and they loved expressing themselves this way. When I joined the team, I showed up with my small Fender Champ amp and Gibson Melody Maker and added some power chords and tasty licks to the makeshift bands.

I think all of us appreciating and loving music so much is what made CBS Records such a special place. The artists knew we genuinely cared about them, and the music they were making. We'd always hang out with them before and after their shows.

One of my favorite people at the branch was Randy Brown, a good-looking guy sporting a perfect light brown 60s mop-top hairdo. He looked like the football star John Elway. Randy worked for Epic and was a big-time fisherman. He built his own fishing flies and was always asking us to keep the lead wrappings from the champagne corks we popped so he could fashion them into weights for his flies. Even though Randy worked for Epic, one of his favorite artists was Taj Mahal, who was on Columbia. Randy and I would go backstage to hang out with Taj, and invariably Randy would sheepishly ask him a question.

'Uh . . . hey, Taj, could you please—'

'Play your favorite song?' Taj would interrupt.

'Yeah,' Randy would say, feeling a bit embarrassed.

'Sure, man.'

And Taj would pull out his beautiful silver Dobro guitar and start singing 'Fishin' Blues.

> *Betcha' goin' fishin' all o' da' time,*
> *Baby goin' fishin' too . . .*

And that's what it was all about. An artist like Taj Mahal might be about to go onstage or might have just finished a set, but he would still sit down, have a chat, and play a song just for two record guys who loved him and were a part of his family of music.

One day, Taj showed up at the branch with a giant Austrian flat-backed acoustic upright bass. It was unusual for an artist to bring such an instrument to a sales office—that sort of thing usually happened down the street at CBS Recording Studios. But he dragged it right into the mailroom and started playing. The whole office stopped, listened, and looked at each other.

What the f—?

I thought it was really cool, so I got out an acoustic guitar, went in, and somehow had the balls to start jamming with him. Every so often I'd look up, see who I was playing with, get starstruck, and just stop. After about thirty minutes, Taj looked up and spoke to me.

'What's wrong with you? You seem like you know where you're going, and then all of a sudden you stop.'

'Yeah, well, that's because when I look up and see that it's *you* I'm playing with, I get nervous.'

'Well, hey,' he said, 'that's *your* problem.'

I didn't understand this at the time, but years later, I got to play alongside some of the greatest artists in the world—Little Feat's groove master bassist Kenny Gradney; Steve Perry from Journey; and David Gilmour, Nick Mason, and Richard Wright from Pink Floyd. What I learned was that no matter who it is, when you are playing, it's just musicians talking to each other in music-speak—if you're a good enough player, they view you as an equal. You just have to get past the starstruck part and play, because they're not even thinking about that—they're just lost in the music.

I remember once, being at a rehearsal with Perry when he was making a solo album.

'Come on, Rap, grab one of my guitar player's axes, I know you can blow.'

It made me feel like a million bucks and put everything into perspective.

'Okay, here we go, blues in A-minor . . .'

• ● •

The LA branch's salesmen were fabled, too—in fact, they had a nickname, 'The Wrecking Crew.' They worked hard and they partied hard. The oldest of them was Clyde Jackson, aka 'White Moses,' who sported a decent amount of beautiful silver hair wrapped around a slightly tanned bald head. Clyde had worked for Columbia for so long that he remembered the days when someone would order albums and he'd have to glue the covers together and place the vinyl inside before delivering them.

Neil Hartley was a well-rounded family man, probably old enough to be my dad. His son, Mark, was my age. and he became a local Columbia promotion man and was one of my early running mates. Even though he was older, Neil was so cool that I always asked for him to be my roommate at our national conventions. He could cut loose with the best of them, and he used to run with Willie Nelson and his gang. He was also known as one of the all-time greatest salesmen Columbia Records ever had.

Two of the younger guys about my age were Mark Kohler, a very savvy salesman, and Leroy Smith. Leroy was a singer/songwriter in his own right who used to perform now and then. We nicknamed him 'U-Roy' after the famous Jamaican reggae artist.

The job of a salesman was more difficult than I knew. One of the first things I did as a local promotion manager was to travel with each one to their accounts to see how the other side lived. Lee Lawrence, who drove a Mercedes and seemed to have the world by the tail, took me to the Wherehouse Record Store chain headquarters one day. The buyer there brought out a giant book as thick as two Webster's dictionaries stacked on top of each other. This book contained the store's entire inventory. It was easy to get them to take the established catalogue items that consistently sold well, but Columbia's lifeblood, like all the other labels', was new artists, and there was only so much space available in each of their stores.

'I want you to take a good amount of this new band we have, Mott The Hoople,' Lee said excitedly. 'We have a real good chance of breaking through with them.'

'And what if you don't?' the salesman replied, before pointing out a half-dozen other new artists that Lee needed to place in the Wherehouse stores. No matter how much helpful information Lee gave the guy about the radio airplay or great press we had, nothing moved the buyer unless Lee gave him a good deal on other tried-and-true records we had. There was no emotion, no particular feel for the music—it was all strictly business.

There were many methods of sales know-how. Once, at a sales meeting, we were discussing a particularly challenging project when the branch manager asked Kohler how the hell he was able to attain the numbers he needed from a very tough account buyer we all knew.

'Simple,' he said, 'I double shipped him!'

Told you he was savvy.

My favorite sales story was when I traveled with Tom Reany (pronounced *rainy*) to his Tower Records account in San Diego. Tom was from the South, or at least I thought he was, because he had this kind of Southern drawl in his speech. Tower Records was 'Tar' Records.

So, Tom and I go down to Tar Records in San Diego, and here, word for word, is how Tom sold a new Miles Davis album.

BUYER: 'Hi Tom, how's it going? What have you got for us today?'

TOM: 'We've got a Miles Davis album coming out.'

BUYER: 'Is it old stuff, or new stuff?'

TOM: 'Does it matter if it's old stuff or new stuff?'

BUYER: 'Yeah, the old stuff sells better than the new stuff.'

TOM: 'Okay, then it's old stuff.'

BUYER: 'Fine, I'll take two boxes. Let's go to lunch.'

Relationships were everything in our business. If you really needed something, and you had treated the people you did business with well in the past, chances were excellent that you would get what you needed in return.

· ● ·

As I've said already, the LA Branch worked hard, but we also partied exceptionally hard, and no place harder than at our annual conventions.

CBS Records held two national conventions a year: a very large one that took place in the summer, which included all personnel from across the country, plus key execs from the label's international offices from around the world; and a second convention, held in January, that was about half as big. They were always held in fun cities like Miami, Vancouver, Toronto, London, Hawaii, and New Orleans. There were meetings and product presentations all day long to rev up the troops, and at night there were dinner shows where many of the new artists were showcased.

Our dinner table was notorious for always being the loudest and most unruly in the room. We were so proud of our achievements, like breaking Loggins & Messina out of the West Coast and selling hundreds of thousands of albums, that we felt like we needed to let the world know who we were. As the ZZ Top song goes, '*We're bad and we're nationwide.*'

Our table was always strategically placed at the back of the room because the people in charge knew that after we were appropriately inebriated, someone would invariably start throwing dinner rolls, which would soon escalate into spoons, forks, and sometimes even knives. At two consecutive conventions, we even set our table on fire, which of course became the hit of the night and the thing we were most known for. An official 'business meeting' was called to discuss the fact that the LA branch would no longer be allowed to set their table on fire at conventions. Fascinatingly, half the staff rebelled, demanding to know, *Why not?*

To be clear, we did get a fair amount of work done during those conventions. One of the things I'm most proud of was our 'one-on-one' meetings. Because we operated like a family, each year at the larger conventions the heads of the different promotion departments would split up the local staff and meet with each person individually. The discussions centered around their personal lives—how was the job going, did they have any complaints, did they need anything more from the national office in the way of help, were their families okay, how did they view their future? Were they still happy doing local promotion, or was there another job they had their eye on in the record company? Caring for employees was a priority. You had to fuck up royally to get fired. The 'Family Of Music' concept wasn't just empty words—it was real.

One of my favorite stories is about the time famed head of promotion Ray Anderson ('Raymo' to us) was having a one-on-one with a new gal who had just taken over the local promotion job in New York. It was a sunny day in Puerto Rico, and they were sitting outside on the balcony of our hotel, about twenty floors up, having coffee. The girl had taken off her shoes, and Ray accidentally kicked one over the side. She went pale.

'Uh . . . Ray, those are Manolos. I'm sorry, I have to leave our meeting and go see if there's anything left of my shoe.'

Ray, being the suave, debonair fellow that he was, picked up the other shoe and threw it over the rail.

'Don't bother!' he told her. 'Buy a brand-new pair and send me the bill.'

That kind of flair epitomized Raymo, who was also blessed with movie-star handsomeness. Once, after a wild Grammy party, still in his tux, he followed Patty LuPone home to her Greenwich Village apartment and could be heard serenading her from the alley, singing, 'Evita, I love you.' Ray showed up the next morning for work still in his tux. Damn that guy—he looked as handsome and cool as he had the night before.

The sales, marketing, and press people also held meetings during the day at our conventions to discuss ways to improve. We even had guest consultants who helped train us in ultimate team building. CBS Records had some of the brightest minds in the music industry, and as a company it continually led the way with innovations that were followed by the rest of the labels. But after hours, look out!

Besides the LA branch story, I was trying to figure out a way to describe how out of control things could get at night when I came across an email that pretty much sums it all up. Larry Reymann, our former local promotion man in Seattle, had sent it to a bunch of us one day when we were reminiscing.

A few of those stories were about John Fagot, our VP of Top 40 promotion, who was passionate about his work, universally beloved . . . and also out of his fucking mind in the best possible way. Promotion men and women often went to extreme lengths to get their records played, and in John's case this once meant chaining his young children to a program director's desk and telling the guy he'd be back after he added the record John was promoting.

'You'll have to feed 'em, but they don't eat much.'

At one of the Hawaii conventions, some of the guys rescued a pig's head from a luau and secretly put it in John's toilet. At the end of the night, John returned to his hotel room, made a beeline for the bathroom, pulled his pants down, went to sit, looked down, and immediately jumped four feet into the air. As Reymann put it, 'Mr. Fagot's shriek when he went to the bathroom will echo forever.'

Larry's email reminded me of other misadventures. In Vancouver, at a popular establishment where young ladies removed clothing to music in a shower sequence, an inspired VP spontaneously took to the stage and stripped to George Michael's 'I Want Your Sex.' An entire Canadian Province must have abruptly taken a synchronized vow of celibacy.

At the Royal York in Toronto, we threw a birthday party for Johnny Rivers in the Epic Records suite. Mike Atkinson, in a three-piece velvet suit, flicked some chocolate cake at Randy Brown, who was dancing on a chair. Randy jumped down and buried Dr. A's face in the cake, which began an epic food fight. Outside in the hallway, several executives were pushing a branch manager wearing a fireman's hat on a food cart, each carrying emergency fire hoses they were unwinding along the way. There was chocolate cake on the walls, the furniture, doors, carpet, lights, curtains, windows; truly impressive. When the boys finally passed out, Roz Blanch, the person in charge of the convention, calmly wrote a check to hotel management.

Food cart capers seemed to be a repeating theme. At the 1972 convention at Grosvenor House in London, a salesman had passed out in the hallway. Rather than walk him to his room, his buddies thought it better to lay him out on a food cart and put a lampshade on his head. Then they wheeled him into the back of an elevator, pushed the down button, and watched him disappear. The hotel's other guests rode up and down on the thing for over an hour, trying not to notice the guy on the food cart with the lampshade, until someone finally had the sense to rescue him.

An evening dinner show at our second Grosvenor House convention in 1977 featured Boz Scaggs backed up by members of Toto. The audience got so rowdy that they started using the hotel's fine silver serving trays and bowls as percussion instruments, beating them with large spoons to play along with the music. The bill for all that ruined silver almost broke the bank.

This last recollection is a bit embarrassing, but here you go. Another of our conventions was held at the Century Plaza Hotel in Los Angeles, and my roommate was my buddy Michael Klenfner, the renowned music business heavyweight who also plays the president of Clarion Records in *The Blues Brothers*. We'd gotten a hold of some very good cocaine one evening, and around two in the morning, we were desperately trying to fall asleep.

'Michael, the furniture in here isn't placed right,' I announced, looking around the room. 'Don't you think the bookcase would be better over there, the beds over here, the desk and TV over there?'

Michael replied in the affirmative, so we got up to rearrange the room. One problem: all the furniture was bolted to the walls. But it was nothing that a little Peruvian marching powder couldn't handle.

Feeling superhuman, the two of us pulled together and yanked all the furniture completely off the walls, leaving large gaping holes. Drywall dust and plaster filled the room. Coated in white flecks and coughing like mad, we moved everything around to how we thought it should be until we were finally exhausted enough to go to sleep.

Every room in that hotel was laid out with the same floor plan. I often wondered what the maids thought when they came in the next day to clean and saw the only room with a brand-new, 'customized' furniture arrangement. Did it mix them up? Interestingly, we never heard a thing about it. Roz probably just wrote another check.

AGENTS OF FORTUNE

IT WAS JANUARY of 1972, and I was in my second year working for Columbia. One of the cool things back then was that, aside from working the priority projects, the higher-ups didn't mind if you decided to go out on your own to see if you could make something happen. In fact, they appreciated it.

Columbia released a lot of albums in the early 1970s, and not all of them came with a marketing or promotion plan. One day, I was sitting at my desk in Hollywood when a new stack of albums was brought in. As I looked through them, I came across a cover that stopped me cold: a black-and-white, M. C. Escher-esque rendering of what looked like an endless number of little rooms or prison cells that seemed to go on to infinity. Way in the back against the backdrop of a pitch-black evening sky, illuminated by hundreds of shiny stars, was the band's logo, which looked like an upside-down question mark. The cover was stark, mysterious, and scary. The band's name, Blue Öyster Cult.

Holy fuck, I wondered. *Who are these guys?!*

I was even more intrigued when I saw some of the song titles: 'Transmaniacon MC,' 'Cities On Flame With Rock And Roll,' 'Before The Kiss, A Redcap,' 'Workshop Of The Telescopes' . . . I put on the record, and the music was like nothing I'd ever heard before. It was hard rock with a heavy metal attitude, but not in the traditional Black Sabbath sense. Some of the guitar phrasings and riffs were so unique they sounded as if they came from another world. The songs sounded like the album cover looked—deep, menacing, trippy—and the lyrics were poetic and alluring. I loved it.

I immediately took the album to my new friend Ron McCoy, who was the program director at KNAC-FM in Long Beach and also did a daytime shift on the air. Serving the Long Beach and Orange County areas, KNAC did not have to compete with LA's more tightly playlisted FM stations, like KMET and KLOS, so Ron was more amenable to playing new bands he liked and turning his audience on to new music before it became popular.

McCoy had an ear for good things. He was a very talented guitar player in his own right, and he had been a child star as a country artist with his stage 'sister,' with whom he recorded and toured under the name The McCoys. Chet Atkins produced their sessions for RCA. Ron was from Dallas, and he was the first Texan I'd ever met (Willie Nelson would be the next). He always wore cowboy boots—the ultra-cool kind with shiny metal tips on the front, which I'd never seen before.

At that time, I was getting heavily into that little ol' band from Texas, ZZ Top, and I had a jean jacket I'd been thinking of embroidering with an image of the Lone Star State on the back. I didn't want to feel like a poser, though, so I asked Ron his opinion, him being from Dallas and all.

'Paaaul,' he said excitedly, in his modest Texas drawl, 'you get that jean jacket of yours and you embroider the great state of Texas on the back, and, by God, be proud to wear it!'

I had a notion McCoy would be impressed with Blue Öyster Cult, and he was. Upon hearing the album, he added a couple of songs to his daily show. He got some decent listener responses to the music, but the game-changer came when I was sent a test pressing of a live show the band had recently recorded. The performance was so hot that the label decided to release its own bootleg EP of four live tracks. Among the four was a searing instrumental called 'Buck's Boogie.'

Blue Öyster Cult had been a good introduction to the band, but the live stuff was over the top. Aside from how talented all the musicians were—Joe and Albert Bouchard on bass and drums, respectively, and Allen Lanier on keys—two things were abundantly clear. Eric Bloom was a badass frontman, and when lead guitar player Donald 'Buck Dharma' Roeser was let loose to improvise solos, he was destined to be a guitar God. Usually, that combination leads to rock stardom.

The *Blue Öyster Cult Bootleg EP* was released right on the heels of the album. When Ron heard it, he added all four tracks to his playlist and began to play the living hell out of 'Buck's Boogie.'

With all that BOC being played on KNAC, we began to sell albums in the Long Beach and Orange County areas. I knew the next step to breaking the band would be an in-person live performance. But rather than trying to have an agent book them in a club or as an opening act, I proposed to Ron and the station owners, Jim and Claudia Harden, that since they had taken a chance on a new band and were reaping success from the airplay, they should consider promoting the show themselves and enjoy the benefits of the ticket sales. If they had skin in the game, I reasoned, it would result in more promotion and more airplay.

I thought Claudia and Jim would rent out a club or a small theater, but they liked the idea so much that they did me one better—they rented out the Long Beach Arena! They made the show into a real event. Tickets and BOC albums began to sell like hotcakes. Now I was excited. With the radio station also being the promoter and needing to sell as many tickets as possible for a hall of that size, airplay and promotional announcements for the band's southern California debut performance exploded across the KNAC airwaves.

I figured that if the label was going to go to the effort of flying the band and their equipment from New York to California for this show, we should do another one in San Diego. I had made a new friend down there as well, Mike Harrison, who was running KPRI-FM. He'd built the station into a monster and liked what he saw happening in Long Beach. He added the music and rented out Golden Hall, which held six thousand people, for a show to be held two days after the Long Beach Arena date. Now I had two stations playing Blue Öyster Cult in heavy rotation, and both of them were selling concert tickets.

The Long Beach Arena show was the first time I staged a large-scale marketing stunt. I wanted to do something so big it would draw citywide attention. I loved the band's logo, which is a cross between the astronomical symbol for the planet Saturn and the Greek symbol for chaos. I wanted to project it, huge, on the side of the Long Beach Arena on the night of the show, just like Batman's Bat-Signal, to gather attention from those driving by and perhaps even spawn more walk-up ticket sales.

The kinds of projectors you'd use to accomplish something like this today simply didn't exist back then. The only way to do it would be to cut out a steel plate with the logo and put it inside a Super Trouper spotlight, which ran by burning a hot carbon rod inside. Steel was the only metal strong enough to withstand the heat thrown off by that kind of spotlight.

Winos drummer Alan Albert turned me on to a fellow with his own foundry. There I met Jake Monroy, who was quite a character in his own right. He was a man of small stature but was built with a husky frame. He wore very thick glasses and was dressed in dirty blue overalls. His hands looked like they were perpetually dirty (even after he'd washed them) from years of metal dust and foundry work. I explained what I needed.

Jake thought about it for a moment, did some calculations, and then told me, 'Something like this has never been done before'—music to my ears. The problem, he said, was that for a steel plate to withstand that kind of heat, it would have to be a certain thickness. 'Steel is the hardest metal,' he continued, 'so it is the hardest metal to cut, and you're asking for a specific logo. This will be a challenge, but I really want to try it because . . . *I love steel*!'

Jake Monroy was the man for the job, and he pulled it off all right. On the night of the show, I gave the thick metal plate with the cutout logo to the man working the huge Super Trouper on the outside of the arena. He placed it inside the lighting tube, lit the carbon rod, focused the lens, and there it was: the BOC logo, lit up well over fifty feet high and just as wide, beaming across the arena wall. All the kids still waiting in line outside went nuts and started cheering. Cars in the parking lot started honking their horns. All of a sudden there were chants of 'BOC! BOC! BOC!' The Blue Öyster Cult Bat-Signal was so huge you could see it from Ocean Boulevard, the main drag in front of the arena. With so much traffic around, curiosity brought a fair number of people to the venue, and plenty more drove past wanting to know what it was all about.

The band killed it that night. It was the first large venue they'd ever played, and they showed they could handle an arena stage. We knew we probably wouldn't sell out the entire venue, but I think the final count was close to eight thousand seats, which was a huge success.

Two nights later, BOC repeated the feat in San Diego, where they played two sold-out shows at Golden Hall. Our budget was tiny—Harrison was selling tickets at the door himself, and I was high up in the hall, giving lighting cues to the union spotlight operator:

'Okay, follow the lead singer…and switch to the guitar player…NOW!'

With all this action, the larger radio stations in LA proper began to play the band's music, and soon Blue Öyster Cult were established as a new and exciting act in the southern California area. Promoters across the country took notice too and began to book the band in healthily sized theater venues.

Not only were Blue Öyster Cult truly on their way, my reputation began to grow as well—and not just in Los Angeles but within the Columbia label as someone who could make big things happen.

A year later, the band came back for a second tour. I came around to a rehearsal to say hi and get reacquainted. I loved talking guitars with Buck, and I was always interested in what new models he was playing. Outside the rehearsal hall, the band's manager, Sandy Pearlman, sat me down and told me to open a black Gibson guitar case that was sitting in front of me. There, lying like a sleeping princess surrounded in deep purple velvet, was a vintage 1962 red-wine Les Paul Jr, replete with a shiny black P-90 pickup.

'Go ahead,' Sandy said. 'You have Donald's permission to check it out.' The guitar had a gorgeous neck, a little wider and thinner than a typical Les Paul Standard; the action was incredible, and it played like butter.

'Wow,' I said. 'Buck's one lucky guy. This thing's amazing!'

'You really like it, huh? Well, it's yours—a present from me and the band for everything you've done for us.'

I was dumbfounded, speechless, as I went around and thanked every member of the group. A bond had developed, and our friendship continued to grow over the years. We remain close to this day.

I had so much fun going on the road with BOC. One of my favorite things was watching their roadie, Eric Weinstein, who Sandy affectionately named 'The E Factor' ('Special Effects Factor,' or 'Factor' for short), load flash powder into the eight pyrotechnic pots strung out across the front of the stage. It was a ritual he performed before each show. Then I'd stand back and marvel at the explosion and smoke generated when the pots were ignited, creating a rousing beginning to each performance.

A typical Blue Öyster Cult show would start with a big announcement, sometimes including a few lyrics by The Doors or whatever the announcer wanted to say that would get the crowd excited. Then he would shout, 'Here they are from New York City—the amazing Blue Öyster Cult!' That was the cue for the lighting tech to push the switch and set off the flash pots. Simultaneously, the band would hit a power chord and bring their arms up to shield their faces from the flash.

One night at the Winterland Ballroom in San Francisco, I went down to the stage before showtime to watch Factor load the flash pots. But this time he was doing something very odd. Usually, he poured a couple of tablespoons of powder into each pot from the brown bottle the stuff came in. He would generally use one bottle for all eight pots. This time, however, he was emptying an entire bottle into each pot. I thought maybe he was high or that something else was up, so I pointed this out to him, as it seemed rather dangerous.

Factor looked down from the stage and spoke to me in a loud, deep, gravelly voice, slowly stringing out his words.

'I . . . hate . . . San . . . Fran . . . cis . . . co.'

'Factor,' I replied, 'what do you mean, you hate San Francisco? *Nobody* hates San Francisco. Everybody *loves* San Francisco! *If you're going to San Francisco, be sure to wear some flowers in your hair,* dude.'

Factor scowled and kept emptying the bottles of flash powder. I went back to the soundboard to warn Sandy.

Of all the characters that flourished in the late 60s and 70s, Sandy was one of the most eccentric. Having originally sported a blond, Beatles-esque hairdo, he would later adopt a fitted black military cadet cap (kind of like Fidel Castro's) that he never took off. An exceptional writer and poet, he had been one of the first rock critics for *Crawdaddy* magazine, and he co-wrote many of Blue Öyster Cult's songs. He also became their co-manager alongside Murry Krugman, another character in his own right. He would go on to play a key role in the punk scene, producing The Clash's *Give 'Em Enough Rope* and co-producing (with Murray) *The Dictators Go Girl Crazy!*

Sandy was famous for incurring huge overtime expenses in the recording studio, which drove record companies nuts. He was always experimenting with different microphone techniques, and he could take forever just tweaking the knobs on a single vocal performance. Once I was in a studio where the engineers had been working on an Eric Bloom vocal for an entire day, attempting to refine the mood with EQ and compression. They were exasperated. Sandy walked in, listened to half a song, and said, 'Sounds a bit strident to me.' How do you fix *strident*? Another time, he heard a track and asked the engineer to 'make it sound more green.' For those of you not familiar with the recording studio, there isn't a button for *green*.

Sandy and I became friends. He appreciated good authentic food, and one of his favorite things to do in LA was to stop at Burrito King on Sunset and Alvarado on the way to a BOC show and scarf down a quesadilla and a machaca burrito. I'd have the latest Blue Öyster Cult album cranked up to eleven on the way to the show, and he'd say, 'Believe me, I've heard this enough. Do you have any Wagner?' He knew his classical composers, and luckily for me, I had a Columbia Records *Wagner's Greatest Hits* eight-track tape in my trunk at the time, so we blasted 'Ride Of The Valkyries' on the way to the show.

Sandy definitely lived in his own world, but I believe he bordered on genius. You could ask him about almost any subject, and he would know *everything* about it. When I was touring with BOC in Canada, we found ourselves eating a lot of incredible Chinese meals. At one dinner, I blurted out, 'Why is the Chinese food so good here?' Sandy informed me that the Chinese were the ones who built the great Canadian Railroad, and that they'd stayed on in the area. And then he went on to give me the *entire history* of the Canadian Railroad.

Whenever I saw Sandy, he always had his nose in a book, but it would never be the latest spy novel. It would be the history of a particular war or the writings of a great existential philosopher. He went on to become a professor of music and philosophy, teaching at McGill, Stanford, Harvard, and UC Berkeley. Not exactly your usual fare for a heavy metal manager.

Back at the soundboard, I reported in.

'Hey, man, get ready. Factor has overloaded the flash pots, and it's gonna be a *way* bigger explosion than usual.'

The announcer wound up the crowd, and then we heard the familiar line, 'So here they are, from New York City, the *amazing* Blue Öyster Cult!'

The pots went off: KA-FUCKING-BLAMMO! The flash was so bright that everyone in the room was blinded. Then came the heat—you could feel it from the stage all the way back to where we were standing by the soundboard. Then came the concussion from the explosion. I swear to God, I thought we'd killed the band and taken out the first three rows of the audience.

When our eyes adjusted, you could see smoke rolling across the ceiling and coming our way. It looked like a hydrogen bomb cloud. I thought for sure they were going to have to call the fire marshal. I watched Sandy in a daze, wondering how scared he must be for the band's safety—not to mention the audience, some of whom could be seriously injured.

Sandy just looked at me with a big grin, as if this was business as usual. In his best nonchalant *Mr. Peabody & Sherman* voice, he declared, 'Wow ... positively nuclear.' Still smiling, he told the soundman to ride the guitars heavy and loud, as if nothing out of the ordinary had happened at all. Then he looked at me and said, 'You know, sometimes I think all anyone wants to hear from this band are the guitars.'

I shook my head, happy that we hadn't been arrested for arson.

When we went backstage after the show, we saw that the 'positively nuclear' flash had singed the eyebrows of two members of the band. Buck looked up, with very little eyebrow remaining, and yelled, 'WHAT THE HELL WAS THAT?'

It was rock'n'roll as it oughta be.

A ROLLING STONE
& A MONKEY

IN THE BEGINNING of FM radio, the format was freeform. Each disc jockey picked their own music to play on their show. Often, the shows were as creative as the music they played, and they were usually centered around a theme: great guitarists, outlaws, politics, even the weather. Most importantly, the presentation by the jocks could be a show in and of itself. Fading out from one song and into another, known as a segue, became an art form—many DJs would fit music together, not only in theme but in similar tempos or keys, and they knew which parts of some records would blend well with others. Listening to FM in those days was like taking a musical journey.

The first station of its kind in Los Angeles was KPPC-FM. It was like a private secret—only the hippest knew of its existence. It broadcast a rebellious style of entertainment amplifying the counterculture thoughts of the day. Music shows were interspersed with far-out satirical comedy bits by a group of guys known as The Credibility Gap. One of the founding members of the group, Richard Beebe, was an original Beatnik turned LA radio personality. He discovered Harry Shearer, Michael McKean, and David L. Lander, who all went on to have very big careers in movies and television. (Think *This Is Spinal Tap*, *Laverne & Shirley*, *The Simpsons*, and *Better Call Saul*, just for starters.)

Teenagers like me were fascinated by this wholly new sound. We felt rebellious by nature, and it seemed like this radio station was made for us, speaking directly to our generation and sharing the new kinds of messages and music we were seeking. The challenge was trying to get a clear signal from a very small radio station operating with limited power. I was able to receive it on my little pink-and-white, gold-trimmed transistor radio if I angled it in just the right way. Other folks were forming makeshift antennas out of coat hangers or whatever they could find to try to capture the signal.

FM was a new style of authentic communication where the jocks talked *with* us, not *at* us, as was the traditional Top 40 style. The new approach was captivating. I loved listening to Jeff Gonzer, who would later become a very good friend, and another cool cat who called himself Mississippi Fats. But my all-time fave was 'The Obscene' Steven Clean.

Every FM jock had his or her own style. Some were funny, others were incredibly philosophical, and some created imaginative tapestries of sound through the way they chose to program their music. Steven, whose real last name is Segal, was a true genius on the air, imparting important, thoughtful cultural messages via spoken word intertwined with just the right music to help bring his points to life. Kids would cut school early to listen to him, just to make sure they didn't miss anything important. They exchanged cassettes of his radio shows, which were like works of performance art.

Steven might begin with some sociological or political message or a question that could make you wonder where he was going. Then he would take you on an incredible journey through music and speech that would all come together at the end of the show and completely blow your mind. He would do crazy shock-jock stuff too, but not just by uttering provocative innuendo over the air. He was much more creative, cerebral, and brilliant.

Moving from KPPC to KMET, Steven once had the UCLA superstar basketball player Marques Johnson dribble a basketball behind him in the studio every time he opened the mic to talk. The experience was like listening to the blues, jazz, or beat poetry. Marques punctuated Steven's speech with different tones and tempos of dribbles—some short, some staccato and loud, others long, quiet lobs—all of it just beyond.

According to Steven, 'It was my all-time favorite show. UCLA had just won another championship the night before, and it was especially amazing because they'd done it without the benefit of having some of their former big-time superstars. I had a friend who was an intern at the station. We were both UCLA basketball fanatics, and he knew one of the players, Dave Meyers. He gave me Dave's number, and I left a message on his phone telling him what a big fan I was and how much I'd enjoyed the last night's game. Dave called back and said, Oh my God, you're my favorite DJ! I told him if he wanted, he could come down to my show to celebrate—be DJ for a while, and play whatever music he liked. He was ecstatic and asked if he could bring some of the team. The next thing I know he shows up with Marques Johnson and Pete Trgovich. Glenn Frey had been listening to the show, and he got all excited and called in: *Hey, can I come down with the guys?* Then all the Eagles showed up!'

Steven was so popular that even his crosstown competitor's girlfriend listened to him. My buddy Jim McKeon was the program director of KWST-FM in Los Angeles at the time. His afternoon jock was Richard Kimball, who had become widely known from his days at KMET. Richard's girlfriend was a hairstylist, and McKeon went to see her at Richard's prodding. When Jim walked into the salon, she had the radio on, but she wasn't listening to Richard on KWST—she was listening to Steven Clean on KMET.

McKeon was shocked. 'You're not listening to your own boyfriend's show?' he asked.

'Yeah, I listen to Richard sometimes,' she replied, 'but, you know, you just *gotta* listen to Steven!'

Steven and I became buddies, and my love for big stunts and promotion theatrics fit right in with his way of thinking. Once, I called him with the idea of renting a full-size upright piano and somehow figuring out a way of having it hauled up KMET's very small elevator and into their equally small studios. The Rolling Stones' piano player, Nicky Hopkins, had just released a solo album on Columbia, and I wanted him to be able to play live over the airwaves. Back then, promotion people were accustomed to bringing artists into the studio with their acoustic guitars, but a piano? No one had ever done that before.

Steven loved the idea. Now all we needed to do was somehow get the damn thing up to the studio. The elevator was so small it could barely hold the piano, much less a person along with it. So, the movers stuffed the piano in tightly, crammed their fingers in between the piano and the elevator control panel, and pushed the button up to KMET. Then they quickly bounded up the stairs to pull it out again, just in time before the doors closed. It was hysterical—like something from a Laurel & Hardy movie.

Nicky had a blast, playing a couple of songs from his new solo album and telling some fabulous Rolling Stones stories. Steven was having so much fun, and the piano sounded so great, that he kept Nicky there for his entire four-hour show and had him play intros and outros to and from commercial breaks, just like the bands do on late-night television.

• • •

When I first met Steven, he lived in Laurel Canyon with his girlfriend and a pet monkey—a gibbon, to be exact. If you think cats can have an attitude, try communicating with an ape. One night after a show at the Ash Grove, I went back to the canyon with Steven and his girlfriend for dinner.

Like most of us in those days, Steven had a typical hippie pad—very little furniture, but lots of pillows and tons of record albums scattered about. When we entered, the monkey was on his perch in a corner, giving us the Greta Garbo 'I want to be alone' look. He finally warmed up to me and sat on my knee while we ate dinner. The monkey was hungry, and he looked at me expecting to be fed. The communication between us was incredible. Our eyes locked, and there was a kind of knowing, like we were newfound friends or something. So, one bite for me and one bite for the monkey. His little hands would take the food from me put it in his mouth, and his eyes would light up. An animal as close to a human being as you can get.

Wow, I thought. *Evolution. I get it.*

As creative geniuses go, Steven was also extremely eccentric, and sometimes he had trouble dealing with life's everyday activities. I'm sure the drugs he was experimenting with didn't help the situation—no judgment here, but he reminded me of the gonzo journalist Hunter S. Thompson.

Outside of his radio show, Steven had an odd lifestyle. For instance, if the television in his apartment broke, he wouldn't bother having it fixed or even throwing it out, he'd just buy another one and stack it on top of the old one. Once when I visited his apartment, I saw that he had amassed three television sets, one stacked on top of the other. Sitting atop the mountain of televisions was a marionette of the American evangelist Kathryn Kuhlman. I mean, forget about the three TVs for a second, where the hell does someone get a marionette of Kathryn Kuhlman? Moreover, who would *want* a marionette of Kathryn Kuhlman?! (Later, Steven told me he was enamored with television evangelists and kept it as kind of a mascot.)

Once, I was hanging out in the KMET music library with a good friend, music director Kathy Kenyon, when Steven called to tell her he was going to be late to his show. She looked up from the phone to get my attention.

'Hey, Paul, do you mind running out and picking up Steven? He ran out of gas on his way here.'

'Sure,' I said.

When I found Steven, he had 'run out of gas' not more than twenty yards from a corner that had not one but four gas stations on it.

'Steven, really?'

'Aw, Rap, you know how I am.'

Cars were like the television sets to him. Steven would never bother to take them in to be serviced, and when one broke down he'd leave it wherever it had stopped and buy another. Or, better, have the radio station buy him one, and just continue on his merry way.

Jim McKeon tapped Steven from KMET to round out his great on-air staff at KWST. I was listening one day when he played an Aerosmith track. Afterward, he complimented the band but continued to speak about their four platinum albums, subtly letting the audience know that the rock business was fast becoming one of '*come and get your bucks*'—a reference to the band Redbone's song 'Come And Get Your Love.' Not yet finished with his social jabs, and just to make sure we understood that the music business was straying from the hippie culture we once knew, he continued, 'Soon they'll be an Aerosmith *monster movie* . . . the Aerosmith from Mars!'

'I can see it now,' he added, probably referring to his far-out brain, or perhaps his drug-induced state. 'You'll be able to see it later. You're listening to KWST, the pulse beat of Los Angeles and all of Southern California, all the way to Alaska and down to Prima Donna, one of the countries down in South America.'

Charles Laquidara, the renowned morning man on the legendary WBCN-FM in Boston, and a major league character in his own right, once called Steven 'the most brilliant disc jockey that ever existed.' Now that's saying something! Steven, himself an original WBCN-er, would eventually move back to Boston, where he continued his wacky merriment and mischief for many years to come.

CHILI DOGS FOR BREAKFAST

IN JANUARY 1973, we had just released Aerosmith's first album. Today, of course, their sound is recognized throughout the world, but back then they were cutting their own groove, and it took radio, press, and retail a little while to get used to that sound, appreciate it, and get behind them.

In fact, it was like that with most bands who had a unique sound and personality. It's not like radio stations automatically added every decent band to their playlists. To the contrary, we always had to *prove* to radio, and the rest of the media, why they should get behind a band. Sometimes this took considerable work, even for acts like Bruce Springsteen and Billy Joel.

The day I took Aerosmith's first album over to my beloved friends at KMET, I was told that their music was 'too loud' and 'too raunchy.'

Isn't loud and raunchy what rock music is? I thought.

No matter, I immediately took the record over to my buddy Ron McCoy at KNAC, who proceeded to play the living shit out of it. The audience responded in kind, and before you knew it, we'd established a good foothold for the band. It wasn't long before all the other FM rock stations in LA came around.

Record labels were always coming up with tchotchkes or trinkets to give people to put on their desks, or T-shirts to wear, to keep our focus on an artist or band and let everyone know we were serious about breaking them. At Columbia, we had some of the best. One day, about a thousand Aerosmith-branded balsa wood gliders arrived at the LA branch from the New York offices. They were good quality, too—these were no cheap knockoffs. They had the band's name painted in big red letters across the wing. Being a big kid cleverly disguised as a responsible adult, when I saw those airplanes, I immediately knew what had to be done with them. Take them to the radio stations and record store folks? Uh, not quite yet.

I was unpacking the planes in the mailroom, along with my buddy Ron Simms, aka 'Spider' (a nickname that dated back to his Little League days, probably due to his lanky build).

'Spider,' I declared, 'we gotta fly these planes off the roof of our building! It's fourteen floors up—they'll go for miles!'

Ron is a great music guy with a warm, infectious personality—a guy you want to share a beer with. He was grinning from ear to ear.

'Yep, Rap . . . that's exactly what we need to do.'

We each grabbed a handful of planes, took the elevator up to the fourteenth floor, and bounded up the stairwell to the roof. From our rooftop overseeing Sunset Boulevard, you could see plenty of Hollywood as you looked right and left. Facing forward, there was a great panoramic view of the Hollywood Freeway as it made its way through town, up and over the Hollywood Hills on its way into the San Fernando Valley. And as we peered over the five-foot ledge of the roof, there was an unexpected surprise of warm air swirling upward.

'With these thermals, I'll bet I can hit the freeway with one of these,' I said confidently.

'I'm going for the Hollywood Bowl,' Spider countered.

And thus began the big competition—who could get their glider to go the farthest? Over the next few weeks, we sent scores of Aerosmith gliders flying high over Sunset Boulevard as far as the eye could see. We kept changing wing configurations and adjusting for different weather conditions. Sometimes we invited guest pilots to join in the fun—not only other Columbia Records' personnel but recording artists as well.

One day, Elton John came to visit his old friend and former road manager, John Babcock, who was now working with us at Columbia. John, aka 'Johnny Bags,' was another major league personality with a big bunch of long black curly hair and a thick mustache who looked very much like John Oates in his heyday. Bags appreciated the soothing part of getting high. He was a wonderful person, universally loved, and his favorite line, which he repeated far too often, was 'Get Down!' He'd say it once and then say it again with a long loud drawl, '*GET DOWWWN*,' to really bring extra emphasis. If he felt he hadn't quite made his point, you'd hear,

'GET . . . FUCKING . . . DOWWWN!' Imagine that on a combination of Quaaludes and marijuana, and you get the idea.

After Elton and Bags had a nice reunion chat, we took him to the mailroom, where we kept a large stockpile of our latest album releases. One of the things we always enjoyed was taking a guest in there and letting them pick as many records as they liked to take home with them.

Elton looked just like you'd imagine—big fancy glasses, bell-bottom pants, and huge platform boots. A wonderful guy who loved music, he gathered a stack of albums so high he could barely see over them. Then Spider posed the question.

'Hey, Elton, we've got these great gliders that we've launching off the roof. Wanna come up and be a guest pilot?'

Elton's eyes lit up under his big rose-colored shades and he was reduced to feeling like a child again. So up we went. We figured that having co-written 'Rocket Man' and 'Take Me To The Pilot,' Elton would be a natural, but turns out he was a way better songwriter and piano player than a model glider pilot. His planes didn't go very far, but Spider and I made light of it to make him feel at home, and we all had a great time.

With so many gliders being launched off the roof, it was amazing that we didn't cause any car accidents on Sunset Boulevard. For all the successful flights we had, plenty of those planes nosedived right down to the street, and I often wondered what it would be like driving down Sunset and all of a sudden have a glider or two appear out of nowhere and slam into your windshield. We never found out, but every day on our way home from work we saw scatterings of balsa wood splinters in the street.

• ● •

No one was more passionate about music, artists, and fighting for them than Steve Popovich. Steve never went to college, but he worked his way up the ranks from the record warehouse to becoming head of promotion at Columbia.

While Bob Moering was my first boss, Steve was my mentor. He could talk about any genre of music and had an innate feel for all of it, whether it was Neil Diamond or Barbara Streisand or Bruce Springsteen or Boz

Scaggs. In fact, the main reason Boz wound up having such a big career was because of Steve.

Disappointed by the sales of his first four albums, Columbia had decided to drop Boz from the label. Many of us were shattered—we were all huge fans. Steve stepped in and begged the A&R staff and even the president of the company to keep Boz on for just a little longer. He knew deep down inside that Boz had the talent to go all the way. The record company listened to him, and Boz's next offering was *Silk Degrees*, which spawned hits like 'Lido Shuffle' and 'Lowdown' and sold over five million copies.

Boz was such a cool guy and one of our favorite artists to hang out with. I loved going to San Francisco to see him play and then join him afterward for a late-night meal, with margaritas, at La Rondalla in the Mission District, along with Steve and some of the other San Francisco branch Columbia folks.

Pops was a good-looking guy who constantly fought his weight. He looked like a handsome hockey player. He had a cherubic face and a big warm personality that lit up any room he walked into. His mind was constantly working, cooking up new promotional schemes or trying to figure out how to help make each member of his team better.

He defined the word *workaholic*. He was so consumed by the business that he worked 24/7. The record business was so much fun that it became like a drug for many who just couldn't get enough of it. At a big label like Columbia, there were so many artists to deal with and people to take care of that Steve found himself totally hooked. He would constantly preach to us to make time for our families as he struggled to do the same.

Living the record business lifestyle to the fullest, Popovich was famous for staying up all night at New York headquarters, taking an upper or drinking copious amounts of coffee, then calling the troops in the middle of the night to crank them up and get them excited about forthcoming projects. He was an incredible inspiration and energizer, his excitement naturally contagious.

A middle-of-the-night conversation would go something like this:

'Hel . . . lo?' I answer, half-asleep.

'Hi, Rap,' says Steve, amped out of his mind. 'How you doing? You sound a bit fuzzy—are you stoned?'

'No, Steve, it's three in the morning. I'm sleeping.'

'Are you sure you're not stoned?'

'Yes, Steve, I'm sure. I've been sleeping.'

'Is Sharon there?'

'Of course. She's right next to me.'

'Put her on the phone.'

'Hi Steve,' says Sharon, sleepily.

'Hi, Sharon, how you doin'? Is Rap stoned?'

'No, Steve, he's sleeping. It's three in the morning.'

Steve, acting like it's midday, has a long conversation with Sharon— how has she been? How's life in sunny Southern California?—and I fall back to sleep. Then Sharon pokes me to wake me up and says Steve wants to talk to me again. I ask Steve if this is going to be a long conversation, to which he replies in the affirmative. I tell him to let me make some coffee and I'll call him back in twenty minutes.

On the surface, you might think this is crazy, but getting a call from Steve Popovich at 3am signaled that you were one of his go-to guys— one of the main men whose mind he values, and who he wants to discuss creative promotional ideas with. And, honestly, scheming with Steve in the wee hours of the morning was a fucking blast, and a ton of stuff got accomplished. By the next morning, you were revved up and raring to go, to do your job at one thousand percent. A call like that from Steve could keep you pumped up for a month.

Our lifestyle in the biz was like one long movie. Pops would be visiting LA, and I might get a call like this at 7am:

'Hey, Rap, get up and meet me and Boz at Pink's for breakfast!'

Pink's is the legendary pink-and-white hotdog stand on La Brea Avenue, near Melrose, famous for their Chilidogs. 'Breakfast' could only mean that Steve and Boz had been up all night, drinking and planning his career, and at about 7am chilidogs sounded perfect, so I'd come down during a chilly LA morning wearing my jean jacket with the collar up to keep out the cold, and have 'breakfast' with the boys outside Pink's.

'Hey, Pops, do you mind if I have tamales and milk? It's a little early for me to wolf down a couple of chilidogs.'

I learned so much from Steve. When I met him, one of the very first things he said to me was, 'Rap, I am going to put a lot of pressure on you to get records played. Whatever I tell you, I never want you to give any money or drugs to a program director or disc jockey to get a record played. You need to do everything above board and remain a class act.' I wouldn't have done so anyway, but hearing that from my boss just made me idolize him all the more.

Once, we were in a hotel room at a convention somewhere, and we were talking about how you keep your credibility as a promotion man. You can't tell radio folks that every single record you are working is great.

'What do you do when a record is just plain bad?' I asked.

Steve answered with incredible wisdom.

'Rap, you can always find at least one good thing about a record. If it's not the vocal performance or the musicianship, maybe it's the song itself, the message it conveys. Or, if not that, maybe the production is exceptionally done well. But there will always be at least *one good thing* you can find. Find that thing, and talk about that.'

I used that advice throughout my entire promotion career.

For any of you Meat Loaf fans, Steve Popovich went on to start his own label, Cleveland International. He and his partner, the great record man Stan Snyder, discovered Meat, and in collaboration with composer Jim Steinman and producer Todd Rundgren, they recorded and released a little ditty titled *Bat Out Of Hell*. That album sold over forty-three million copies worldwide, becoming one of the biggest sellers of all time.

Steve Popovich was not only one of the most talented record men I ever met but one of the greatest human beings I ever met. He was instrumental in my growth as a promotion man, and as a man in general as I made my way through life.

BIG GREEN LIGHT IN THE SKY

WITH FM RADIO growing rapidly in popularity, and more music being created to fuel the airwaves, the executives at CBS Records felt they needed someone to give full-time attention to the format. They wanted an FM rock specialist, and because of my passion for the music, my accomplishments with the format, and being positioned in Los Angeles, I got the nod. I would become the first full-time regional FM rock album promotion man in the country.

Now I'd be traveling to new interesting cities—Portland, Seattle, Denver, but most excitingly of all, San Francisco, the epicenter of the countercultural movement, home of the Grateful Dead, Jefferson Airplane, Santana, Sly & The Family Stone, Creedence Clearwater Revival, Country Joe & The Fish, and more. I'd also be working with one of the most famous FM rock radio stations in history, KSAN. The program director there, Thom O'Hair, was a visionary, and music director Bonnie Simmons had an exceptional ear for music. I'd also be rubbing elbows with another living legend, promoter Bill Graham.

The kicker was that the company wanted me to work not only Columbia records but also the ones being released on our sister label, Epic, and all the other associated labels as well. I was thrilled, of course, because it meant I got to concentrate solely on promoting the music I was passionate about. It turned out to be one hell of a great job. But the downside was that there were so many records to promote all at once that I could barely keep up. I'd just finish getting a bunch of albums launched and on their way with airplay at the now eighteen or so FM stations I was working, and then, as I was about to take a breath, I would get a call from another manager—like, say, Irving Azoff, who was looking for *immediate action* on one of his acts.

Irving fought for his artists in a no-nonsense, totally in-your-face way, and he was rapidly making a name for himself as one of the most notorious screamers in the business.

My assistant would tell me Irv was on the phone, and this is how it went.

'Hi, Irv, how ya doin'?'

'I want KLOS and I want it now!'

'Yeah, I'm sure you're referring to the new Dan Fogelberg album. Anyway, how's about a nice *Hello, Rap, nice to talk to you* first?'

'I want KLOS and I want it now!'

'Yeah, okay, got it. I just received the album this morning, and I ran it right over to the station. It's going to take them a second to listen to it.'

'I want KLOS and I want it now!'

'I played them the advance, and I know they like it a lot. I am sure they will add it this coming Tuesday.'

'I want KLOS and I want it now!'

'Okay, got to go now, Irv. I'll call you as soon as they add the record. Have a good day.'

'I want KLOS and I want it now!'

Click.

Believe it or not, that is, word for word, how that conversation went. I'm not sure if Dan Fogelberg was sitting in his office at the time and Irv was just trying to show off, but Irving Azoff quickly became a legendary terror to deal with. There were no compromises—he demanded what he wanted, and that was it. He also became the manager of the Eagles, and what he did for them, and for Don Henley as a solo artist, was unprecedented and mightily impressive.

It was only much later, when I got to co-produce a *Live By Request* TV special featuring Don, that I finally figured out Irving's MO. He pushed one of our executive producers to the brink, causing the guy to say, 'Okay, I quit, the special is off.' I realized then that Irv will push you until you break, or are just about to. It's then, and only then, that he knows he's gotten *everything he can* and can go back to his artists, look them straight in the eye, and tell them he did everything it was humanly possible to do for them. At any rate, he's always been on my side, and later on, after he'd mellowed (a bit), he helped me figure out a couple of things when I was in a tight spot. I've been especially appreciative of that.

· ● ·

Things were going great, but my schedule was grueling. Traveling in the most efficient fashion meant visiting four cities in four days and making the most of every minute. A typical day would find me in my hotel up at six, having ordered breakfast the night before to be delivered by room service by seven. Often, I'd be a tad late, just out of the shower, meeting the waiter at the door in a towel. Not a problem unless the waiter was a woman, and then I was embarrassed, not wanting her to think I was looking to pull any James Bond-type moves.

I'd treat myself to whatever fancy breakfasts they had—blueberry pancakes, me—and copious amounts of coffee. The coffee was sorely needed because chances were, I hadn't gone to sleep until two or three in the morning the night before. Then I'd hightail it to the local airport by nine, turn in the rental car, and be in the next city by eleven the same morning. I'd rent another car, drive directly to a radio station for a quick meeting, and then go to another and take the program or music director out to lunch. After lunch, I would check into my next hotel and make some phone calls. If I had time before dinner, I would visit a key record store in town to enquire about the hottest-selling albums and check out which promotional displays were up—not only for Columbia but to see what the competition was doing as well. A good part of the record business happens locally, in the streets. I wanted to know what was going on, everywhere.

After visiting the record store, I'd meet another program director, and often his wife, for dinner at the fanciest restaurant in town. In fact, I learned to be a connoisseur of fine food and great wine via the Columbia Records expense account. After dinner, it was not uncommon for me to head back to the radio station or to the PD's home to hang out for a bit longer. I'd be back at my hotel at two, and up again at six.

You can imagine, after four days and nights of a schedule like this, counting all the drinks and other stuff, that I was pretty whooped. Because I'd change cities and accommodations daily, the road would play tricks on me. One of the funniest things was when I'd get up in the middle of the night to go to the bathroom, still half asleep, and walk smack into a wall because my mind was remembering the room configuration from the hotel the night before.

I'd get home at the end of a long week and just collapse for a good twelve hours. And those were just the trips I took on my own, not the ones where I'd be traveling with an artist on a promotional tour. That would be a whole other adventure.

• ● •

Things were going great when, all of a sudden, I hit a speed bump. The head of West Coast A&R at Epic Records had signed some bands that were having trouble getting any substantial FM radio airplay. Not wanting to face the fact that perhaps he hadn't made the best choices, he decided he needed to blame someone, and that someone was me. He called me into his office and told me I wasn't doing a good job, I wasn't traveling enough, and perhaps I was the reason his bands weren't getting the airplay they deserved. I showed him my intense travel schedule and tried to point out that other records I'd worked had been quite successful in the FM format, and that my work ethic was to give an equal amount of attention to every project. It's just that some new records were better accepted than others. He didn't like my answers, and he intimated that maybe a change was needed—meaning that if things didn't begin to look brighter for some of the bands he'd signed, he was going to try and have me replaced (fired). It was a clear threat.

I was very proud of the job I was doing, and I was beginning to get an excellent reputation in the new cities I was traveling to, but I was still very young in the business. Epic's head of A&R was my senior, and I really didn't know how to handle the situation. I left work that day quite upset and came home that evening and told Sharon all about it. Then I told her my plan.

This guy had a penchant for model airplanes, and he had some beautiful replicas hanging from the ceiling in his office that he clearly loved.

'So, hon, tomorrow I'm going to storm into this guy's office, give him the stink eye, start yanking his model planes down from the ceiling one by one, and break every goddamn one of them into tiny little pieces, right before his eyes! And when I'm done, I'm going to march out and slam his door so hard it comes off the hinges. Then, I'm going to pop my head back through the broken door and say, Send me the bill. Whaddya think?'

'I think you need a drink.'

'Fuck this guy, honey . . . I'm gonna—'

'Paul, take a breath. Take ten breaths. That is *not* how you're going to handle the situation. Talk to Del.'

It's great to have a down-to-earth, well-focused life partner. Sharon has always set me straight when I go off the rails.

Enter Delmer Costello.

Del was the head of the entire western region sales force and promotion team, and he was an amazing man. He was a bit older than the rest of us, and you could tell he knew a lot about life and the general lay of the land. He'd been there before, and he had the wisdom of those extra years under his belt. He was tall and thin, wore fancy cowboy boots, and had a balding head with a naturally red ponytail. He looked cool, but he could talk business with the best of them. He could also get down with his troops and party hard. Del's philosophy was this: *Just do your job and don't create problems that I have to fix.* He was another one of those great characters whose individual persona was applauded by all.

When Del tried to make a point, every other word was a curse word. They just flowed out of his mouth. He was a lot like the Al Swearengen character in *Deadwood*—tough, sometimes crude, always loveable. Our favorite expression of Del's was 'Jesus Christ!' but he had trouble with some of his pronunciation. His voice would amp up to a high register and become a bit nasally, so it came out as 'Jesus Keist.'

'Jesus Keist, Rap, you look uptight,' he might say. 'When was the last time you had your pecker sucked?'

Yep, Al Swearengen to a tee. But his crudeness was part of his charm. Everyone loved and revered him. As roughly hewn as he could be, he was never that way with any of the women in the office. Long before the #MeToo movement, Del knew what was appropriate and what was not, and he was always a perfect gentleman. And although at times he could be quite a lady's man, I actually think women intimidated him a bit. He always seemed to get quiet and kind of shy around them.

Being in charge of the entire sales force and promotion teams in the western region was no easy task. It wasn't just about making quotas on record sales—Del had to manage all of these people, and these people all had larger-than-life personalities themselves. It was like managing a basketball team full of superstars. When he promoted some people to higher-level jobs, he had to explain to others why they weren't quite ready to move up yet. In a business where everyone has a big ego, this could be especially hard. How do you dash someone's dreams and then, in the same breath, figure out a way to keep them motivated? Del could do it.

Another Del attribute was that he took care of and protected his people—something you never see enough of in the business world. The morning after my meeting with the head of A&R at Epic, I poured my heart out to Del, then stayed in his office while he called the A&R guy. I thought it was going to be a diplomatic talk designed to diffuse the situation. Del was an expert at diplomacy.

'I hear you're giving one of my star players some real shit.'

I could hear the guy's voice on the other end of the phone as he tried to explain.

Del interrupted, his voice getting louder.

'Uh, huh. Uh, huh. WELL LISTEN, MOTHERFUCKER, IF YOU UTTER ONE MORE BAD WORD ABOUT MY GUY TO ANYONE, I'M GONNA COME OVER THERE AND BEAT THE LIVING CRAP OUT OF YOU! I'LL BREAK YOUR MOTHERFUCKING JAW, YOU MOTHERFUCKING ASSHOLE! YOU GOT THAT?'

Situation diffused. I never heard from the guy again. And I learned that intercompany politics could be handled in a myriad of ways.

Thank you, Del.

· ● ·

When I got promoted to the FM rock regional job, Del threw a party for me in the conference room. It took place after one of our weekly sales meetings. Nothing too fancy—some finger sandwiches, crudités, crackers and cheese, fresh fruit, a cake, and plenty of champagne. The corks started popping, and people dove into the food. Before long, we were all pretty juiced. Someone threw a cracker at someone else and laughed. Then a radish flew back across the table in retaliation. All of a sudden, the fruit started to fly, and before you knew it . . .

'Food fight!'

The long conference room tables were immediately separated, turned on their sides, and used as barricades, one on each side of the room. The fighting forces split into naturally formed teams based on whoever happened to be sitting where during the meeting. Food was flying at a furious pace—tomatoes, rolls, crackers, cheese squares, celery sticks, radishes, carrots. Champagne bottles were being squirted across the room like flamethrowers. Then people began to lob handfuls of cake (which was a shame, as it was really good cake). And what a mess—the carpet was beginning to get soggy.

In a capture-the-flag move, we launched our empty champagne bottles across the room like hand grenades and rushed the enemy's barricade. Diving over the top, we grabbed Del and proceeded to wrap him up head to toe in rolls of sales printouts—he looked like a mummy. We were laughing our asses off. Pictures were taken, but Del made sure they never saw the light of day.

We left the conference room in a total shambles—walls covered in cake and champagne, the carpet soggy with smooshed food and cake icing. The next day, someone declared the carpet totaled and replaced it. Word got out, and for a good month, wherever I went, people would give me a sly smile and say, 'I heard about your party.'

· ● ·

When you got a promotion at CBS Records, you also got a new office. Since I was now representing the entire western region, they wanted to move me closer to Del. But as the company was growing so fast, they were running out of office space. The only place left near Del's office was a large closet that was used to store records. Del told me that they had plans to move our offices to a new location and asked if I could please make do for now and build a small office in the closet.

Of course, I said that would be fine—what else was I going to say? But since I was going to be in a closet without a window, I decided to have some fun. One day, I got hold of Sharon (who had since gotten a job in Columbia's press department, right down the street where the recording studios were) and my buddy Spider from the mailroom, and took them both with me to Pier 1 Exports.

We had a field day in there and came back a ton of stuff, which we used to decorate my closet office like a South Seas fishing shack. The walls were covered from floor to ceiling in bamboo. Tiki masks, hand-painted Polynesian leather shields, and large Koa wooden spears adorned the walls. Fishing nets holding colored glass-ball floats and starfish hung from the ceiling, and very large shells sat on the front of my desk and on the guest table as well. When you walked in, you could swear you'd been transported to Tahiti, or at the very least the Florida Keys. I also had plans to buy a projector and show surf movies within a wooden frame behind my desk in place of a real window.

My new office was a huge hit with colleagues and visitors alike. Sharon put out a press release to the trade magazines, and we even made the *Hollywood Reporter*. Everything was going great until one day when I spied Jack Craigo, the New York headquarters' VP of sales and third in command of the entire company. Jack was a real heavyweight in the business and a very serious man who liked everything buttoned up.

Good grief, I thought. *I can't let him see this office. He's not going to get the joke—I'm gonna get fired.*

I tried to get up quickly to cut him off at the pass before he got a glimpse of my Tiki hut digs, but it was too late. I couldn't get up from behind my desk and out of the room in time to meet him before he stepped in.

Jack walked in, stopped in amazement, and slowly looked around. I tensed up and held my breath.

Here it comes, I thought.

He looked at me with his jaw dropped, and then started to laugh out loud. He had a funny kind of measured laugh. It came out in an exact cadence. Something like *ha—ha—ha—ha—ha*. He was grinning from ear to ear.

'Hey Rap, how are they runnin'?' he belted out. '*Ha—ha—ha—ha—ha.*'
Whew. I exhaled all the pent-up air in my lungs. I quickly tried to
explain, but Jack put his hands up to let me know that everything was okay.

'It's fine, Rap,' he said, still chuckling. 'I get it. Have fun with it.'

Then he sat down, and we had a long serious conversation about the
state of the record business, FM rock radio's role in helping to establish
new artists, and the power it was gaining in spurring album sales. Even
surrounded by what looked like props from *Gilligan's Island*, it was nice to
be treated professionally and taken seriously.

• ● •

It didn't take long for CBS to appreciate the results of having an FM rock
specialist. At the end of my first year, the company decided to form two sets
of staff for FM regional album promotion, one for Columbia and another
for Epic and the other associated labels. Since I was already in place, I had
my choice of label, and naturally I chose Columbia because of the huge
roster of rock legends that I would continue to get to work with.

The band I'd helped launch a few years earlier, Blue Öyster Cult, were
beginning to become legendary. Pioneering powerful production effects
to enhance their shows, they had gotten into laser light technology early
and had actually developed a 'laser tunnel' that emanated from the stage,
with two giant beams of bright blue/green light that spread out and then
warped around to create a gigantic tube shape that would completely
envelop an entire arena audience. Talk about feeling like you were on LSD!
It reminded me of the scene in the movie *The Ten Commandments* when
the Red Sea parts and the Hebrews walk between the giant walls of water.
The band used the laser tunnel for a year until the government shut them
down because they were concerned about the bottom light beam hitting
some audience members right between the eyes.

In May of 1976, BOC released the album *Agents Of Fortune*, featuring
the hit single '(Don't Fear) The Reaper.' When I first heard it, I knew I had
to uncork something very special to promote it. Taking a page from the
band's lauded laser-production imagery, I came up with a *Twilight Zone*-
esque scenario.

It's dusk, the night is closing in, and soon the sky will be pitch black. Imagine you are driving down the freeway in Southern California and suddenly a giant, blindingly bright beam of blue-green light shoots across the sky, right over your head. It's huge, and it penetrates the darkness for miles and miles.

You're startled—you've never seen anything like it, and now you're trying to make sense of it, because it came out of nowhere. It continues to glow and is now starting to move from side to side, pulsing as if it's hunting for something or someone. In fact, it looks just like the ray shooting from one of the flying saucers in *The War Of The Worlds*.

Could it be that the Aurora Borealis has somehow arrived in the skies of Los Angeles? Is it some kind of military test? Or, in fact, have aliens finally landed? Your imagination begins to get the best of you, and you begin to sweat. You pull off the freeway into the nearest gas station, where people are already gathered, everyone pointing up to the sky. The huge beam of light seems to be emanating from a small outcrop of hills. A little afraid, you hop back into your car and follow the other people who have begun to drive toward the light. You realize you are headed toward Signal Hill, the highest point in the city of Long Beach.

If aliens *have* landed, you will certainly see them. Hell, you may even meet them . . .

While many people were genuinely frightened by what was going on, others knew exactly what it was and were cheering on the light from the comfort of their own front lawns.

I knew what it was, of course. I was at the light source, at ground zero. In fact, I was the one shooting the light.

It was a lighting effect that no one had ever seen before—a thirty-watt Argon laser cannon developed by a special laboratory in the San Fernando Valley. It was so powerful that it shot for over thirty miles. And because it was a laser light, it was just as bright at the end as it was at the point of origin. I had seen it on the news one evening and thought, *Wow, if I could get hold of that thing and shoot it across a city, it would totally freak people out.* It turned out the lab was excited about renting it to me, thinking the publicity would do them good.

In those days, record companies encouraged creativity, and if you made your case well, they would give you money for inventive ideas. The next morning, I called CBS headquarters in New York.

'Hey, I need four thousand bucks to shoot a laser beam off a mountainside.'

'Of course you do, Rap,' the head of promotion replied.

He was still getting used to my event-style promotion imagination, which had recently included renting a movie-prop version of a Sherman tank for BOC's Eric Bloom and Ted Nugent to ride around on, pre-concert, in the parking lot of the Long Beach Arena. I assured him that all of Southern California would hear about this one.

I decided to bring this promotional stunt back to KNAC, where it all began, so I went to see the new program director, Paul Sullivan, who loved bold, audacious, showstopping ideas.

'So, here's the deal. We shoot this thing off Signal Hill, and we program it to do a light show for each song off the album while you debut the record in its entirety over the air. The light travels for over thirty miles and will be seen by everyone from Long Beach to Pasadena and into Orange County.'

Sullivan loved the idea and was instrumental in making it happen. At that time, giant laser beams burned so hot that they had to be cooled by water. But where the hell were we going to get water on the top of Signal Hill? Well, Signal Hill was developed for drilling oil, and it was covered with oil rigs. Paul made a deal with the Shell Oil Company to use one of their water pumps at the very top of the hill.

On the evening of the event, we mounted the laser cannon—a long glass tube encased in a metal box about ten feet long by three feet high—on top of a shed. We connected two water hoses to it and aimed it out toward the foothills of Pasadena, which were just a little more than thirty miles away. As the two scientists who came with the laser double-checked all the gadgets that made it work, Paul called the station and got them to cue up the record.

'Fire it up!' he yelled, and we turned the thing on.

Holy fucking shit! The light was so massive, and so bright, that it really did stretch all the way from Long Beach to Pasadena. And, as advertised, it was as bright in Pasadena as it was where we were standing. It looked positively unreal, and so scary that our first inclination was to immediately shut it off. We all just stared at the thing in amazement.

'We're definitely going to jail for this one,' I muttered. But I had done all my due diligence. I had even gotten permission from the staff at Long Beach Airport, who were happy that I called, lest a 747 land on us, thinking we were the runway. With a couple of weeks' worth of promotion on air, the kids in the know were ready, lying on blankets in their front yards, drinking beer, smoking dope, and staring up at the sky, all set to enjoy the music and the biggest light show they'd ever seen in their lives.

All was going swimmingly until something happened that we hadn't counted on. You, the curious person driving your car to the light source along with a few others, were not alone. Hundreds of other people had gotten in their cars and driven up the winding road to Signal Hill to check out the mysterious light. All kinds of cars were appearing and parking haphazardly around the shed. Most of them had their windows down, blaring the radio station playing the new album. Kids started to get out of their vehicles, creating a huge crowd. Yikes. We had no security. Who'd have thunk?

Some of the folks who were fascinated by the light started throwing their car keys in the air to see what would happen when they hit the beam. I had to shout down to them from atop the shed to stop, because the refraction from a light this powerful could blind someone, and it might even melt their keys. Other people had brought their party along with them, drinking beer and smoking dope. Now, I really was convinced we were all going to jail.

As the laser-beam party got into full swing, with music blaring and kids dancing in the oil field, it was time to treat the folks in Orange County to their own light show. Sullivan grabbed his remote microphone and announced over the airwaves, 'Dig this, Orange County!' We focused the beam into a fan shape and swung it around facing south. The light covered so much ground it was hard to believe. It left tracers in the sky—just magnificent.

I thought it was only a matter of time before the police showed up, but they never did. We were about fifteen minutes into side two of the album when the unthinkable happened. Some Shell employee miles away, walking through the main plant, had spotted a water valve open. Because it wasn't tagged, he thought it had been opened by mistake, so he shut it off. Back at the shed, we watched as, all of a sudden, the giant glass tube, thirsty for water, started to rupture from the back—slowly at first, and then quickly, all the way to the front.

C-R-A-A-A-A-C-K!

As instantly as the giant mysterious light had first appeared, it just as mysteriously disappeared, leaving the sky a quiet pitch black.

At first, it felt weird, like something important was missing. Just a second ago, there had been this incredible light show, parting the heavens and creating all kinds of excitement. Now there was just emptiness. Our stunned silence was immediately interrupted as the crowd went crazy with cheers and applause. It was then that we exhaled and shared smiles with one another. Even though we hadn't finished playing the entire album, we'd certainly made our point. We also made the late evening news, having blown minds from Long Beach to Pasadena, Whittier to Garden Grove. Mission accomplished.

DON'T FALL OFF THE PORCH

OVER THE YEARS, I've often heard people make snide remarks about how the artists or bands that make it are somehow specifically chosen by the record company to receive a special push while others are unceremoniously left behind. While it is true that some artists are chosen to be priority projects based on our beliefs in their probable success, it is also true that there are no givens in this business. Some artists that I was convinced were destined for stardom just never resonated with the public, while others that I just didn't get right away went on to have big careers. This is not just true for me but for all record executives, including label presidents with the power to sign artists.

At both Columbia and Epic, we took pride in giving everyone a shot—at garnering as much airplay and press as possible, putting artists out on tour, and making at least one video, all to ensure the widest exposure possible. The truth is that it's the audience's response to the music that dictates who will get a further push forward. Our philosophy was to promote everything and then read the tea leaves to see what the public wanted to hear more of. This also assured each artist that they had been given a legitimate chance to see if they could create enough interest to build a career.

In the spring of 1976, the newly formed regional album rock teams held a famous meeting at the Caribou Ranch in Colorado, about forty minutes west of Boulder. Renowned producer James William Guercio had built a state-of-the-art recording studio there with the money he made from producing Chicago's early albums. It became a haven for artists who really wanted privacy and a totally different feel from recording in a city like New York or Los Angeles.

Unlike major urban centers, Caribou Ranch had no strict rules or union regulations, which could sometimes hinder the creative process. The studio attracted top-of-the-line artists like Michael Jackson, Billy Joel, John Lennon, Elton John, and Joe Walsh, who wrote and recorded 'Rocky Mountain Way' there (as featured on an album with one of the best titles ever, *The Smoker You Drink, the Player You Get*).

At that time, the Columbia rock team was captained by Michael Pillot, an exceptional music man who'd grown up in New Orleans and whose taste in music reflected a fine simmered gumbo packed with many different flavors and spices. Mike loved and appreciated Bruce Springsteen, Elvis Costello, James Taylor, and Wille Nelson just as much as he loved and appreciated The Neville Brothers, Dr. John, Professor Longhair, Wayne Shorter, and Miles Davis. Gil Colquitt, an FM radio vet, was the East Coast rep, and I covered the West Coast. The Epic side was headed up by a fellow named Mike Shavelson, who dressed in hippie overtones and wore a feather earing, while my buddy Jim McKeon, formerly the program director at KWST-FM, had been hired to be my Epic counterpart on the West Coast.

Mac was a wonderful guy with a warm personality. He and I had become close friends while spending many scheming sessions discussing creative promotions over strawberry waffles and whipped cream along with café au laits at the Old World Restaurant on the Sunset Strip. ('An extra terrine of strawberries, please.') He had been going toe-to-toe with the legendary KMET-FM when management started to tinker too much with his vision. At the same time, I'd heard Epic was looking for someone to cover album promotion on the West Coast, so I asked him if he'd be interested in 'coming to the dark side.' I felt that Mac, with so much experience in programming rock radio (first in Detroit and then in LA), would have an extra special perspective when it came to promoting his peers. Epic took to him immediately, and Mac excelled as a record man.

Harvey Leeds, another former CBS college rep, rounded out the Epic Records squad as the label's East Coast album rock specialist. If most of us in the business are a bit left of center, Harvey lived in a world where no center exists. He was the grand character of all characters, totally outrageous, a rebel with many causes, and the quintessential New Yorker. Not too tall and a tad plump, with his own version of a Jewfro, he loved all kinds of food, talked a mile a minute with no filter, was hysterically funny, and continually came up with outrageous stunts to bring attention to the artists he was working with. Think Mel Brooks crossed with Evil Knievel, and that will give you a glimpse into his personality. He went on to be instrumental in the success of Meat Loaf, Stevie Ray Vaughan, Ozzie Osbourne, and many more. He was, and is, loved by all.

The setting couldn't have been more beautiful. The rolling hills of Colorado in spring; beautiful trees, purple, yellow, and white wildflowers everywhere, the sky a huge cerulean blue with big white puffy clouds; the air clean, fresh, and crispy thin. So far away from the hustle and bustle, we could smoke a joint, enjoy the greatest pancakes and hamburgers (made by the ranch's excellent chef), and then go for a horseback ride.

I don't think Harvey had ever seen a real horse before, much less been on the back of one. We set out for a long ride among the wildflowers. It was jaw-droppingly beautiful. The joke was that during the entire two-hour ride, our usually fast-talking New Yorker didn't say one word—not a peep. He just kept staring all around at the incredible landscape, and every so often he would look down at the beautiful animal he was riding. I think the whole thing was so far from anything he'd ever experienced that he felt like he was in a dream. We enjoyed getting high up there too, though we needed to remind ourselves of our watchwords every time we left the bunkhouse, 'Don't fall off the porch.'

When work started, the idea was to share all the music that was coming out on both labels over the next few months and put our heads together to come up with creative promotion plans for each project. The most memorable piece of music was played by Mike Shavelson. First, he played us a track from Mother's Finest, a new funk-rock band from Georgia who were following in the footsteps of Sly & The Family Stone. They sounded really good, but the song Mike played didn't quite feel like a down-the-pike home run to our ears. Fair enough, some projects were known as 'work records,' and they took a little time to seep in. And, as I say, none of us knows everything.

Mike went on to say that Epic planned to make Mother's Finest a priority, before adding that he also had 'something brand new from a band called Boston.' And then he played 'More Than A Feeling.' The whole room stopped. Wait a minute, sometimes we do know everything. We all looked at each other, stunned, especially me and Mac.

When both labels had finished their music presentations, McKeon and I asked, 'Hey, can you play that Boston song one more time?' When the music came blaring out of the speakers a second time, Mac and I looked at each other, knowing we'd just heard the next big thing. Somehow, a guy named Tom Scholz had reshuffled the deck of guitar riffs and created something unique yet something that sounded familiar at the same time. The guitars were stellar, and the vocals were even better.

'Point of order, please,' Mac said. 'Mike, that's an astonishing piece of music. If the rest of the album is that good, it's gonna blow big, I mean *really big*. With all due respect to Mother's Finest, I don't get how they'd be our #1 priority after hearing this.'

Mike went on to talk up Mother's Finest, who in all fairness were a great live band who were already known for upstaging bigger, more established acts when they opened for them. I'm sure he felt the pressure and responsibility to toe the company line and keep everyone in focus, which was very important, with so many records being released. So, for now, Mother's Finest remained our top priority.

However, because I was the Columbia guy and couldn't get in trouble for rebelling against Epic's wishes, I decided to chime in.

'Mike, you know how this goes. We all make our plans, and then the people decide. You guys can spend every last dime you have on Mother's Finest, and I'm not saying you shouldn't—they're a great band. But when "More Than A Feeling" is played for rock programmers, unless my ears have gone bad, there's gonna be a firestorm like none of us have seen in years. It's gonna explode beyond any of our control, and it's going to take over the airwaves. And that band is going become Epic's #1 priority—and fucking fast.'

Leeds smiled quietly—he knew a smash hit when he heard one. And props to Shavelson: he did his job. But deep down inside, I think he knew it as well.

Mac and I returned to Los Angeles and immediately went to visit our friend David Perry, the music director at KWST. David and his wife, Linda, had a nice apartment in Hollywood, just down from the Sunset Strip. David had hung a giant pair of JBL stereo speakers at one end of the living room that were so big they took over the whole place. It looked funny, but in those days the music ruled, and having such a big setup was not unusual, especially for an on-air disc jockey and music director at a powerful rock radio station.

We sat David down and put him in front of the speakers, like in the famous Maxell tape commercial. We put on 'More Than A Feeling' and cranked up the volume. If there was ever a sound and production that was made for JBL speakers, it's that song. The patio glass doors rattled, and the huge sound of the guitars and vocals blew back David's hair, just like in the commercial. He looked over at us, eyes bugging out, grinning ear to ear like he'd just seen God. And he had.

'When can I play this thing?'

A week later, the project was given the green light, and Perry cracked open the mic at KWST to debut 'More Than A Feeling.' Shortly after that, so did KMET, KLOS, KNAC, and every FM station across the country. Phone requests were ringing off the hook. Boston blew up faster than a speeding bullet and proved more powerful than a locomotive. Within just a few weeks, the band became Epic's top priority. The audience had spoken. The train had left the station.

• ■ •

As the music business continued to grow, so did our promotional teams. At Columbia, we added Bill 'Billy B' Bennett in the South, Dave Remedi out of Chicago to handle the Midwest, and Ed Climie for Texas and the surrounding areas. With his Texan drawl, Climie had his own way of saying things. Once, after we'd finished discussing the business at hand on a phone call, he announced, 'Rap, I'm gonna go get some groceries, go home, get wet, get prone.' That meant, *I'm going to go out to dinner, head home, take a shower, and go to sleep.*

Because we were continually bringing famous artists, disc jockeys, and other music-industry wheelers and dealers into the happening restaurants around town, we became local celebrities ourselves. We wielded sizable power because we were the force that made things happen at radio, which turned into millions of record sales. Artists' managers courted us, knowing that we were a major key to their bands' successes.

On the East Coast, the Young Turks—A&R man Mark Spector and promotion and marketing men Michael Klenfner and Rick Dobbis— frequented the Palm Steakhouse so often that their caricatures were painted on the walls. On the West Coast, we were an especially proud bunch. Notorious for our swagger and for drinking copious amounts of Dom Pérignon to celebrate our successes, we became known as The Magnum Force. There was me, Warren Williams (West Coast Top 40 in LA), Bob Conrad (Phoenix), Burt Baumgartner (San Francisco), Larry Reymann (Seattle), and Greg Phifer (Denver). We even had our own T-shirts printed, depicting a smoking .57 Magnum handgun next to a bottle of Dom. And it is with this swagger in mind that I recount the following story.

CBS had an expense report form that included separate lines for everything: in-town expenses, travel, entertainment, and so on. I hated filling out these reports. It was very time-consuming, and, as mentioned, I am terrible at math. I was constantly missing five cents here or ten cents there, and the report had to add up exactly. I could easily spend an extra hour or more trying to find where those few extra pennies had disappeared. Beyond that, filling out a month's worth of expenses required a lot of writing—explanations of travel and business meetings over breakfasts, lunches, dinners, and drinks, denoting who you were with and what companies or radio stations they represented.

One day, in a frisky mood, I thought I'd have some fun. I decided to write every single letter, number, comma, and dollar sign with a different, brightly colored pen. Using blue, black, red, green, purple, orange, and yellow, it took me a good five hours to complete the form. When it was done, it looked like a painting by Georges Seurat—so many little characters of color, sitting side by side in such a joyful display. It was blinding if you tried looking at it for too long.

The expense department was run by a wonderful woman named Helen Katsaros. She was very friendly, had a big heart, and was always extremely helpful. Most of us were usually a couple of months behind with our expenses, and Helen would send a gentle reminder or call our assistants to give us a friendly kick in the pants to get up to date. She had an entire room full of people who sat at desks and went through the expense reports of every single employee in the company. That's a lot of paper.

I mailed in my Seurat-style expense report and waited for a reaction. Not a peep was heard from the New York office. Nothing. Total silence. My check was processed and sent back to me in the normal fashion.

About eight months later, I was in New York for some long-range planning meetings. I decided to say hi to Helen, as I had never met her in person. I walked into the room with all the people sitting at their desks, and Helen came up to me.

'Hi, Helen,' I said. 'I just wanted to meet you in person.'

I guess she figured that I was one of the album rock guys by my looks, as I was still sporting the big Afro, mustache, and goatee.

'Are you Mike Gussler?' she asked, referring to one of my colleagues from Texas.

'No, I'm Paul Rappaport.'

'*You're* Paul Rappaport?' she asked. 'The guy who sent us the Impressionist expense report?' Then she turned to the room full of desks and people and said, 'Can I have your attention, please? *This* is Paul Rappaport!'

I got a standing ovation.

HEADS DOWN, FREAK 'EM OUT

ONE OF THE GREATEST perks of my job was that I got to go on the road with the artists I was promoting. Sometimes that just meant a straight promotional tour designed for radio interviews, or perhaps the artist playing a couple of songs with an acoustic guitar live over the air. Often, when you traveled with a band on tour, you'd invite radio and press to the show and to hang out with the artists backstage afterward.

This was most important at the beginning of an artist's career, when seeing someone like Bruce Springsteen, Elvis Costello, or Billy Joel live in person was so impressive that it answered any lingering questions a radio programmer might have about whether or not to play their records. But whether it was a promo tour or a concert tour, traveling with an artist was always an adventure. You entered their world and became part of their lifestyle. By spending quality time together, long-lasting bonds were formed. Here are three of my fondest memories.

A listen to The Kinks' 'Life On The Road' will put you in the mood. That song pretty much sums up everything.

• ● •

I loved Mott The Hoople—glam rock with real groove and slash guitar, played first by the great Mick Ralphs and then by the twisty Luther Grosvenor, aka Ariel Bender. I also got a kick out of the adorable groupies that followed them from city to city. Every night I had to let them in through the backstage door, as I didn't have the heart to turn them away after seeing the distances they'd traveled.

'I just saw you in LA last night. How the hell did you get to Phoenix?'

'Oh, we drove all night. Please let us in, we just *looooove* Buffin [the band's drummer], and we *must* see him!'

They were very sweet indeed, and I remember Buffin having a field day with all the young ladies.

I was with the band for their tour in support of 'All The Young Dudes,' their hit song written by fellow glam-rocker David Bowie. My favorite member of the band was the bass player, Pete 'Overend' Watts. It was fun watching him get dressed in his stage clothes. Every night he put on huge over-the-knee, thigh-high platform leather boots, which he wore outside his pants. They were so long and so stiff that the roadies had to put them on with Watts lying back on a couch, legs stretched straight out, while they pulled the zippers all the way up with pliers. Then they'd grab his arms and pull him up, stiff-legged, to a standing position. From there, he could never sit down again, only walk absolutely straight-legged around the stage, without ever being able to bend his knees even an inch. During long evening performances with multiple encores, he would get so tired. After the last curtain call, he would walk briskly back to the dressing room with that very funny, stiff-legged gate, and collapse straight backward onto the couch, begging the roadies to quickly grab their pliers and release him from the bondage.

The mastermind behind Mott was, of course, Ian Hunter, a great songwriter and vocalist with big-time flare and powerful stage presence. He's also a great guy who, although quite proud of his achievements, did not take himself too seriously, which I always found quite refreshing.

Whether it was because we had similar hairstyles or just loved the same music, Ian and I hit it off pretty well, and we enjoyed each other's company. He was fond of a particular red wine at the time that was rather expensive. I remember saving my expense money so I could treat him to a bottle at a dinner we had at the Beverly Hills Hotel. When I went to pick him up the next morning, to take him for an interview at KMET, I walked into his room and found at least eight empty bottles of the exact same wine. I had to laugh. I thought it had been an extra special occasion, but he was living off the stuff!

That morning, Ian was dressed in jeans and a nice shirt. As we were about to leave, he asked me to wait a minute. He went into his bedroom and came back out in black leather pants. Then he had another thought and went back in to put on one of his blousy ruffled shirts. Again, we were about to leave when he went back a third time and finally came out with his black leather jacket that matched his pants. He was now dressed in full stage garb. As we were walking out the door, he added the final touch—the big dark sunglasses that were his patented look. He lifted the shades, gave me a sweet wink, and then, in his deep English accent, quietly admitted, 'Me image, you know.' We both laughed.

After Mott, Ian went out on his own, and we had a pretty big rock hit with the song 'Once Bitten Twice Shy,' from his self-titled solo album. The record featured a searing lead guitar solo by Mick 'Ronno' Ronson, who used to hang out with another guitar great and pal of mine, Earl Slick. When the two of them hit parties together, all kinds of mayhem were sure to break out.

I put together a West Coast press and radio tour for Ian to promote the album. His manager, Fred Heller, a nice fellow who always sported a bowtie, sent his associate director, Sunny Schnier, out on the road with us. Sunny was a beautiful gal, very buttoned-up and businesslike, and also very fashion-forward.

In San Francisco, we had two major interviews: one with Joel Selvin from the *San Francisco Chronicle* and the other with KSAN-FM. The KSAN interview was to take place the night before we saw Joel, and it was a giant step for Ian because, up until this point, the station only played music from the traditional rock culture—the Grateful Dead, Bob Dylan, The Allman Brothers. Playing a song by a 'glam rock' artist was thought of as forbidden, but the night DJ, Norman Davis (aka Night Owl), was a very hip dude, and Mott and Ian Hunter were not lost on him.

The KSAN interview was a real breakthrough for Ian, but while we were driving to the station, 'disaster' struck.

'We have to stop,' Sunny announced. 'I just broke a nail.'

'Sunny, we can't stop. We can't be late for this one.'

'No, really, this is important. We need to stop at a drugstore so I can get something to patch it.'

'Sunny, we really can't stop,' I repeated. I felt bad, though, and not wanting her to think I was an uncaring person, I added, 'But I promise when we get to KSAN, I'll fix your nail for you.'

'Huh? *You'll* fix my nail?'

Sunny sounded very disgruntled, but she could see that I wasn't about to stop.

Once we reached the station and got Ian settled in the studio with Norman, I motioned to Sunny to follow me into the engineer's room, where there were tape machines and editing equipment. When you edit a tape, you place it across a thick metal block with an indentation made for your finger to press down on the tape. You hold the piece of tape in place while you take a razorblade with your other hand, and to the right of that spot, you slash the tape through a slit in the block that acts as a guide. Then you make another slash further down the tape where you want the edit to end, and place some white editing tape across both pieces, splicing them together.

I took Sunny's finger with the broken nail and placed it on the indentation, pulled some white editing tape from a reel above, and spliced the two pieces of broken nail together.

'Voila! Fixed!'

Sunny looked amazed. I took another small piece of tape and wrapped it around the back of the nail for extra strength.

'There. That'll get you through tomorrow, and maybe even the next day.'

A rock'n'roll road remedy.

For all promo tours, I was in charge not only of setting up the interviews and delivering the artists to the radio stations but also of initiating all of the travel, including airline tickets, hotels, rental cars, and meals. For all of these things I used my company American Express card. I would use it over and over and over again—I was constantly pulling it out of my wallet. It became a habit, an automatic second sense. Whenever something needed to be done to complete a mission, or there was a hassle, I didn't even have to think. I just pulled out the old AE.

As I mentioned earlier, Ian was fond of his red wine, I was fond of some other things, and everyone was fond of marijuana. Late nights spent with DJs could result in some very hazy mornings. In fact, I remember being in a bit of a haze throughout that entire trip. I got the work done, but sometimes I was on remote control.

Late in the morning after the KSAN interview, I was driving in that same remote-control state as we headed to Sausalito for lunch to do the interview with Joel Selvin. We were a tad late, and I was speeding (helpful hint: don't ever speed in Sausalito). Sure enough, I heard a siren, looked in my rearview mirror, and saw the red lights flashing.

Uh-oh.

It had been a long night and a rough morning. This road trip was beginning to take its toll, and I was feeling like I'd been in one long movie for days and nights that seemed endlessly hooked together.

My brain was in a fuzzier state than I realized. I knew, instinctively, that when you are pulled over by the police, you have to hand something to the officer. I just couldn't remember for the life of me what that thing was. The incident registered as just another hassle, so I pulled out my instant remedy, the panacea for all things, and handed the cop my American Express card. Yep.

The cop peered into the car. He looked at me—big hair, big sunglasses—then over to Sunny, who looked like she'd just stepped out of *Vogue* magazine and into the passenger seat. He looked in the backseat, where he saw Hunter—bigger hair, bigger sunglasses. We were quite a scene, I'm sure. Then he looked down at the AE card, looked at me again, took off his police-style aviator shades, got really close to my face, and began to speak very softly.

'Son, I don't know where you're from, but here in Sausalito, we don't take bribes.' Then he screamed in my face, 'AND IF WE DID, DO YOU THINK WE'D TAKE AMERICAN EXPRESS?!'

I was the laughing stock of the car for the next two days.

• ● •

The Jamaican reggae musician Peter Tosh had been one of the core members of The Wailers, but in the mid-70s he sought to establish himself as a solo artist. In 1975, Columbia put out his album *Legalize It*, featuring a cover image showing Peter sitting in a field of marijuana, smoking a large pipe painted in Rastafarian green, yellow, red, and black. We had a hit on album rock radio with the title track, so I put together a promo tour of the West Coast for Peter, who was traveling with a funny little sidekick named Ozzy.

When I toured with an artist, I tended to sidle up to their lifestyle while we were together. If I was with Roger McGuinn, that would mean waking up at noon every day and having a cheeseburger and a beer for breakfast. There could be no radio morning show interviews. Everything had to be planned for after the cheeseburger/beer combo. If I was with Mick Jones from The Clash, I would enjoy an afternoon cup of Typhoo tea. A few years later, I would go on tour with Ron Wood and Keith Richards and The New Barbarians, and during that week, I hardly ate or slept at all. More on that later.

Going the road with Peter Tosh meant smoking ganja, as he called it, and a fair amount of it. The day I met Peter, the first thing he did was take a vile of cocaine I had with me and throw it away—literally.

'Hey! That's fifty bucks of coke you just tossed!'

'Rrrrap,' he replied in his beautiful, deep Jamaican accent, 'thees is very bad for you, mon. Only smoke ganja. Very good for your body and soul.'

So, while I traveled with Peter, I found myself living on ganja, nuts and berries, and green mint tea with honey. That was the other big thing: Peter didn't want me drinking coffee. 'That bad for you, mon. Always drink mint tea with honey.' He carried his own little plastic honey-bear jar with him wherever he went. 'No stress, no anxiety—just peace.' He told me you should always travel with mint teabags and a little container of honey, and then, on an airplane, all you had to do was ask for hot water and you were set.

I must admit, after a week on the road with Peter, I did feel an awful lot healthier.

Peter dressed in army fatigues with boots and wore a black beret and very large dark sunglasses that looked like goggles. Honestly, he looked very scary and dangerous, like a military or revolutionary figure. Although he was a very peaceful character, that get-up put a lot of his fellow airplane passengers in a heightened state of anxiety. I know we were followed by plainclothes law enforcement of some sort because I saw the same guy sitting not too far from us reading a newspaper in every airport we visited.

Being a Rastafarian, Peter used marijuana to gain wisdom, open spiritual doors, and become closer to Jah (God) and creation. Unaccustomed to being in America, he kept pulling out large spliffs and tightly packed balls of marijuana from his pockets at inappropriate times. Once, we were on our way to the *Cashbox* magazine offices in Hollywood, and right on the corner of Sunset and Cahuenga, in broad daylight, he pulled out a baseball-sized package covered in brown paper and opened it up to show me.

'Good ball that, mon!'

'Jesus Christ!' I yelled. My hair stood on end. 'That may be the best ball in the history of the world, Peter, but the Hollywood police department is one block away, behind us, and if you don't put that thing back in your pocket right away, the only promo tour you and I will be taking is to Federal Prison!'

'Okay, okay. Can I smoke a spliff at *Cashbox*?'

'NO!'

'*Billboard*?'

'NO!'

'When we go to KMET?'

'Yes,' I smiled. 'You can smoke a *big* spliff at KMET! In fact, they have a special room for it.'

Certain radio stations were more relaxed than others when it came to smoking dope in their offices. KMET was one of those, but no place was more relaxed than KZEL in Eugene, Oregon. When it came to smoking marijuana, these people were professionals. And because it played such a big part in their lifestyle, everyone at the station was looking forward to meeting Peter.

All along the two-hour drive from Portland to Eugene, Peter, Ozzy, and I were gaining all sorts of wisdom, and at a rapid pace. Halfway to Eugene, totally baked, we saw a huge rainbow. Peter made us stop the car, convinced this was a sign from God. We pulled over to a field where Peter got out and started running around with his hands in the air, shouting, 'Jah, God! Jah, God!'

When we finally reached KZEL, we were really hammered. Jamaican weed is pretty powerful stuff. But the folks at the station were so happy to meet Peter that they immediately wanted to start sharing their best crop with us. Yikes. They all wanted to get high with Peter Tosh. Can you get *too high* on marijuana? I found out the answer on that day: yes, you can. I waved it away, but Peter, wanting to be kind and sociable, smoked every joint put in his mouth. He also wanted to share some of his own Jamaican wonder with his newfound friends.

We did the interview with talented woman disc jockey and supreme musicologist Chris Mays. I remember Peter being so high that he was rambling for a good part of that interview—lots of stream-of-consciousness stuff. It was all very interesting—about his culture, Jamaican history, the part ganja played in all of that, and so on—but he was clearly gone, gone, gone, operating in another galaxy. He played at least one song on his acoustic guitar, but he struggled, and he had everyone laughing, including himself, when he tried to record a simple live promo for the station. He just couldn't get his words to go in the right order.

Past that, and the fact that I spent some time hanging out with my good buddy Stan Garrett, the program director, I don't remember a fucking thing. I'm sure we must have had a great party that evening, but there's just a big blank space there. And I don't remember how we got back to Portland the next day either.

• ● •

Elvis Costello's first tour of America was an exciting one. We had gotten an excellent response from the FM format to his debut album, *My Aim Is True*, and both the folks in the music industry and his new fans were looking forward to seeing him perform for the first time with his band, The Attractions. I first saw him along with some rock radio friends I'd had invited down to his debut at the Whisky A Go-Go in Hollywood. His performance was riveting, and we all realized we were witnessing something new and exceptional.

After the show, I met Elvis and his colorful manager, Jake Riviera, plus The Attractions band: Bruce Thomas on bass, Pete Thomas on drums, and Steve Nieve on keyboards. It being their first time in America, I remember asking Elvis what his plan was.

'Heads down and freak 'em out,' he replied, making clear his desire to make a big impression.

Good plan. It worked like a charm.

When they came back for an expanded second tour of the States, America was still quite new to them. It was fun to see their reactions to American culture. I remember taking them for a Mexican dinner in Portland, Oregon. I believe it was the first time they'd ever experienced Mexican food. Pete looked at Bruce and asked, in his thick English accent, 'Would you like to split a *burr-ito*?' He had no idea what it was.

One day, Steve walked out of a five-and-dime store looking curiously at the pack of Lifesavers he'd just bought.

'You don't know what those are, do you?' I asked.

Steve shook his head. I realized he had a sweet tooth, just like me, and as a kid growing up in the 50s and 60s, I was extremely well versed in American candy. So, every day on the tour, I took pleasure in buying Steve a new treat and explaining what it was.

'Steve, this is an American legend, a Three Musketeers candy bar—it's chocolate with fluffy nougat inside.'

'This is a Milky Way—similar to Three Musketeers, but with a caramel layer on top.'

'This is a Snickers bar. Same thing as the Milky Way, but add peanuts.'

'And this . . . *this*, Steve, is an Abba-Zaba!'

On a healthier note, I'm not sure if it was the Mexican food, but Elvis started to have a real jones for avocados.

While we were in Portland, Oregon, something happened to the equipment truck, and we were told that Steve's Vox organ wasn't going to make it to the show.

'Well, that's that,' the road manager said sadly. 'We're gonna have to cancel tonight's performance.'

Elvis's first concert in this great music town was going to be crucial to the building of what would become a long-lasting career. Missing his debut at the Paramount Theater was not an option.

'Before you do that,' I said, 'give me a minute.'

In those days, rock radio was a real community, everyone dedicated to the advancement of the new music we all loved so much. I called the local rocker, KGON-FM, and asked the afternoon jock if he could do us a favor and announce our predicament. Could he ask his listeners for any volunteers who owned keyboards and might lend them to us for the evening, and could they please bring them to the backstage entrance of the Paramount at 6pm?

I explained to Steve that Portland was a passionate music city and that I could guarantee that at least one keyboard would show up, though it might not be the kind he used. He said he would make do.

At 6pm, Steve, the road manager, and I went around to the back entrance of the theater. Lo and behold, there were three guys with keyboards, all set up and ready to go. To our surprise, one was a Vox organ, the exact same model Steve used onstage. We offered to pay the young man for the use of his keys, but he refused the money. He just wanted to lend a hand to a fellow musician. This was another sign of how things were back then—a generation of like minds, all putting our best foot forward for the sake of the music.

That show turned out to be one of the highlights of the tour. After an extended applause asking for a third encore, it appeared Elvis wasn't coming back. The house lights went up and the black curtain backdrop was hoisted, revealing the raw brick back wall. The audience started filing out of the theater. But then El surprised us by coming back for yet one more song. The crowd went nuts, and everyone who had already gone out of the theater started rushing back in. It was pandemonium—forget finding your original seats, everyone just stood there, beaming and loving the performance of a new young artist who wanted to give his all for his fans. No mood lighting, no production, just four guys under the bright house lights, warts and all, playing against a brick wall for the people.

A real bond between artist and fan was created that night. It was one of those moments you never forget.

I loved traveling with artists when they were shopping for instruments or other musical items. One time I'd gone with David Bromberg to look for old violins, and another time with Rolling Stones keyboardist Nicky Hopkins, in search of bootleg albums that were recorded from his side of the stage so he could hear himself play. Now, Elvis Costello was in search of a Rickenbacker six-string guitar.

The Rickenbacker has a jingle-jangle sound and is especially great for rhythm, but many musicians who bought Ricks wound up swapping out the original pickups for other styles so they could obtain heavier and more versatile tones. Elvis wanted to buy one with original pickups—he loved that true Rickenbacker sound. We had a devil of a time finding one. In fact, we couldn't. He was about to give up when I told him about my mine, which was sitting under my bed collecting dust. Since Frank Shargo had given me that Gibson Melody Maker and I was well into playing the blues, I hardly picked up the Rick anymore. And I would never switch out the pickups. I never liked switching any parts of guitars to change them into something they were not meant to be. I've always believed each guitar has its own soul, and my Rickenbacker's soul was totally intact.

I told Elvis I'd give him my Rickenbacker. He was taken aback by the gesture. Guitars become friends, and they can be hard to part with, so he suggested that he at least buy it from me. I thought about it for a second, but over the years I had been given a few guitars as gifts, and I felt like in some way it was my turn to give one back to someone else. Because I was such a fan of his music, and the fact that we'd formed a genuine friendship, I told Elvis it would mean more for me to give it to him as a gift. So, I did.

Upon the band leaving the West Coast, I loaded their tour bus with a fifty-dollar assortment of candies for Steve, and a crate of avocados for Elvis, along with my Rickenbacker. Later that year, I got a call from him in England.

'Rap, wait until you hear my new album, *Armed Forces*. Your Rickenbacker is all over it!'

I was blown away. Now my old friend, the red Rick that I'd bought at Downey Music when I was seventeen years old, was about to be heard all over the world, on what would become one of Elvis Costello's most celebrated albums. Every time I hear songs like 'Accidents Will Happen,' 'Oliver's Army,' or '(What's So Funny 'Bout) Peace Love And Understanding,' I get a huge smile on my face. Sometimes I choke up a bit.

Back then, we were making a lot of things up as we went along. But on a higher level, it seems like some things were written in the stars. Between saving the Portland date and having my Rick ensconced in rock history, I began to feel like I was put here for a reason.

For a few years running after *Armed Forces* was released, Elvis would call around Christmastime and say, 'Hey, Rap, I'm so sorry, but it's been a very cold winter, and we ran out of firewood, so I had to . . .'

He'd say it in a way that really had me wondering. Damn that British humor.

TOUGHER THAN THE REST

IN THE 1970s, Bruce Springsteen began to capture our hearts and souls with his purposeful songs, important sociological messages, and the just-plain-fun stories he told onstage. His incredibly moving performances transformed the biggest skeptics into religious zealots helping to spread the word. Bruce Springsteen was your friend, your confidante—he stood for everything you did, and he was your voice, speaking your truth, and speaking it to millions of others who felt just like you. For so many people around the world, he still does. Whether you've seen Bruce perform a hundred times or it's your first concert, you walk away feeling exalted, joyful, fulfilled, and with a smile planted on your face guaranteed to last for at least a month.

I had a lot of cool adventures with Bruce and The E Street Band. I started working with him right at the very beginning, with his first Columbia release, *Greetings From Asbury Park, NJ*. I loved the songs and imagery and was immediately attracted to the music. But it was when Sharon and I first saw Bruce live, at the Troubadour in 1973, that we realized Bruce was something *extra* special.

The Troubadour show was so powerful that the next morning I fired off a telex to the New York offices, trying to capture the excitement that everyone in the audience had experienced that night. Before the age of computers, we had a machine called a TWX. You typed your message on one end, and it came out on the receiving end, just as you'd typed it.

Bruce was known for playing a Fender Esquire guitar, which was quite unusual among rockers, so it became a trademark for him. I made my poor assistant type the message in the shape of that guitar—with only one word across for the headstock, perhaps two on the neck going down, and the rest following the curves of the body as I had traced it for her. It drove her nuts, but when the telex printed in New York, it looked exactly like Bruce's Fender Esquire, and it blew the folks at headquarters' minds.

Without a doubt, the phrase 'hardest working man in show business' describes Bruce Springsteen to a tee. Of all the people I've ever worked with, I've never seen anyone as driven as he is. Not even close.

In the early days, I enjoyed watching him rehearse the band at soundcheck. At around 3pm, the E Street band would be onstage, and for large, arena-size shows, Bruce had an extra-long wire attached to his guitar. It had to be one hundred feet or more so that it could stretch all the way from his amplifier down the center aisle to the soundboard, three quarters of the way back in the hall. Bruce rehearsed the arrangements while at the same time working on getting the sound right, twisting knobs this way and that. I'd never seen such detailed attention to the control of the overall sound of a band by the artist like that before, and I've never seen it since.

A typical soundcheck could last two hours, and I remember one that lasted for three—that's easily four or five times longer than any other artist or band I've ever witnessed. Then the band would take a break come back at eight o'clock and do a four-hour show. For anyone who's ever seen Bruce, that's four hours of constant athleticism, running up and down the stage, sliding on his knees, and being passed around the auditorium on his back by his loving fans. After the show and a good forty-five-minute towel-down, Bruce would come out of his dressing room to meet, shake hands, and talk with all the radio, press, and retail personnel, along with any lucky fans who happened to have made it backstage. And this was no hurried affair. Bruce took the time to have a meaningful conversation with each person who was there to meet him. Sometimes, these meet-and-greets could go on until one o'clock in the morning, then Bruce would finally head back to his hotel, get a few winks of sleep, and get up and do the whole thing all over again, city by city by city.

At another concert later on in his career, after his traditional three or four encores, Bruce came backstage looking totally spent. Dripping with sweat, he looked from behind the stage curtain to see if any audience members were still standing and clapping. Also backstage that night was Columbia's head of sales, Tom Donnarumma, who looked quizzically at Bruce and said something like, 'Gee whiz, Bruce, you've already done way more than anyone would ever expect of you. Are you actually thinking about going out there again?'

'Donnarumma,' Bruce rasped, looking back at him, 'I'm in the business of the unexpected.'

In his autobiography, Bruce talks about not feeling the support of the Columbia label in his early years. That was certainly true of the higher-ups, but there were others among us who understood right away that we were witnessing rock'n'roll history. We strapped on our armor, held our shields high, and drew our swords to go out into the world like gladiators, ready to fight to the death to help make his career happen. In the beginning, his four biggest fans were the aforementioned Mike Pillot, Peter Philbin in A&R, Glen 'Brahma' Brunman from the publicity department, and me.

It was hard for Bruce at first because he was cutting his own musical groove. Artists who do that can go on to have long careers, but they often take longer to get there, simply because it takes a while for people to absorb something new. I was having an especially hard time on the West Coast as most of the radio folks just didn't get Bruce. I would hear complaints like, 'He's an *East Coast* artist. He's singing about giant Exxon signs—we don't have Exxon here.' I couldn't believe they could hear Bruce's incredible lyrics and come away with just that. Other folks had written him off as a Bob Dylan copycat.

Despite all my hard work trying to spread the word about what I was hearing and what I'd seen at the Troubadour, only two disc jockeys in Southern California played any of the music from Bruce's first two albums, *Greetings From Asbury Park, NJ* and *The Wild, The Innocent & The E Street Shuffle*. They were Steven Clean and Mary Turner, both at KMET. Mary especially took a liking to Bruce's music, and one of my favorite memories is that wonderful interview they did together. Bruce agreed to very few interviews back then, so this one was going to be a big deal. When Mary put her stamp on a new act, it gave that artist instant credibility. And she was now playing Bruce Springsteen at least once or twice every evening.

When I arrived at the station to meet Bruce, he was at the guard gate, fuming. At the time, he didn't dig the rock-star limousine thing at all—he liked to drive himself everywhere. On this occasion, he'd pulled up in a rental car wearing blue jeans and his patented rolled-up flannel sleeve shirt, and the guard at the gate, who was a friend of mine, didn't believe this was really Bruce Springsteen.

The guard apologized and said that every other artist who ever came to KMET would pull up in a limo, so he was skeptical. I tried to explain that to Bruce, but he was really pissed.

'Get in,' he said, motioning for me to get into the passenger seat of his car. He burned rubber as he drove us into the parking garage, his anger turning to road rage as he tore around each corner as we worked our way up to the roof. The tires were squealing, and sometimes I thought we were riding on two wheels. I held the armrest for dear life. I remember thinking, *There's a fifty/fifty chance that we could fly off the edge of the garage, have a bad accident, and die.* The only silver lining I could muster was, *Well, if we do die, at least I'll be remembered for going out with Bruce Springsteen.*

When we got into the station and started to settle down, I popped a bottle of champagne to try to loosen everyone up. It really helped, and pretty soon Bruce was lighthearted and talkative. The best part of the interview came when Mary asked Bruce what his band did while he was out doing all the public relations stuff.

'*My* band? My band is probably back at the Sunset Marquis, catching all the television sets the English bands are throwing out the window!'

The E-Street Band were musicians like I'd never met before. They were somehow made of tougher stuff than most. I guess that came from playing all those long sets in bars together and all being from New Jersey and the New York area. I had fun hanging out with them, mostly with drummer 'Mighty Max' Weinberg and bassist Gary Talent, who were quite approachable.

The sax player, Clarence Clemons, was a riot. I was once on the road with the band for about a week. Every day of that week, Clarence wore the same outfit—a light brown Mercedes mechanic jumpsuit. We were on a plane going to one of our final destinations when I finally got up the courage to ask him about it.

'Hey, big man, you've been wearing that exact same Mercedes jumpsuit for five days in a row now. Pretty soon, it might start to get a little funky—how long are you gonna wear it?'

Clarence looked down at me with that big ol' grin of his.

'I'm going to wear it until someone gets the *idea*,' he said, shooting an eye toward Bruce and his manager, Jon Landau. Money was starting to roll in, and the big man was looking to upgrade.

Also joining the band on the road was another soon-to-be friend, the talented writer Dave Marsh. He always carried a little white typewriter with him to capture the rock history being made. On off-hours, I loved watching him play pinball. He had a sixth sense about where the ball was going before it got there, and he banged the hell out of the machines using powerful hip action, urging if not demanding the ball go where he wanted. Watching him play pinball was a show in and of itself.

Those innocent days are always the best, when it's all about the art and the mission. After the big money rolls in, things get complicated, especially for the artist. I once found Bruce sitting on a curb with his fist curled under his chin like Rodin's statue *The Thinker*. Bruce is not a happy-go-lucky kind of guy; he's not brooding, either, just kind of even. But on that day he looked unusually down.

'What's wrong, Boss?' I asked.

He looked up at me as if he'd had a lightbulb moment.

'I just figured out that if I'm gonna make more than five hundred dollars a week, I'm gonna have more than five-hundred-dollar-a-week problems.'

I would go on to learn the same lesson.

When Bruce released *The River*, he had a shot at having his first Top 40 hit single with 'Hungry Heart.' In those days, you could sell plenty of albums just off rock radio airplay alone, but if you also had a song that crossed over to the Top 40 format, you got a whole lot of new fans. A million-selling album could quickly multiply into a four-million seller. I was backstage at a show in Cleveland when I was informed by the New York office that 'Hungry Heart' was poised to become a big hit.

I walked up to Bruce after the show, excited to share the news.

'Great news: you're about to have a big hit Top 40 record! Ka-ching, ka-ching!'

'Man, that's great,' he replied, looking at me wide-eyed. ''Cause you know my 'vette? I've been lookin' for a set of wheels for it for the longest time!'

At the time, Bruce was driving a cool-looking blue Corvette.

'No, Bruce,' I said, 'I'm talkin' about *buying the whole Corvette factory* kind of money!'

Bruce just looked at me like I was nuts, shook his head, and walked away.

Another time, Bruce and I were out eating pizza together, reminiscing about the Roxy show, when the subject suddenly changed to surfing. He told me about his early surfing days on the Jersey shore. It being a common interest, we shared some great surf stories.

'And Clarence surfed too!' he exclaimed. 'Can you imagine the big man on a surfboard?

'At one time I lived in the back of a surfboard shop for three months,' he added. 'The resin fumes drove me crazy for the first two weeks, and then I got used to it.'

Bruce looked up at me with eyes wide, like he'd just realized something major.

'Do you think that affected my writing?'

'Gee, I don't know, Bruce, but you've written some of the greatest songs ever, so who cares.'

He pondered my answer in classic deep Bruce thought, then went back to his pizza.

YOUR PURSE IS ON FIRE

BY 1979, THINGS had changed in New York. CBS had a new director of album rock promotion, Fred Humphrey. The company had switched around some responsibilities, and I got promoted to become Fred's second-in-command as national director of album rock promotion based in LA.

Columbia had recently signed Ronnie Wood as a solo artist, and he was about to release his first album, *Gimme Some Neck*. Woody was also putting together a band to tour the album, featuring Rolling Stones mates Keith Richards and Bobby Keys, as well as some other stellar musicians. I was excited—I had been a fan of his since The Faces, featuring Rod Stewart and himself, while Keith Richards had been my all-time rock hero ever since I became a Stones fan during my teenage years. He personified everything about rock'n'roll to me.

The Faces were a total blast to see live. At the concert I attended, the first thing they did was come out onstage and build a makeshift bar next to their amplifiers. In between songs, band members would go over to the bar and have shots of whiskey or whatever else was displayed on the shelf. This proved very effective in guaranteeing a rip-roaring performance. And as the band got more lit, the more rockin' they became. In fact, the greatest move I ever saw was when a gal in the audience threw one of her high heels onstage. Rod picked up the shoe and was about to throw it back when his eyes lit up with a great idea. He went over to the bar, grabbed a bottle of whiskey, and returned to centerstage. There, he filled the shoe with whiskey, held it high over his head, and then tilted it back, letting the stream of golden liquid pour into his mouth. Having drunk from the girl's shoe, he tossed it back into the approving crowd, who went bonkers. Now, that's rock'n'roll.

Woody's unique style of rhythm guitar was the engine that drove The Faces. Keith Richards's rhythm style is what drove The Rolling Stones (together with Charlie Watts, of course). And the interplay between the two guitars—the 'weaving,' as Keith calls it—is what makes The Rolling Stones' sound. The New Barbarians would excel as a band by featuring these two driving forces in perfect rock step with one another.

Woody and Keith were the first two Rolling Stones I met, and it could not have been more perfect. I'd heard Woody was in our West Coast art department, approving the album cover for *Gimme Some Neck*. I thought it might be a good opportunity to hop down a floor and introduce myself. And no sooner had I walked through the door when he came right up to me.

'Hi, I'm Ronnie Wood,' he announced, bright-eyed and bushy-tailed, as if he had a notion that somehow I wouldn't recognize him.

Of course, you are, I thought. *Who the hell else would you be, with that chiseled face and bird of paradise hairdo?*

'I know,' I laughed.

We immediately hit it off. Being a guitar player helped create a bond with many of the artists I met. We all speak the same passionate language about the instrument. And, at the end of the day, celebrity aside, all of these guys are just players at heart, and they all love to talk guitar.

The next thing I knew, I was being invited to a rehearsal, which was held on a large soundstage at a movie studio lot in Culver City. Aside from Woody's wife at the time and a gal who was taking care of Keith, I was the only other person there who wasn't a band member. And what a band it was. Besides Woody and Keith, it featured Bobby Keys on sax, Ian McLagan (who'd played with both The Faces and The Rolling Stones) on keys, jazz-fusion giant Stanley Clarke on bass, and Zigaboo Modeliste, an absolute cannon from The Meters, on the drums.

As soon as I arrived, Woody came running up to me excitedly.

'Hey, Rap, come here, I want to introduce you to Keith.'

Wow, I thought. This was going to be a big moment. We walked over to the drum riser, and all of a sudden standing right in front of me was my all-time rock idol. I was stunned. Rolling Stones songs, albums, and live shows flashed through my brain. But even more importantly, this was the guy I'd emulated—unabashedly copied—for years while learning how to play electric guitar. His music was a part of me, and I have to admit to being a bit starstruck. Okay, *a lot* starstruck.

Keith immediately put me at ease. He was unexpectedly approachable and totally down-to-earth. He didn't seem to have any false airs, and he made me feel right at home. I guess he figured Woody wouldn't let just anyone into the fold. He was dressed in black jeans, white T-shirt, and a black leather jacket. With a guitar slung over his shoulder, he looked . . . well, perfect.

'Hi, nice to meet ya,' he said. 'Wanna do a line?'

He pointed to the drum riser nearby, where four long lines of cocaine had been laid out side by side, like rails on a railroad track.

'S-sure,' I said, a bit timidly.

I was certainly no stranger to cocaine. The drug had become widely popular within the music industry, and I found myself under its spell along with everyone else. Using it had become a social thing. Many people I knew carried a vial or some other fancy container with them, in the same way people carried their private flasks during prohibition days. Sharing a couple of lines or small hits via a tiny coke spoon was akin to offering someone a swig or two of whiskey from their flask. It was that kind of warm offering Keith was extending. And here I was, doing it with my hero.

Okay, I thought, *I'm done now. I can retire.* Then I sat down and watched one of the most remarkable events I've ever seen in music: Keith Richards teaching Stanley Clarke how to play rock'n'roll. Stanley, an incredible visionary on bass with monster chops, came from the jazz-fusion world and had been a founding member of Return To Forever. He had a funky style, and he played a lot of notes. Rock'n'roll is pretty simple by comparison.

The band would start a song, and then Keith would wave his hands, signaling the guys to stop. He'd look evenly at Stanley and then tell him, in that familiar deep, gravelly voice, 'No, Stanley, that's too many notes.'

They would start again and then immediately stop again.

'Stanley, it's not be-bop, da bump, bump, bump . . . it's wah-a-wah, a-wah-a-wah. It's simple, very simple.'

I could see Stanley getting frustrated.

Well, if you want Stanley Clarke, this is Stanley Clarke, he must have thought. *If you only want wah-a-wah-a-wah-a-wah, why did you call Stanley Clarke?*

This went on for some time, until they reached what seemed like a compromise. It was amazing to watch two giants of music having to work something like this out.

I was sitting next to the gal who was traveling with Keith, a pretty, short-statured blonde. I smelled something burning, looked over, and noticed smoke rising out of the green leather drawstring bag sitting by her feet. She appeared to be having a fire in her purse. Yep, a fire in a purse.

I have to say, in all my rock'n'roll adventures, I'd never seen a fire in a purse before, and I haven't seen one since. This gal was supposedly there to take care of Keith, but as the rehearsal wore on, she was getting more blasted than him—or anyone else, for that matter.

'Hey,' I said, leaning over and whispering in her ear, 'I think your purse is on fire.'

She looked up in a daze.

'Do you want me to help you put it out?' I asked.

She nodded yes.

'I have to dump the contents of your purse out on the floor. Is that okay?' Again, she nodded.

I quickly opened the drawstring, picked up the bag from the bottom, turned it upside down, and gave it a few hard shakes. A flood of matchbooks hit the floor, all different sizes and shapes—some regular cardboard ones, plus numerous small boxes of wooden stick matches, each in a different color, bearing a unique name and logo. She had evidently been collecting matchbooks from every bar, club, hotel, and restaurant that she and Keith had been to in the last month, and I guess with so many matches in her bag, somehow one of them had rubbed against a striker, and *whoosh!*

I swiftly stamped out the fire before it spread. The fascinating thing was, other than a few feminine items (use your imagination), the only things in her purse were these matches. Well, again, that's rock'n'roll for ya. If I hadn't caught it in time, God knows what would have happened.

I joined up with the tour on its West Coast swing. My wild-man colleague from Texas, Mike Gussler, had been put in charge of the tour, and he had somehow talked the label into commandeering a private jet for The New Barbarians to travel on. And barbarians they were. I was no stranger to drug culture, but the quantity of consumption blew my mind.

When you traveled on Barbarian Airlines, as you walked through the cabin, you'd find Stanley Clarke and his crew upfront with their health food bars, fresh juices, and all kinds of nuts and berries. Stanley was not only new to rock'n'roll music but also new to the rock'n'roll lifestyle, and he wanted no part of it. But as soon as you walked through the curtain to the rest of the plane, it was total debauchery. The first thing that came to mind was the Dupont Chemical company slogan, 'Better living through chemistry.'

There were roadies at the back of the plane, mining giant cocaine rocks as big as your fist. They would take these large chunks of coke, put them into professional green plastic laboratory grinders, and crush the stuff into extremely fine powder. A couple of tray tables could be seen piled high with weed, blow, and all kinds of liquor. Keith's favorite was something called Rebel Yell—one hundred percent proof alcohol, available only in the South. It tasted like lighter fluid to me.

I hope the pilots are more like Stanley's crew, I remember thinking.

On one trip, I was sitting across from Woody, who kept offering me more coke. Wanting to be polite and respectful, I told him, 'Hey, Woody, you're being quite a generous host on this tour, but I want you to know that I am here to work and not to do all your blow.'

'Rap,' he chuckled, 'it's fine. It's *endless*, don't worry.'

And it was endless, so I ceased to care. I also didn't sleep much for seven days and nights straight.

The way the tour was planned, we would fly to a major city, like Dallas, and everyone would unpack and set up a home base. From there, the plane would fly like spokes on a wheel to the various concert dates in that particular area of the country, then back again after each show. It certainly made life much more livable than constantly flying from city to city, continually having to pack and unpack again. But I think the real reason was that once these guys unpacked and made themselves at home, it would be next to impossible to gather up all of them and all their gear again on a daily basis.

Late at night, one might find Keith wandering the hallways, swaying this way and that, slurring his speech in that deep Keith Richards timbre that we've come to love so much. He could never remember my name, so he called me CBS. He'd saunter up to me, and say, 'Hey, CBS, wanna come to my room and listen to some reggae?'

The whole tour was like one giant, never-ending party, with the actual gigs seemingly a secondary thought—it was the lifestyle that took precedence. A typical day would go like this. Get up at four or five in the afternoon, have something to eat, and leave for a private airport at six. Then you'd board the plane, and the party would start—that is, of course, if you were behind the curtain. Then, once we were properly 'tuned' for the gig, we'd arrive at another private airport, get in long black limousines, and sometimes there would be more party in the car (possibly including a quaalude or two on the way to the local arena). From there, each band member would go to their dressing room, warm up for a bit, and hit the stage.

The shows were truly great. How could they not be? Two of rock's greatest guitar players, weaving phrases and notes between them; Woody singing his heart out; Bobby Keys wailing on sax; McLagan tickling the ivories; and the bottom held steady, with Stanley and Zigaboo laying down grooves you just had to tap your foot to. The audience loved it. If you were a guitar player, the show was especially rewarding. With no Mick Jagger out in front, taking your attention away, the guitar players were the stars of the show.

The traveling rule was, when you heard the encore, the Stones' 'Jumping Jack Flash,' that was your cue to get back into the limo and be ready to leave. The guys would come offstage and immediately be wrapped in terrycloth robes and whisked into the limousines, which would take off like a shot. We'd be out of the arena and on our way back to the airport while the audience was left still standing and clapping, hoping for one more song. The Stones had used this ploy for years to avoid the huge crowds waiting for them at backstage entrances for autographs and photos, making it almost impossible for them to leave.

In Denver, a well-known photographer for *Rolling Stone* magazine was traveling with us in Keith's car. The show ended, and I was waiting in the car when Keith hopped in.

'Go,' he told the driver.

The photographer saw us and started running toward the car, yelling and waving her hands. I turned to Keith as the driver started to leave.

'Hey, what about—'

'She knows the rules.'

We drove right by her, leaving her to fend for herself. She never made it back to the plane on time, of course, and she had to spend the night at Denver airport before catching a commercial flight back to Dallas the next morning. When I saw her back at the hotel the next day, at first, I thought perhaps Keith had been a bit mean. But then I thought, *Hey, you're on tour with The Rolling Stones, or at least two of them. Rules is rules.*

Back at the hotel after a show, the party would continue—in fact, it would kick into high gear. More of everything, nonstop. Band members, tech crew, and other guests would meet in someone's room where there'd be music blaring, cassettes strewn about all over the floor, lingerie hanging from lampshades. It would go full blast all night.

At most music-business parties, the lines of coke would get shorter as the wee hours of the morning approached—as if somehow that would make any difference to being able to fall asleep—but not this time. Nope. New rails of coke almost as long as the coffee table itself would be laid out as fast as they'd disappeared up the noses of the guests.

Very early in the morning, someone would walk over to the window and peek out behind the curtain. If it was still dark, a member of the crew would come into the room and pass out 'reds' (barbiturates) to help everyone go to sleep. If perchance the sun had come up, someone would invariably shout, 'Let's stay up until the gig!' And then the medical grinders would magically appear again. Newly awakened, the entourage would return to their rooms, clean up for a bit, then go shopping.

While I admittedly found the use of cocaine provocative as long as I kept a lid on it, I just couldn't do the whole thing of going up with coke and then using a red or a quaalude to ease you back down again. That lifestyle threw me—it was like living life upside-down. So, when I returned to my room, I'd put the red cap in a row next to the others that I'd been saving each night (or, more precisely, each morning). I'd stay up until the party subsided around six or seven in the morning, then try to sleep during the day, which wasn't easy with so much speed in my system. Then I'd get up at four in the afternoon and be hungry, but I didn't know if I wanted breakfast or dinner.

I had planned to work this tour like the others I'd done before—see my radio friends during the day, do some work, and then take them and other industry folks with me to the shows at night. But I had been sucked into this wild lifestyle, and it was everything I could do just to hang on.

On the flight to Denver, I noticed we were an hour late, so I pointed it out to Woody.

'It's okay,' he told me. '*They wait.*'

'They wait?' I replied. 'Hey, that used to be me! Sometimes I waited for you guys for fucking ever! I always thought you were backstage getting high. The truth is, you probably weren't even there yet! And this whole leaving the arena immediately after the performance thing—shit, I would be there clapping like crazy, thinking you would hear me and the rest of the screaming crowd and come back for another song if only we clapped loud and long enough. But you were already gone! Fuck you guys!'

Woody got a big kick out of that one.

On the flight home that night, however, things got a bit rough. Keith had misplaced his bottle of Rebel Yell, and he sauntered up and accused me of stealing it.

'You . . . YOU stole my Rebel Yell!'

He was clearly out of it, and it was hard for me to see my hero like this. Even harder to find myself on his wrong side.

'Keith, I didn't steal your Rebel Yell. We're on a plane, for God's sake—where the hell would I hide it?'

Then things got a bit comical, me and Keith crawling around the floor of the plane, searching under the seats, until I finally found the bottle and handed it to him.

'See!'

He grabbed it, scowled, and walked back to his seat. Sometimes, meeting your heroes can disappoint. That one hurt.

After five days of living this scene, I became a bit worried for both Woody and Keith's health. Fun is fun, but this was way too excessive. Both guys were looking a bit crispy, Keith especially. Every afternoon on the way to the gig, his valet would stuff him into the limousine, hiding under a little pork pie hat. If you looked closely, you could see his complexion was gray. I loved the guy so much, and I didn't want to be around if this was going to be his time of passing into the next life. Years later, when I met him again, he would apologize for his behavior on this particular tour, and we would have the conversation I'd always dreamt about. But for right now, it was hard for me to see my hero in such bad shape.

I decided to talk to Woody about it that night.

'Hey man, this is going to sound like the most un-hip thing, and may even come off like a Jewish grandmother, but I love you guys, and I'm worried about you. I know Keith's your hero too, and you're trying to be like him, but you can't—there's only one of him, and he's somehow bionic.'

Little did I know at the time that Ron Wood actually *could* go toe-to-toe with Keith Richards in all things drug and alcohol related (and that's saying something).

'This is just way too much blow, Woody,' I continued. 'Forget about all the other stuff.'

Then he gave me his Ron Wood logical answer.

'Don't you see, Rap? We have the secret.'

'The secret?'

'Yes,' he said excitedly. 'You see how fine a powder the coke is ground up to? When we do it, we only do it through these very small cocktail straws, never with a rolled-up dollar bill or a regular-size straw. The coke is ground to such a fine powder that we can never burn out our septums!' (The story went that Fleetwood Mac's Stevie Nicks had put a hole in her nose from having small rocks of coke lodged in her nasal cavity, and it had affected her voice.)

I collared Woody and brought him closer to me.

'Woody, I'm not worried about your septum, I'm worried about your fucking bloodstream!'

He just looked at me like I was crazy and went on his merry way.

The most amazing thing was, no matter how fucked up they got, The New Barbarians played great every single night. Somehow, Keith Richards had finetuned this kind of lifestyle. No matter how bad he looked in the afternoon, by showtime his color was back, and so was his energy, and his guitar playing was brilliant. Better living through chemistry? Who knows.

As of this writing, Ron Wood is seventy-seven years old, Keith is eighty, and The Rolling Stones are back on tour!

I did wonder, though, if I was the only one having trouble sleeping. One night after a gig, I dropped off Ian McLagan at his room and told him I'd pick him up the next morning to escort him to the airport. I slept as best I could, got myself together the next morning, and went by Mac's room to pick him up. He answered the door in the same black suit and crisp white shirt he'd been wearing the evening before. He was holding a bottle of shoe polish in his hands, along with a toothpick.

'You gotta see this!' he said, looking up at me. 'I've been up all night working on it and just finished it in time to leave for the airport.' He pointed to a mural that was about three feet by four feet, hanging over the bed. It was your basic hotel kind of art—a lithograph of a black-and-white pen-and-ink drawing, depicting an overhead view of a big park in a fun cartoon style. There were all kinds of trees and scenes of kids with balloons, parents walking with strollers, people playing baseball, a carousel, popcorn vendors, and so on.

'So?' I asked.

Mac told me to look closer. He had stayed up all night, doctoring every illustration with black shoe polish, using the toothpick as a small brush, to make every scene totally pornographic. Gals were now going down on guys, the popcorn vendor's shlong was hanging out of his pants, dogs were doing it doggy style—anything and everything lewd and erotic you can think of was now being depicted in what appeared to be the same black ink drawing style as the original art, except the 'new and improved' park scene was obscenely, jaw-droppingly hysterical!

The funniest part is that mural might still be hanging over the bed in that hotel room, because unless you looked close up and paid attention to the details, from a distance it just looked like a normal black-and-white illustration of an innocent park scene.

My question about everyone else staying awake at night was answered, but at least Mac had found something constructive to do with his extra awake time.

The New Barbarians left their mark, one way or another, in every city they visited. When the tour was finally over, because Woody had made himself so available for all of our promotional needs, I talked the company into buying him a thank-you gift. I paid a visit to Red Rhodes Royal Amplifier Service on Cahuenga Boulevard in Hollywood—the same Red Rhodes I used to watch as a kid on those Cal Worthington *Country Music Time* TV shows. Since then, Red had become a famous pedal-steel session player, performing on albums by The Beach Boys, James Taylor, The Byrds, The Monkees, The Carpenters, and more. Now he had this very hip shop where he fixed amps, developed custom pickups for guitars, and always had a few very nice instruments hanging around the store. I'd befriended him and his son Michael, who were the only ones I trusted to give my guitars a GP (grind and polish) and set them up properly.

'Hey, Red, I just got done working with Ronnie and Keith on that New Barbarians Tour.'

'And you're still alive? I heard all about it.'

'Yeah,' I laughed, 'it was pretty wild. Listen, I need something very special as a present for Woody.'

Red walked over to the guitars hanging on the wall.

'How about this?'

He handed me a beautiful blonde 1956 Fender Stratocaster. It was a bit worn, but still really in great shape. If memory serves, it had gold parts on it. I played it, and it seemed special.

Me, Gussler, Obi-Wan, and a few other Columbia execs presented the guitar to Woody in his Hollywood hotel room at the end of the tour. It blew his mind—he was very touched. And that's one of the legacies of Columbia Records. Yes, we were record executives, but we were music people first, and lots of us were musicians who could relate firsthand to the players we were working with. We were a family.

Keith came down to Ronnie's room to see the guitar. He loved it, and I could see in his eyes that the feeling was not just for the guitar. He saw the relationship—the love and admiration that Woody's record company family had for him, and I think he was very moved by that.

I DON'T LIKE MONDAYS

BOB GELDOF IS a force to be reckoned with. If you want to talk about characters, he takes the proverbial cake. He is quick-witted, often talks without a filter, and is funny as hell. I once reached out to him to see if he'd call into the Jim Kerr *Rock And Roll Morning Show* at Q104.3 FM in New York to wish Jim a happy birthday. Bob's reply was something akin to this.

'Rap, I'm in fucking Africa, but sure, I'll fucking call all the way to the fucking United States to wish Jim fucking Kerr a fucking happy birthday. But let me ask *you* something, who's going to fucking call *me* and wish *me* a happy fucking birthday when it's my fucking birthday?'

While I enjoy the use of the word 'fuck' as much as anybody and have introduced it into my everyday vocabulary, no one enjoys it more, or even comes close to using it more, than Bob Geldof. He is also one of the smartest and most well-read people I've ever met. He can talk circles around almost anyone when it comes to discussing history, politics, and socioeconomics, and he's often invited to heavy-duty think-tank meetings with high-level world leaders. Most interestingly, if you start talking to him about his gargantuan achievements—Live Aid, Live 8, Band Aid, 'Do They Know It's Christmas?' and so on, or the fact that he's been knighted by the Queen of England—he seems very unimpressed with himself. But as soon as you turn your attention to The Boomtown Rats, he becomes extremely animated and will talk FOREVER about the band and his involvement. Indeed, once Bob is on a charge, there is no stopping him. And when it comes to the Rats, he's got good reason. You see, The Boomtown Rats blew the lid off Ireland and put that country on the map in much the same way as Bruce Springsteen made New Jersey famous, opening the door for other Irish artists to be better recognized, including U2, Sinead O'Connor, and The Cranberries. Bono will tell you that the Rats were a huge influence on

U2 and gave them the belief that another Irish rock band could make it big.

Fred Humphrey had been spearheading the charge for The Boomtown Rats since 1978 along with the band's product manager, Jonathan Coffino. I'd first met Coffino when I was a college rep. He was one of the new faces making things happen at Columbia Records—a hard-core New Yorker and a direct, no-nonsense kind of guy.

I first met Bob in his hotel room at the 1978 Columbia Records convention in Dallas. I was planning a West Coast promotional tour for him and Boomtown Rats keyboardist Johnnie Fingers, and I wanted to get to know Bob a bit before we left. I remember thinking that he was quite a bit taller than the usually slight figures I'd met from Britain. He looked classy in his pressed jeans and sharp dark blue blazer, and he had the coolest-looking acoustic guitar sitting on the couch. It was a beautiful deep green—the first colored acoustic guitar I'd ever seen.

Bob had a bit of a swagger and was more sure of himself than most new artists. I would soon find out that the reason for this was that Bob and the Rats were not new at all, only new to America. They were already established as huge pop stars in Britain and Ireland. With 'Rat Trap,' they'd become the first Irish band to have a UK #1 hit, and their over-the-top punk-rock performances were blowing audiences away. At a recent awards ceremony in London, Linda McCartney had strolled over to their table and asked if the band would be kind enough to take a picture with Paul.

'Our kids love you guys,' she told them.

'Sure,' they replied, looking up at her in shock, 'but shouldn't this be the other way 'round?'

Having gone through the star-maker machinery in Europe, Geldof was to some extent a seasoned vet. He knew the ropes and he understood that his job extended beyond making records and performing onstage. He was always on time for his interviews, and, most importantly, he had vision. He knew how to grab attention for the Rats. But it was still hard for him, having become a superstar in another part of the world, to now come to America, where no one knew him or the band at all.

The Boomtown Rats had worked their way up the ladder the old-fashioned way, playing clubs, building an audience over time, and learning how to make great records. The thought of now having to do it all over again, in a country as big as the United States, was disconcerting. Bob and the Rats had been spoiled. They wanted success in the US, and they wanted it quickly.

I first saw the band in a club, and I was blown away. They had been promoted as a punk/pop band, but what I saw had much larger overtones. The rhythm section was so great, and Geldof was so strong as a frontman, that I felt they had a Rolling Stones kind of longevity in them, far beyond where any hit record could take them. They were explosive onstage (and, as of this writing, still are).

The challenge I faced was that the songs they were writing made sense for Europe but didn't resonate here. We had a great live band to promote, but we were only able to obtain so much airplay on rock radio. On that West Coast promotional tour, I explained to Bob that the music that resonated deeply in this country was being made by artists like Neil Young and Bruce Springsteen, who wrote about American culture.

One of my favorite Boomtown Rats songs is 'Mary Of The 4th Form,' but no one in this country even knew what the fourth form was, so I told Bob he would do well to write something more universal that could give the Rats a sense of relatability in the States.

On our promo tour, Bob and I sat in the front of the car, with Fingers in the back in his patented striped pajamas. He wore them day and night, onstage and off. He was quite a sight. He always reminded me of John and Michael Darling, Wendy's brothers in *Peter Pan*. As I drove, my right ear would be getting a real workout from Bob, who'd be complaining nonstop about everything under the sun.

'Rap, Fingers and I just played a few songs for the LA branch with me on acoustic guitar and he on the keyboards, and they thought we were a fucking duo! A FUCKING DUO!'

'Bob, maybe a couple of sales guys weren't all that hip to the Rats, but I guarantee you most of the branch knew who the fuck you were.'

'And stop talking to me about Bruce fucking Springsteen! The guy's a fake, *it's fucking Hollywood on vinyl!*'

I believe Bob has quite a different opinion of Bruce now, but at the time he was full of piss and vinegar about *everything*. There was no consoling him. I had to calm down and take a deep breath, being a huge fan of Springsteen and having played an important role in his career.

'Bob, you are welcome to your opinion about Bruce, and whomever else, but whatever you do, *do not* mention that opinion to anyone in radio during our interviews, or to anyone in the press. I've already been through it with Elvis Costello. I know you guys are passionate, and I respect your opinions, but sometimes they're just not helpful to your career.'

We were able to do some very cool things with The Boomtown Rats. Bob had it in his mind that he wanted to play Frederick's Of Hollywood, a famous lingerie store. *Hey, this will get some attention*, we thought, and it did. We closed off Hollywood Boulevard, put the band inside the store, and they rocked the entire neighborhood. Accustomed to making all kinds of promotional swag—jackets, T-shirts, belts, and so on—we decided to make some promotional panties. Frederick's, of course, in black with a chartreuse green Boomtown Rats logo across the front. I even once met an industry gal who was wearing them. I got all excited to tell her that I was the guy who'd made them, thinking I'd score some points, but she just looked at me sideways and walked out of the room. I never saw her again.

Not long after that, in late January of '79, Bob, Fingers, and I were doing some promotional work in Atlanta. We were at a college radio station, WRAS, when the news came in that a sixteen-year-old girl, Brenda Spencer, had opened fire on a bunch of school kids with a rifle in San Diego. We were all in shock. There had been a handful of school shootings in the 1970s, but they were few and far between. The idea of a young teen shooting at elementary school kids was horrifying. The story came across the telex machine, and the woman program director had asked to see it. She read the news report aloud, including the part about Spencer being asked why she'd done it.

'I don't like Mondays,' Spencer had replied simply. 'This livens up the day.'

Bob asked the program director for the piece of paper. I couldn't for the life of me figure out why. He folded it up, put it in his pocket, and we left. When we got into the limo, he uttered something off the top of his head, as if he was just pondering it. Something like, *Hmm, I guess the silicon chip inside her head must've switched to overload.* Then he chuckled darkly.

Wow, I thought. *That's kind of cold.* But Bob is a deep guy, and often whatever he's saying on the surface has a more profound meaning. I dropped him back at his hotel. He was going to be visiting the Atlanta office that evening, and I had to get to some meetings back in Dallas.

It couldn't have been more than two weeks after that incident that Bob called to tell me he'd written a new song about what had happened that fateful day in San Diego. It was called 'I Don't Like Mondays,' and he wanted to play it for me over the phone on his acoustic guitar. I was floored. At first I thought, *Wow, is this too soon? Is this guy so hungry for success that he's taking advantage of a bad situation to create some kind of sensationalism?* But then I realized that Bob had been hit by something very powerful, and the song had come to him honestly and very quickly, as many songs do when inspiration strikes.

'Does this work?' he asked, sounding a bit unsure of himself.

'Wow,' I said. I took a breath. 'Actually, I think it's pretty amazing, and I think you should start playing it immediately for folks on your acoustic guitar, whenever you have the chance. It's going to build your credibility in this country as someone who is feeling what we are all feeling and haven't been able to put into words.'

Powerful circumstances had just given Bob Geldof and The Boomtown Rats genuine authenticity in the United States. Playing the song early for people, before it was recorded, would bring immediate attention to this fact, and by the time an album version was released, most folks in the industry would already know that they were more relevant than ever—a force to be respected.

• ● •

A few months before the release of *The Fine Art Of Surfacing*, which contained the recorded version of 'I Don't Like Mondays' along with some other great songs, we put a plan together to have the Rats play the Lee Abrams 'Superstars' Convention. Lee had become the leading consultant for the FM rock format, and his clients included more than sixty radio stations that patterned their formats after his vision. Lee took all the best music from the freeform days of jocks picking their own songs and reasoned that if he made a basic playlist of all these songs, the ones that fans never tired of hearing, and programmed them where they fit best during a twenty-four-hour period, he could develop a tried-and-true format that would keep listeners constantly glued to their beloved rock radio stations. He was right.

At the time, many of us thought that Lee had ruined freeform radio. But the truth is, this kind of idea was destined to happen—it was a natural evolution. If you think about it, Lee created the Top 40 version of rock. At any rate, the good news for Bob Geldof and the Rats was that Lee liked them and was up for helping to break them in America. We figured that with the band being so great and Bob being such an over-the-top frontman, it was a slam dunk. Just invite Lee's sixty radio programmers to a concert one evening during their convention, and as soon as they saw the band play, they'd fall in love with them. Then, when the record came out, they'd all add it to their playlists with Lee's blessing.

Everything went swimmingly until Bob decided to push a few buttons, which he always enjoyed doing. About halfway through the concert, he asked the audience, 'What do think about the state of rock radio these days?'

Some applauded, of course, but many others booed.

'Well, if you don't like what you're hearing,' Bob continued, sounding like he was at a protest rally, 'you can talk to all those guys sitting in the back of the hall wearing the satin jackets. They are the ones who are running rock radio all across the country.'

This, of course, invoked more boos as people turned around to give Lee's guys the evil eye. I think Bob meant it as nothing more than a friendly headbutt—a way of serving up a little punk-rock notice to radio in general. But it did not go over well at all.

Undeterred, the band carried on with a great performance, and then Bob introduced 'a new song' that was especially poignant because it was written about an event that happened in San Diego, which coincidently was exactly where this year's Superstars convention was taking place. The Rats then gave a powerful performance of 'I Don't Like Mondays.' It moved everyone in the audience—even the Abrams guys who were still feeling chafed by what Bob had said earlier.

The band got a standing ovation, and from that we knew they would do well on tour, but some of Lee's guys were grumbling as they left the building. Trying to downplay what had happened, we looked at Lee and threw our arms up in the air, as if to say, *Whaddya expect?*

Backstage, Bob looked at me with a half-sheepish, half-devilish grin.

'I didn't fuck that up too bad, right?'

The next day, we flew to Seattle. Jonathan Coffino was on the road with the band too, and he had witnessed the San Diego incident the night before. He was also tight with Lee, and he was not happy. We met at the Seattle branch offices, where he told me we needed to set up a national live broadcast of The Boomtown Rats to counteract what just happened.

I could see he was panicked, but I told him that this was probably the *worst* thing we could do right now. What we needed to do was the opposite: take a breath, take some heat off the Rats, and let everything die down. I told him that time, and me talking to any aggrieved programmers in my own way, would take care of it. And it did. By the time *The Fine Art Of Surfacing* was released that October, 'I Don't Like Mondays' was flying on the radio. It became a big hit in no time.

Coffino was cool. He'd trusted me. In fact, at Columbia, everyone was so good at their particular job that we all trusted each other. We were like a great sports team, blocking for each other, passing the ball to someone else when needed, and always covering for one another. We were a force of nature. The record company with the well-known red labels on all our albums and singles became known as the Big Red Machine.

But no matter how successful The Boomtown Rats were becoming, Geldof was always pushing buttons. At the California World Music Festival at the Los Angeles Memorial Coliseum, where the Rats were on the bill with Ted Nugent, Cheap Trick, Aerosmith, and Van Halen, Bob said something that riled up the fans, and a few folks started throwing things at him. One of them hit Bob on the side of the head with a can, prompting him to stop the show and address the audience in that brilliant Irish brogue.

'You may not agree with everything I say, but I didn't come all this way, *t'ree t'ousand miles*, to get hit in the head with a can!'

Someone in the audience answered back, and the next thing I knew, Geldof was having a conversation with fifty thousand people. I've never seen anything like it. After that, the band played 'Mondays,' and in the end, they got a big ovation.

When Bob came offstage, I thought he'd be happy, having conquered this prestigious festival, but he started raging about another new-wave band that was getting a lot of attention, The Fabulous Poodles. Bob liked to rant and rave, but he had a charming way about him that made it lighthearted and sometimes even funny.

'Rap, what's all the fucking fuss about the Fabulous fucking Poodles? Why are they getting more attention than us? We're THE FUCKING BOOMTOWN RATS! Fuck the fucking Fabulous fucking Poodles. What are they anyway? What the fuck do they mean? I'll tell you what they fucking mean: absolutely fucking nothing.'

Bob was pretty amped, and even though I was chuckling inside, my poor ears, which had suffered plenty already from Geldof fire and brimstone, were hurting again. I was getting a headache. One thing was for sure, though: from then on, The Fabulous Poodles would hence be known as *The Fabulous Fucking Poodles*.

'Bob,' I tried to explain, 'sometimes one band gets more press than one or another, a quick flash of media blitz. But I guarantee you, at the end of the day, it's The Boomtown Rats that will be remembered, not the fucking Fabulous fucking Poodles. Oh, by the way, you just got a huge applause from fifty thousand kids in Los Angeles.'

If you're reading this, my friend, I was right: no one today gives a shite about the motherfucking fucked-up Fabulous fucking Poodles!

• • •

The Boomtown Rats made quite a big splash in America, but it didn't last as long as any of us would have liked. Taking a break from the band for a while found Bob Geldof raising $190 million for famine relief in Africa by spearheading the song 'Do They Know It's Christmas,' which led to

'We Are The World' (featuring many great superstars all singing together as one), followed by Live Aid, which was watched by 1.9 billion people around the world. The Live 8 concerts followed in 2005, to mark Live Aid's twentieth anniversary, and subsequently Bob was knighted by Queen Elizabeth II for all his efforts.

Fast-forward about twenty years, and I'm in England on business. I've been invited to David Gilmour's birthday party, a nice event held in a big hall with a pretty big stage at one end. There are large round tables with fancy centerpieces, and hors d'oeuvres are being passed around before dinner is served. It reminds me of a bar mitzvah party, except that the band that's gonna play is David's! It's the band being assembled to tour his new album, *On An Island*. And, needless to say, it's going to be the best birthday party band any of us will ever see.

Besides family, the crowd included lots of rock royalty. Bob was there, now much older, his hair gone gray. He and I hadn't seen each other in years, but when I approached him, he gave me the biggest hug. It immediately felt like old times.

I started to congratulate him.

'Bob I'm so proud of you—Live Aid, Live 8 . . . you're a fucking knight, for God's sake.'

'Yeah, yeah, yeah, but guess what? The Rats are getting back together. We've just released a greatest hits package, and we've got all kinds of other things in the works!'

He was going a mile a minute, like no time had passed, and it was all about The Boomtown Rats. Once again, he seemed unimpressed with all his other accomplishments. I was taken aback by his humbleness. At the end of the day, what really got Bob excited was being the frontman of The Boomtown Rats.

PART TWO

FEATURING

TOMMY TUTONE

BILLY JOEL

LOVERBOY

BOB DYLAN

PAUL MCCARTNEY

PINK FLOYD

THE ROLLING STONES

CHRIS WHITLEY

THE GRATEFUL DEAD

TOMMY CONWELL

JUDAS PRIEST

BRUCE DICKINSON

JOURNEY

ALICE IN CHAINS

THE TWELFTH FLOOR

IN THE SPRING OF 1979, out of the blue, I got a phone call from Columbia's head of promotion, Ed Hynes. Fred Humphrey was leaving his job as head of album promotion, and they wanted me to come to New York and run the department for a little while.

'We know you're an LA guy and have no desire to move to New York, but we need you to come here and run the department while we look for someone to take over. We're all Top 40 people, and we don't have a clue about how the album thing works.'

'Sure Ed, I'll come ASAP.'

I told Sharon I was heading for New York and that the company was going to put me up in a hotel. She could follow in a few weeks and stay with me. Spring is a wonderful time to be in the city—Central Park and tree-lined streets are blooming, and the tulips are out in massive display on Park Avenue. I showed up to work at Black Rock, the famous CBS building on the corner of West 52nd Street and Sixth Avenue, which was home not only to the record company but also to CBS Broadcasting. William Paley had built the Columbia Broadcasting System from a small radio network into one of the largest radio and television network operations in the United States of America. His office was on the top floor. The Columbia offices were on the twelfth floor, which became famous in its own right.

The building got its nickname because of its dark gray granite-sheathed outer structure, with its narrow vertical support columns protruding between gray tinted windows. It looks very unique among the other skyscrapers that surround it—a Black Rock, indeed. The interior was distinctive as well. The walls and doors were made of metal and were movable. This design allowed the walls to be moved at will, whenever a reconfiguration of space was needed. The funniest thing about it all was that whenever you wanted to hang something, it had to be on a magnet. The walls were painted a soft gray, the doors were black, and the company provided flat black magnets about four inches square, with ample-sized silver hooks on them. The ones on the back of your office door, to hold heavy coats, were larger. Given how many gold and platinum record plaques we accumulated over the years—not to mention all the framed photos and posters—there were a lot of fucking magnets around.

I quickly began setting up projects, creating promotional strategies, and learning how the charts worked. On the album side of things, rock radio reported airplay as 'light,' 'medium,' or 'heavy' spins. The life of a record on the charts was all down to math. As stated, not my strong suit, but this one was easy to figure out.

Steeped as I was in the art of promotion, I had already made long-lasting relationships with many rock radio programmers, and now I was rapidly making more new friends across the country. By working closely with them, gaining credibility, and helping them to achieve their goals of more devoted listeners by offering very large promotions with our superstar acts, I had their ears. I realized that a successful week of promotion meant that each album project we were working needed to acquire at least ten new radio stations per week, and the others that were already on the charts needed to continually move up in numbers of rotations. I created weekly goals for each record to ensure their healthy growth on the charts. It became like a game to me. I became a chart-manipulating motherfucker.

I did not do this all on my own. Columbia Records had the greatest local promotion team in the history of the record business, full of acclaimed record men and women from coast to coast. Each had strong relationships with the stations in their markets and would relay to the national office how each project was faring. The national team and I made calls whenever our people needed extra backup. We also hired key independent promotion people, ensuing that every artist we worked with got a legitimate shot to see if their music would fly on rock radio.

Within three weeks, I was having so much fun, and affecting such big change, that I didn't want it to end. A kid who grew up with a bit of an inferiority complex was tasting what one could do with real power and the money to make things happen. I was able to help my beloved music heroes, and new heroes yet to come. I had a lightbulb moment: *I was meant to do this*. Now, I had to talk them into giving me the job, full time.

I put the idea to Ed Hynes, reminding him how quickly I'd gotten a handle on things. He thanked me for my work, but it seemed like my laid-back West Coast surfer boy reputation wasn't helping me here.

'Rap, this is the NFL. The heat and the pressure are tough, and the politics are very real. You're a great promotion man, but you will get chewed up and spit out here. Be smart. You have it knocked on the West Coast. You do your thing and nobody bothers you.'

His reply made me second-guess myself, and I wondered if going back to the West Coast wasn't the best idea after all.

I called my dad in California. He had always given me the best advice.

'Hey, pop, I have this opportunity to do a really big job,' I began. Yadda, yadda, yadda. I told him everything, and also that I had to take into account my easy mortgage on the cute little house Sharon and I had bought in North Hollywood, and the fact that we'd just planted four peach trees.

'Paul,' my dad boomed in that loveable, burly, Brooklyn barrelhouse voice, 'we are a close family, and it would be hard for me to see you move all the way to New York. But in a couple of years, those peach trees will become boring. Opportunities in life don't show up that often, and when they do you have to take them. Go for the job. And don't worry if you can handle it, I know you. You'll do great.'

Dad's belief and those few sentences set me on a path that would change my life and Sharon's forever, and in the most dramatic and amazing ways.

That Sunday, I drove over to Ed's house in Connecticut to try to convince him I was right for the new job. It was an interesting trip. First off, he lived in the countryside and the directions were like, *make a right where there's a big oak tree that's been split by lightning . . . go by a muddy fork in the road where there's usually a badger hanging out . . .*

The other thing that took me by surprise was when I got lost in the town of Darien, just east of Stamford. At the time, most of the town was very conservative, and it was known for being severely racist. I parked up and walked into a general store to ask to use their pay phone.

TOP LEFT Howdy! Me on horseback, aged five. **TOP RIGHT** My sister Ruth. You won't find a bigger heart on the planet. **ABOVE** Sharon and me, sitting in the notorious bunk #5 at Camp Ramah in Ojai, California, known for shaving cream wars and the biggest pranks in camp. **RIGHT** My Super Parents, Walter and Vera Rappaport.

ABOVE The Jades gone mod and in our stride, with new member Ed Meyers (far right) on Vox organ and guitar, and me sporting my new Rickenbacker. **LEFT** The Jades in our surf-band early days. Left to right: Frank Shargo (bass) Ron McCarrell (drums), me (lead guitar), and Mike George (guitar and vocals).

SAVAGE YOUNG WINOS

EVOLUTION OF A ROCK BAND
BIG BEAT PERFORMANCES

MOGAN DAVID AND HIS WINOS

TOP LEFT Me and the fabulous Tony Bennett, the night he changed my life. **ABOVE LEFT** The Savage Young Winos album. **ABOVE** My first gold record, with Loggins & Messina. They took TP and me out to lunch to thank us and presented us with these. We were all like a family in those days. **LEFT** Me outside the Whisky A Go Go in the Winos days, with my Gibson Melody Maker and slide guitar great Jesse Ed Davis on the marquee.

LEFT Firing up the 30-watt argon laser cannon to launch Blue Öyster Cult's *Agents Of Forturne*. It shot for 30 miles! **BELOW** Backstage with BOC and KNAC's Ron McCoy.

OPPOSITE TOP With Roger McGuinn of The Byrds and my KMET-FM DJ friends Mary Turner and Jim Ladd. **BOTTOM** With Sandy Pearlman, BOC songwriter, producer, and co-manager.

RADIO STATIONS

KRDS - Randy Morrison
1900 Folsom, Boulder, 80302
KRNW - Peter Rodman
1426 Pearl St. Boulder Colorado 80302

KLOS - Tom & Paula
3321 S. La Cienega
L.A.
663-3311
HOT - 870 / 1033
462-5728
1901

KMET - Joe Collins
5828 Wilshire Blvd.
L.A. 464-5638
937-0117
935-1463

KNAC - Ron Paul Fuhr
320 Pine Butclay EP Hines
LongBeach, Ca. 90812
775-8172 Hot - 432-2766 1501
437-0366
John Graziano   Jessie Bullet Co.

KPRI - Mike Keith Allen
11585 Sorrento Valley Rd.
#104   Cecile
San Diego, Ca
(714) 452-8181
565-6006   KPoL - 466-4/23

KDKB - Linda HAWK
P.O. Box 4227
Mesa, Arizona 85201
(602) 833-4261   834-4493
HOT - 834-7578

KGB -
4141 Pacific Hwy.
San Diego, Ca 92101
(714) 297-2201 Valerie MacIntosh
Rick Libert Program Mngr.

KSAN - Bonnie
Bonnie Simmons Hot - 986-2825
Tom-O'Hair
211 Sutter St.   345 Sansome
San Francisco, Ca 94104
(415) 986-2825
Weekend 397-7677 (Hot)

KOME - Dawa Jang
Cliff Feldman 1245 S. Winchester
1694 Alameda
San Jose, Ca 95126
(408) 246-6811   6312 Night
KSJO - 408-246-6600 KATE
Don Wright   Lobster Paul

KZAP - Robert
Robert Williams Bruce Meier
924 9th St.
Sacramento, Ca 95813
(916) 444-2806

KYA FM STEVE
MTJUCK KTYD - 805
RADIO STATIONS 963-1601
397-2500
HOT-7696 HELEN McLINE
KWST - Mike Cooper
8833 Sunset Blvd.
Hollywood, Ca Paul Sullivan
657-6130 620-5478X
HOT - 657-5461
KISW - Lee 624-4305
Lee Michaels FM 100
Seattle, Wash.

KZAM - John Kertzer 206-454-
HOT-454-1541
KINK - Scott
Scott Carter 15th &
5101 S.W. Jefferson
Portland, Ore Miko
(503) 224-8620
226-5080 KZAM
KZEL - Stan
Stan Garret
P.O. Box 1122
Eugene, Ore
(503) 747-1221

KFML
Don Zukker RdE
Bill Ashford Gunner
290 Fillmore 6675 E. Tennessee
Denver, Colo 80206-80224
(303) 398-1390 757-1390
Tom Travell PD 757-1333
KBPI - FRANK - P.
Ken Kohl Jeff Roylock
Frank Felix   John Bradly
4460 Morrison Rd.
Denver, Colo. 80219
(303) 936-2313

KYMS - LINDA
1601 N. Bristol
Santa Ana, Ca 92706
(714) 835-1063

FM-90 - Dave Moore
Royal Inn
1355 Harbor Dr.
San Diego, Ca 92101
(714) 238-0022

KTIM - Clint 456-1009
Clint Weyrauch
1040 "B" St.
San Rafael, Ca 94901
(415) 456-1510

KFIG - (209)
485-7762

KCROCK - 578-7067-68
BELAIR SANDS - 476-6571
KCBS - 415-982-7000
K101 - (415) 956-5101
KZEL - STAN GARRET
P.O. Box 1122
Eugene, Ore. 974
(503) 747-1221
KVAN - 286-5738
P.D. Bob Brooks
KGON - Mike Johnson
P.O. Box 22125
Portland 97222
(503) 655-9181

KZOK - Norm Gregory
1426 Fifth Ave
Seattle, Washington
(206) 223-3911
Jeff Salgo
MD. Bruce Murdock
KREM - Rob Glendenny P.D.
South 4103 Regal
Spokane, Wa 99203
(509) 534-0423
Cal Walker (Jack)

CKLG - Bob Morris
1006 Richards
(604) 681-7511

KBZY - Bill Struck
123 Speer Blvd.
Denver, Colo.
(303)

KPFK - Earl O'Tarr
3729 Cahuenga Blvd West
No Hollywood, Ca
877-2711
759-5600
David Cloud
KWFM - Alan Browning
199 No. Stone
Suite 210 Hot-623-9335
Tucson, Ariz 85701
(602) 624-5588

SEATTLE -
(206) 763-2450
515-0931
DENVER -
(303) 623-6668
837-8333
770-4413
SAN FRANCISCO -
(415) 495-6910

KATE HAAS Branches -
VANCOUVER
(604) 327-0291

792-9292

ACR
441-0606

OPPOSITE My 1970s western-region rock radio call sheet, depicting the frequent personnel changes at radio and my penchant for color.

RIGHT Don't fall off the porch! Columbia and Epic Rock Promotion teams at Caribou Ranch Recording Studios. Left to right: me, Michael Pillot, Harvey Leeds, Mike Shavelson, Gil Colquitt, and Jim McKeon.

ABOVE With Terry 'TP' Powell and Bob Moering. These guys taught me the record biz. **RIGHT** At KSAN-FM in San Francisco with Elvis Costello and *My Aim Is True* producer Nick Lowe. Music director and DJ Bonnie Simmons received the Red Shoes Award (taken from the song title) for helping to break Elvis in the Bay Area. Left to right: Michael Pillot, W.W., Nick, Bonnie, E.C., George Chaltas, and me.

ABOVE With The Bangles. Everyone said they were a great girl band. I always thought they were a great band that happened to be women. *Photo by Lester Cohen.* **LEFT** Tres hombres: me, Chris Whitley, and Billy Gibbons. Those two hit it off big time, and I learned some new licks.

YOU CAN'T START A FIRE
WITHOUT A SPARK.

COLUMBIA
RECORDS

Rapper!

Budgeted Year to Date
20,304.00

Actual Year to Date
19,625.97

what a good boy you
are!

$ 678.03 left to
spend $ $

TOP LEFT I was constantly bringing industry folks to meet Bruce for his autograph. When he became a big star, I finally asked if I should get one. We laughed our asses off, then he handed me this. **TOP RIGHT** Getting hugged by the Big Man, Clarence Clemmons, was a BIG deal. **ABOVE** An 'official' expenses report on Columbia Records letterhead created by my assistant, Gail 'Brueser' Bruesewitz. I especially appreciated the silver ribbon and #1 Jewish Star. **LEFT** Brueser decided that we should switch stereotype places for this photo, with me sitting on her lap, taking dictation. For the record, she never sat in my lap.

ABOVE With two of my biggest heroes, Adam Rappaport and Keith Richards. **FAR LEFT** Rappy and Woody. **LEFT** Adam attempts to hustle Bill Wyman at pool. **BELOW** Left to right: Debbie Samuelson, Phil Sandhaus, John Fagot, Mick, me, Amy Strauss, and Marilyn Laverty.

OPPOSITE TOP The greatest record company promotion team ever assembled, Palm Springs, 1982. Front row, sitting and kneeling: Jim McKeon, Mike Martucci, Ray Anderson, Sal Ingeme, Bob Sherwood, Michael Scurlock, Herb Gordon. Second row, standing: me, Sheila Chlanda, Buddy Bengert, Tom Chaltas, Gail Bruesewitz, George Chaltas, Linda Kirishjian, Burt Baumgartner, Dave Remedi, Richie Tardanico, Tim Burruss, Jim Del Balzo, Kevin Knee, Mark Westcott. Back row: Jay Miggins, Bob Conrad, Larry Reymann, Al Stann, John Fagot, Alan Oreman, Ritch Bloom, Marc Benesch, Gene Denonovich. **BOTTOM** Some of the gang at a convention in Hawaii after a few cocktails. Back row: Jack Lameier, Sheila Chlanda, Jim McKeon, George Chaltas. Front row: John Fagot, me, Michael Scurlock, Ray Anderson.

LEFT Adam in Judas Priest stage garb. The band gave him some of their performance gear to play as a knight with his neighborhood friends.
BELOW En garde! Bruce Dickinson and I go toe to toe down the hallways of Columbia Records.

OPPOSITE TOP Promoting Tommy Tutone's debut album with a '57 Chevy at Hollywood's popular drive-in, Tiny Naylor's: Jon Scott, me, Tommy Heath, Chuck Randall of KROQ, Jack Snyder of KMET, manager Paul Cheslaw, Jim Keller. **BOTTOM** Backstage with Ann and Nancy Wilson of Heart, visiting with Journey after their sold-out Seattle concert.

OPPOSITE TOP My assistant, Rasa, with Steve Perry, celebrating three full days of ColumbiaCast rock radio interviews. **BOTTOM** Two favorite music business heavyweights, Herbie Herbert and Michael Klenfner.

RIGHT The one and only Harvey Leeds's holiday card. They broke the mold that broke the mold that broke the mold. *Photo by Bob Gruen.*
BELOW Paul McCartney at a *ROCKLINE* live syndicated radio show featuring listener call-ins. Left to right: Jim McKeon, Dennis Lavinthal, Ray Anderson, Lenny Beer, Rachel DiPaola, Howie Gillman, Paul, Cindy Tollin, Mark Felsot, Jimmy Hite, Tommy Nast, me, and host Bob Coburn. *Photo by Lester Cohen.*

OPPOSITE TOP The Pink Floyd airship prepares to launch. *Photo by Jimmy ienner Jr.* BOTTOM Floyd manager Steve O'Rourke announces *The Division Bell* album and tour at the Rose Bowl, Pasadena, California.

ABOVE Me onstage with Pink Floyd, London Arena, 1989, playing the encore, 'Run Like Hell.' RIGHT A young Sam Rappaport takes the controls of the Floyd airship.

OPPOSITE TOP Josh Rosenthal and me with the incomparable Leonard Cohen. **BOTTOM** The guys, dressed for the Grammys. Left to right: me, John Fagot, George Chaltas, and Jimmy Mac.

RIGHT My bandmates for one song, Pink Floyd's Nick Mason and David Gilmour. Two of the finest artists I ever worked with. **BELOW** Billy Joel is the only artist I ever worked with that I could easily enjoy listening to for another hour after a three-hour show.

OPPOSITE TOP Magic! Me with Penn & Teller. *Photo by Charles Miller.* **BELOW LEFT** A signed photo of my mentor, the Master of Misdirection, Tony Slydini. **BELOW RIGHT** Pulling music exec Pam Edwards's head out of a graduation cap. It took me a moment to put her all back together.

ABOVE With Adam at a party to celebrate Alice In Chains getting halfway to a gold record. Note the half cake. **RIGHT** Adam with Sean Kinney, Layne Staley, and Mike Starr. Yikes. Maybe Boy Scouts would have been a better choice?!

LEFT My heart and soul. Adam, Sam, and me, holding our new surfboard model, the Sharon Rappaport.
BELOW Cowabunga! Me at my favorite break, Pipes, just south of Swami's, Encinitas, California. *Photo by Sam Rappaport.*

OPPOSITE Sharon and me. No explanation needed.

FOLLOWING PAGE Keith's simple lesson in open-G tuning. *Photo by Henry Diltz.*

To Paul,
(5. Strings
3 Notes
2 Fingers
1 ass-hole
love

The whole place just stopped and stared at me. The men there looked their stereotype, all dressed up like Orville Redenbacher in striped shirts, bowties, and suspenders. What it took me a second to figure out was that when they saw *me*, with my mustache, goatee, big Jewfro, and large nose, they'd pegged me dead to rights—a Jewish hippie. They were wondering first, what the hell was I doing in Darien; second, how I had the balls to walk into their store; third, did they even want me to touch their phone; and fourth, could they get away with lynching me?

I'd never been stared at like that before. Daggers were coming out of their eyes. My dad had told me that there was plenty of anti-Semitism left in the world, but coming from a background of peace, love, and rock'n'roll, I'd just blown it all off. But here it was, as real as could be—stark, heavy, and right in my face.

I walked to the back of the store to call Ed for some final directions (I must have missed seeing the badger). While I was on the phone, the guys at the front of the store were deep in conversation. I was seriously scared. I didn't know what they were planning. Perhaps they'd slash my tires, forcing me to stick around long enough to get rousted? Or maybe just take me out back and shoot me, then disappear me in one of many muddy creeks around those parts? It was no joke. I walked briskly past them, hopped back in my car, and sped away.

'Hey, wait a minute!' I heard them shouting.

Wait a minute my ass. I was shaking.

I finally found the muddy fork in the road and made it to Ed's house. Nice spread, nice family. It took me an hour to convince him to give me a shot.

'I'll tell you what,' he said. 'Why don't you fly Sharon in, do the job for a little longer, and let's see if you two even like living in New York.'

I thanked him profusely and told him he'd never regret it. I asked for directions back without having to go through Darien.

Sharon flew in for a visit. Within two weeks, we had fallen in love with New York City. I often describe it as Disneyland for adults. There's Upper West Side Land, Midtown Land, Times Square Land, Little Italy Land, Greenwich Village Land, and on and on. And, just like Disneyland, all those areas of the city have completely different personalities, different kinds of food, different architecture, and the people who live in those varied parts of town dress uniquely to their particular surroundings. I have always found that fascinating. Go to Midtown and everyone is looking sharp, buttoned-up, wearing the latest fashion; just thirty blocks south, down in Greenwich Village, everyone is wearing black and looking hip. You'd think you were in a different country.

The electricity in the air is discernable. With so many people around, so much culture, and so many wonderful, unique stores, as soon as you leave your apartment or hotel and your feet hit the pavement, you know you are bound for a great adventure. New York feels like a big small town. Even with so many people living there, it's not uncommon to find some friends standing in line to see a movie. I love to visit LA, see family and friends, eat real Mexican food, and surf some of the greatest waves in the world, but I doubt Sharon and I could ever leave this place—it's just too exciting.

'We love it here, Ed,' I'd tell him each day when I saw him, 'and I'm killing it. You've got to give me this job!'

While Ed was still interviewing candidates, a beautiful thing happened that was told to me much later in my life. One of the possible contenders was an extremely talented promotion man, Lenny Bronstein. Originally from New York, he was fast-paced and very amped, with an abundance of energy. He had been the national head of album promotion for A&M Records and now was an independent album rock promotion man. He was big in stature too—indeed, his nickname was Heavy Lenny.

Later on in our careers, Lenny told me that he had been invited to interview for the job. He also told me that when Ed started talking to him about it, he interrupted him and asked, 'Why are you interviewing me, or anyone else for that matter for this job? The best album rock promotion man in the world is just down the hall, doing it all for you right now.' Thanks, Lenny.

Ed had to admit that I'd been performing well during my test drive. I made him a believer, and he finally gave me the job.

One of the first things I needed to do was replace myself as national head of rock promotion West Coast. My easy first choice was Jim McKeon, who by now had built a great reputation as an FM rock radio promotion man. He and I had only gotten closer over the years, having shared an office and a similar laid-back promotion style. I knew wrestling him away from Epic Records was going to cause a stir, and lots of heat came my way, as high up as Epic's president, Ron Alexenburg. But Ron, being a great music man himself, ultimately understood. The Columbia roster featured many of the greatest rock artists in the world, and a national gig was going to be a step up for Mac.

It was a magical combination. If Mick Jagger and Keith Richards were the ultimate dynamic duo of rock'n'roll, Mac and I would become the dynamic duo of rock promotion, establishing the bands Midnight Oil, Men At Work, Loverboy, Journey, The Psychedelic Furs, Toto, The Hooters, The Outfield, The Bangles, Scandal, and more at breakneck speed.

One of the first new artists we promoted after I started the national job was a band named Tommy Tutone. Tommy Heath and his partner, Jim Keller, had started the band in 1978 and created a brand of power pop rock that was easy on the ears and made you want to sing along. You'll know them from the big hit '867-5309/Jenny,' but our first single from their debut album was 'Girl In The Backseat.' The lyrics talk about a girl in the back seat of a car '*going down slowly . . . looking for the promised land.*'

My love for big, splashy promotions would really ramp up now that I had a sizable budget to work with, and this was no exception. I was able to buy a two-tone bronze-and-white '57 Chevy in incredible condition from someone in northern California, where the band hailed from, for just over $3,000. The idea was to create a larger-than-life promotion to bring radio programmers' attention to the song. I announced a nationwide contest for all the rock radio programmers and music directors to have a chance to win the car. That got *everybody's* attention!

The first thing we needed to do was drive the car to Los Angeles, where we'd stash it until the contest was over. It's a dirty job, but someone had to do it, so Sharon and I flew to somewhere just south of San Francisco, bought the car, and drove it to LA. We had such a blast, making it our business to stop at every drive-in burger stand we could find. Waitresses in roller-skates were thrilled to serve us, and we got hoots and hollers from plenty of other drivers down the coast.

I hired a beautiful model, and ace photographer Lester Cohen took a picture of her wearing high heels with her long legs sticking out of the backseat window of the car in a provocative position. Of course, you only saw the car and the legs. The model was a very lovely person and a good sport, even if this wasn't the big break she was hoping for.

'I finally get my chance to appear in a big-time record company advertisement,' she'd say, 'and all you see are my legs—no one will know who I am!'

I bought the double-page center spread in the widely read music-industry newspaper *Radio & Records* (known as *R&R*) for an ad showing the car and the girl in the backseat and announcing the contest in very large type. Each successive week, as 'Girl In The Backseat' gained momentum nationwide, I would repeat the image and highlight all the new radio stations coming aboard, along with the upward rotations from stations already playing the record. 'Girl' was becoming a hit—all we had to do was spread the word and keep fanning the flames.

The music director who won the contest—name pulled at random out of a top hat—was a woman from a rock station in Lubbock, Texas, the home of Buddy Holly. Perfect! The town threw a big parade for her, and she drove her prized '57 Chevy down Main Street to the delight of the crowd.

· ● ·

With the Tommy Tutone contest, I realized how powerful a striking trade magazine advertisement could be in helping to build a band's career. If you were clever enough, you could help shape programmers' opinions about an artist by the way you couched your words and the image you created.

Aside from the royal blue logo on the front page, *R&R* looked just like a regular newspaper. All the industry stories were in black and white, along with record company ads announcing a new album, single, or tour. I called my contact at the magazine, Jeff Gelb, to ask if adding color was possible. He checked with his general manager, Dick Krizman, and the answer came back yes—for a few extra dollars. If we were the only record company adding color, I reasoned, our ads would stand out above all others, and therefore add a perceived importance to them.

At first, we just used a bright red to highlight radio station call letters or anything I wanted to call special attention to. But then, when other record companies began to copy my idea, I asked Jeff how many different colors were available. It turned out there were over a thousand! All of the colors available for printing were gathered together as a large stack of swatches in a narrow eight-by-two-inch book that you could fan out like a deck of cards, *The Pantone Book Of Color*. Not only were there endless mixtures available, but there were gradients of the mixtures, and if you printed them in different percentages, you could create fancy shadings. I began creating ads with intricate designs using different colors and percentages mixed together.

A conversation with the art director at *R&R* might go like this.

'OK, this is an ad for the band Judas Priest, showing all the rock radio stations playing their new single in just the first week of release. I need an image of a Gothic church with the headline, *New Judas Priest—Now Testifying At The Following Churches*. Under that, please list all the call letters of the radio stations playing the new single.'

That was the easy part. Then the fun began.

'I want the church in black, I want the band's name in Pantone chartreuse 382 C, outlined in Pantone rhodamine red U, and the station call letters in Pantone deep purple 2597 C . . . no, no, make that Pantone 266 C—it's much brighter. I want all the call letters to look like they're getting stronger as they're listed, so start them with halftone dot pixels at twenty-five percent, then add two percent to each call letter until you reach the last two, which will be printed at a hundred percent.'

The ads looked stellar—real works of art—and I was getting compliments from our artists' managers, radio station programmers, and even folks from other record companies. But I was driving the people from *R&R* out of their minds. This was taking way too much time. When I booked ads over the phone from New York, I would ask them to describe the colors, and then, when visiting LA, I would go over to their offices to see the Pantone book and make notes. Finally—ostensibly to make things easier—Jeff Gelb gave me a Pantone book to keep for myself.

When Dick Krizman found out about this, he exploded.

'You did WHAT?! Giving Rap a Pantone book is like giving machine guns to the Mob!'

Fast-forward a few years, and the color wars between record companies, continually trying to outdo one another by adding fancy colors to their ads, finally escalated into my commissioning the first traditional four-color advertisement in *R&R*. It was stupidly expensive, but everyone followed suit regardless. Before you knew it, we were all living in a very vivid, four-color world. Without realizing it, I had ushered in a sizable increase in advertising budgets, not only for Columbia but for the industry at large. I never got in trouble for it. It seemed like a natural evolution that came under the cost of doing business. The funny part was, we were now all equal again—just spending a lot more money. The *Album Network* tip sheet was actually printed in four-color on nice paper stock, and the ads inside got so outrageous that publication owner Steve Smith, Jim McKeon, and I were nicknamed the Pantone Triplets.

Always wanting to outgun the competition, when Pink Floyd's *A Momentary Lapse Of Reason* came out in 1987, I proposed a 3-D advertisement to *R&R*. I hired the country's foremost 3-D comic-book artist to create the image and paid for 3-D glasses to come with every issue. The magazine's editor, Bob Wilson, loved the idea so much that he waved his longstanding rule of never altering or compromising the newspaper's front-page logo to accommodate a record company advertisement. When that issue hit people's desks, the first thing they saw was *R&R* in 3-D, accompanied by a set of glasses. And when they came upon the image for *A Momentary Lapse Of Reason*, all they could think was, *Whoa! Positively psychedelic!*

THE EVERYMAN

OF ALL THE ARTISTS I've ever worked with, Billy Joel remains the most down-to-earth. He seems the least impressed with himself, and he carries no false airs. If you ever met him, you'd be astonished at how normal he is. If you went to lunch with him, he'd want to talk about your life and how you were doing, or maybe about his love of boats and Long Island. Of course, money and fame have had a big effect on his life, as they would on anyone's, but he remains balanced in a wonderfully sincere way. I wonder if it's because he grew up just another blue-collar kid in Hicksville, New York. I don't know, but he seems to still be that same person to this day.

Years ago, before Billy started doing his Madison Square Garden residencies, Sharon and I went to see what was then his record-setting tenth consecutive sold-out show at the venue. I was so proud and happy for him. We went backstage before the show and found him in his dressing room, reading the newspaper. I greeted him with a big smile.

'Hi, Billy . . . wow, ten sold-out shows in a row—congratulations!'

'Yeah, we're still kickin' around,' he replied, looking quite unaffected by it all.

'Still kickin' around?! Billy, *that's ten sold-out shows in a row* at Madison Square Garden!'

'Yeah, yeah, I know. Relax, sit down. Have a drink.'

Typical Billy.

A few years after that, we went to see him perform for a charity in West Hampton. Again, we went backstage to say hi before showtime. Billy was dressed in blue jeans and a nice black long-sleeve shirt. He couldn't decide whether to tuck the shirt in or leave it out. He looked up at us, tucked the shirt in, and then pulled it out again.

'Whaddya think, in or out?'

'What do I think? I think you're Billy Joel, and you've played thousands of shows in your life all over the world! And you still don't know whether you should tuck your shirt in or leave it out?'

You gotta love a guy like that. He left it out.

I first met Billy and his then-wife, Elizabeth, in Los Angeles, just before the release of his Columbia debut, *Piano Man*. I was so impressed with how many great songs there were on one album. I had seen another piano man, Elton John, make his first Los Angeles appearance at the Troubadour in 1970. Like everyone else in the audience, I immediately knew we were witnessing the next big thing. Three years later, listening to *Piano Man* on my way to Billy's appearance at the Troub, I knew we were all about to witness another next big thing.

After the show, I invited Billy and Elizabeth up to the Columbia offices to get some free records. I remember they were both wearing jeans and T-shirts and looked as poor as church mice. I thought about how much money there *isn't* at the beginning of one's career. I opened the stock closet door, and their eyes popped wide open with excitement. They both walked down the stairs holding so many albums in their arms they could barely see over the top of the stacks they were carrying.

The most fun you can experience with an artist is when they are just starting to cultivate fans at the beginning of their career. It's an innocent and exciting time. At Billy's very first show in Phoenix, he joked from the stage about male rock stars putting a banana down their pants for photos, to make them look more well-endowed. When he returned a year later, he was stunned at how many fans were smiling and throwing bananas onstage to greet him. Touched by this warm and fun gesture, and wanting to endear himself even further to the crowd, he said, 'I can't thank you all enough for coming to my show tonight. I know you could have easily bought tickets to see Rod Stewart, who is playing across the street at the big arena in town. So, for all you people who chose to be here with me instead of seeing Rod, this is for you.' Then he launched into the greatest imitation of Rod Stewart I've ever seen. If you closed your eyes, you'd think you were hearing Rod wailing away on one of his most famous rockers. The crowd went wild—they got to see Billy Joel and hear Rod Stewart all in the same show.

As talented as Billy is, it was hard at first for West Coast radio stations to understand his music. Just as Bruce's early records reflected East Coast imagery, Billy's references to a boy from Oyster Bay Long Island and songs like 'New York State Of Mind' and 'Scenes From An Italian Restaurant' seemed foreign to rock stations steeped in Led Zeppelin and Van Halen. Billy's brand of rock wasn't rock enough for them, and it took me forever to convince the rock programmers that they were making a big mistake by ignoring him.

There was a standing joke between me and then music director of KMET, Richard Kimball. He would literally break any Billy Joel record I brought to the radio station.

'Hey Paul, give me that record. I'll bet you don't know that if you take a vinyl album and hit it on its side against a tabletop, it will shatter into a million little pieces.'

THWACK!

Sure as shit, that's what would happen. I'd bring in a Billy Joel album upon release, Richard would break it, and that would be that. It got to the point where I'd bring in a Billy record, take it out, and immediately break it myself right in front of Richard before he could get his hands on it. It was pretty funny, but deep inside I knew it was no laughing matter.

To compound things, Billy's singles were all ballads, so no one knew how much he rocked. My solution was to take people to a Billy Joel show. Once they saw him live, they got it. I was spending gobs of money from Seattle to San Diego taking entire cities worth of rock jocks and programmers first to dinner at a swanky restaurant and then to the show. Wanting to inform headquarters what I was doing (read: cover my ass), I called the aforementioned Mike Pillot, the head of album rock promotion.

'Hey, P. Listen, I'm spending a lot of money out here taking tons of people to a nice dinner and then to see Billy. It's working, but I just wanted you to know.'

'It's fine, Rappy,' he replied. 'We're *making* a lot of money!'

Those were the days.

The dam started to finally break with *The Stranger*, and when *52nd Street* was released, I was able to negotiate a real breakthrough.

In 1978, KLOS-FM in Los Angeles had become a rock juggernaut responsible for selling thousands of albums. Every rock artist needed KLOS to play their albums to ensure maximum exposure and sales in LA. Billy Joel's airplay and sales picture would not be complete without KLOS playing a track from *52nd Street*. I was heavily soliciting program director Frank Cody to pick a song to add to his playlist. This one *had* to happen. I was getting close when I was called to attend some important meetings in New York. The meetings were scheduled for the end of the following week, so I had that Monday free to make my last case before I left. Blessed as I was with the gift of the gab, I was sure I could convince Frank to add a song from the album before my flight.

My bosses at Columbia headquarters were watching closely. Getting KLOS to play Billy Joel in good rotation was key to breaking him wide open in LA. My reputation was on the line, and the pressure on me was enormous.

Amped up, I walked into KLOS that next Monday only to find out that Frank had been called into a meeting with his general manager and would not be able to see me. My stomach turned upside-down. I really needed this one. What to do? I'd wanted to tell Frank about how many albums Billy was now selling in Los Angeles, and how his ticket sales had grown exponentially, proving his overwhelming popularity. And I'd wanted to do it with a persuasive presentation. But if I wasn't able to talk with Frank, I was doomed. Just leaving him a note, even a long one, wasn't going to cut it. I needed something imaginative—something completely over-the-top to drive my point home.

Luckily, I had a stack of sales printouts with me. The LA branch sold hundreds of thousands of albums, and our 10 X 15-inch weekly printouts were thick. I decided to paper Frank's office with them. Pulling some scotch tape out of his desk drawer, I began to decorate. I covered the walls, his desk, his chair, and even the floor. It looked like a Halloween stunt. I positioned Billy's album sales as the first thing Frank would see when looking down at his desk. I outlined them with a Sharpie, and in huge letters across the top, I wrote, *Billy Joel is selling thousands of albums and concert tickets in Los Angeles. It's time.* Then I flew to New York.

The next day, all the higher-ups were asking if I'd gotten Frank to add the record. All I could do was wait—and as Tom Petty sings, '*The waiting is the hardest part.*' I was so wound up I couldn't eat.

Finally, late in the afternoon, New York time, I called Frank. I closed my eyes and held my breath, awaiting his answer.

'Hi, Rap. You'll be very pleased to know I got your message . . . your *many* messages.'

Then I heard a brief laugh. Thank God Frank Cody had a sense of humor.

'I added "Big Shot" to our playlist today.'

My brain exploded in euphoria. It was one of the happiest moments of my career. My reputation was cemented—I would be a star that week. I looked up at the heavens to say thanks.

'I know you needed this one,' Frank continued, 'but I also want you to know that I think "Big Shot" is a great song and that Billy Joel is good for KLOS.'

Frank was constantly barraged by his bosses back east about what music to play and what music to stay away from. To his credit, he ran KLOS as he saw fit, playing the music he thought was best for his Los Angeles listeners. This upset his bosses from time to time, but they couldn't argue with the ratings. Frank Cody had vision. For all of you in Southern California who hear and enjoy Billy Joel in regular rotation on your classic-rock radio stations, you have Frank to thank for it. After the tremendous success of 'Big Shot' on KLOS we never looked back. Billy Joel was finally established on rock radio on the West Coast. Thank you, Frank.

• ● •

One of the secrets of Billy's success was his band. They adapted the way they played to his lyrics. During recording sessions, drummer Liberty DeVitto would always enquire what the next lines of a song were so that he could add thoughtful drum passages that helped bring a song to life. Along with Doug Stegmeyer on bass, Richie Cannata on sax, and Russel Javors on guitar, that band was a force to be reckoned with.

Once, in San Francisco, I took some of the guys and their monitor mixer,

Jim McGehee, to dinner at one of my favorite restaurants, Marrakech. The restaurant offers Moroccan food that you eat with your fingers and a wonderful red table wine. The ambiance is superb—you even feel like you are in Morocco, surrounded by elaborate geometric architecture, low-lit in purple, pink, and orange lights. Tapestries adorn the walls and large round silver tables are positioned low, with comfy tufted ottomans on which to sit.

The band and crew were staying in Oakland, so we all hopped into a station wagon and drove across the Oakland Bay Bridge into the Tenderloin district. At the front of the restaurant, as we walked in, was a large blue tile fountain spilling into a pool, which made the entrance awkward, because you had to walk around the large fountain and pool to make your way to your seats.

After an incredible feast featuring unique dishes like lamb with roasted almonds and honey, we were all pretty stuffed. We'd also drunk enough of that red wine to sink a battleship. Attempting to get up and leave, we discovered we were more buzzed than we thought. The tell was, as we were walking out of the restaurant, we failed to see the fountain. We walked right through it—sloshing along without a care, our shoes and pant legs getting completely soaked.

Arriving back at the station wagon I was voted the designated driver because I was the least intoxicated. McGehee was riding shotgun, and Liberty, Richie, and Doug were in the backseat, with Lib on the passenger side. As we drove back across the bridge, we saw a row of construction cones all along the edge of the right-hand lane. Liberty piped up from the back, 'Hey, Rap, every time you spot a cone, see if you can get close to it.'

No sooner had I done so when Liberty quickly snapped open his door and knocked the cone clear over the guardrail and off the bridge. Immediately we all shared an inebriated a-ha moment. We continued across the entire bridge, swerving to the right at every cone, knocking them all off the bridge, one by one, into the waiting bay below.

Whack! Whack! Whack!

I was getting into a rhythm, which I'm sure Liberty, being a drummer, appreciated. Then McGehee got into the act. We must have been really high, because no one seemed the least bit worried about getting caught and paying for the ramifications of our actions (reckless driving, DUI, destroying city property . . .). On a positive note, we managed to avoid swerving completely off the bridge and made it back alive.

• ● •

In the early 80s, Billy invited the Columbia promotion staff to his home in Lloyd Harbor for lunch. It was a good-sized house on a corner of Lloyd Neck Beach with a pool overlooking a private dock, replete with a small Boston Whaler. There was also a carriage house with a built-in recording studio upstairs and a large garage with the beginning of a nice motorcycle collection.

Billy pulled me outside at the back of the house and pointed down the beach.

'You see that stone building way down there?'

'Yeah.'

'That's a fort—a real fort from the 1800s. Some people just bought it, and they're gonna make it into a house. Now, that's real money!'

'Real money? What the fuck is all this?' I replied, pointing to our surroundings.

'Yeah, I know, I know,' he laughed. 'I've done okay.'

We laughed and started to talk about how these things are relative. But the one thing that every rock star will tell you is that no matter how much money they have, it can't buy you the most important things in life.

Always true to his fans, Billy would balk every time we told him we were putting together a greatest-hits package.

'Come on guys,' he'd complain. 'These songs have already been hits, now they're used cars. I don't want to take advantage of my fans selling them used cars.'

While we had to admit that part of the idea concerned the bottom line, it's also true that fans like greatest hits packages because it's so much fun to listen to one favorite song right after another. I explained that what he considered to be 'used cars' were forever gems that people would hold dear for a lifetime. Eventually, he'd come around, but his fans are like an extended family to him, and he always wants to take care of them, treating them with love and thoughtfulness.

Billy has always closed his shows with the words that celebrate each human being's right to have respect and belief in oneself, no matter their place in life.

'*Don't take any shit from anybody.*'

During the pandemic, at the Robin Hood Foundation's *Rise Up New York!* TV concert, Billy was introduced by the governor of New York, Andrew Cuomo, before the lights on the Empire State Building flashed in sync with Billy's performance of 'Miami 2017.' You know you're a big deal when you're duetting with the Empire State Building.

At the end of the song, Billy stopped, looked into the camera, and reconfigured his patented closing.

'Stay strong, New York, please wear a mask, and that way you won't catch any shit from anybody.'

It was quintessential Billy Joel—a reminder that whether you're a rock star or the mailman, we're all in this together.

READING THE TEA LEAVES

'RAP, WAIT 'TIL YOU HEAR THIS! It's a new band out of Canada, and they're gonna go all the way!'

Mason Munoz, the son of legendary WNEW-FM disc jockey Scott Muni, and a key marketing manager at Columbia Records, had come running excitedly into my office holding an advanced test pressing of a new album. I took the shiny vinyl LP and began listening. And, honestly, I didn't hear it right away. As good as the record was, it just didn't sink in for some reason. To make matters more difficult it was being released in October, which is when everything starts to shut down for current projects, as radio is focused more on hits and holiday songs. In those days, record stores only wanted to stock up on all the big hit albums they'd be selling during the Christmas season—there'd be little room left for any new music on their shelves.

Let me get this straight, I thought to myself. *I have a rock band named Loverboy, the album cover features a skinny, androgynous-looking teenager, and it's coming out in October?*

Being a professional means giving every record a legitimate push, whether you 'hear it' or not. It's your job to obtain as much airplay as possible, to see if the public becomes enamored with the music. I told Mason that for some reason the record didn't resonate with me, but I assured him I'd promote the hell out of it and find out if we had something.

It was late in the year, and I needed people to pay immediate attention, so I placed large color ads in all the major trade magazines to make a big splash. No more than two weeks later, I got a call from Gloria Johnson, the evening disc jockey at KGON-FM in Portland, Oregon. Gloria was one of those special people with exceptional ears for rock music. In fact, she was so good at identifying new potential rock acts that I'd say she was to on-air talent what the legendary John Hammond was to Columbia Records' A&R department—yes, that good.

Gloria was a wonderful person and a rocker at heart, and when she talked, I listened.

'Hey Rap, how ya doin'? I'm calling to tell ya you have a big hit on your hands!'

'Really? Who?'

'Loverboy!'

'Loverboy?!'

'Yeah, I'm playing a track called "Turn Me Loose," and the phones are ringing off the hook!'

That was all I needed to hear. The tea leaves had spoken. It was time to turn up the heat. I ran down the hall, yelling for Mason.

'I told you so, Rap.'

Our local promotion team started to spread the word as fast as they could—we had a track that was getting huge requests from rock fans. McKeon and I called all our close friends at rock radio, hired the independents, and both Bill Hard and Tommy Nast from their respective influential tip sheets (weekly publications that offered album reviews and programming recommendations) were on board. The heat was on!

'Turn Me Loose' was quickly gaining airplay in many cities around the country and started to rise on the rock airplay charts. It was time for me to call and introduce myself to their manager, Bruce Allen, in Vancouver. I had good news: he and his band were about to have a big hit record.

I would come to learn that Bruce Allen was one tough Canuck, very outspoken, and a force to be reckoned with. He'd previously managed Bachman-Turner Overdrive, and he would go on to steer the careers of Bryan Adams and Michael Bublé, among others.

'Bruce Allen Talent,' his secretary announced chirpily.

I told her who I was and why I was calling. She put me on hold, which seemed to last an eternity. Finally, Bruce picked up the phone, huffing and puffing, sounding out of breath.

'Big office, huh?' I asked, trying to make a joke.

'Whaddya mean?' he said forcefully in his thick Canadian accent.

'I mean, your office must be really big—you got winded running from one end to the other.'

'Naw, naw, nothing like that. I just had a fight with my accountant.'

'Lots of yelling and screaming, huh?'

'No, a *fight*.'

'Like, a fistfight?'

'Yah, a real rough-and-tumble!'

'Shit, Bruce, I haven't hit anyone since the seventh grade.'

I would later learn that Bruce Allen had a large painting of the professional boxer Chuck Wepner hanging over his desk for inspiration. Wepner's nickname was the Bayonne Bleeder. No matter how battered he got during a fight, he would always get up off the mat and keep coming, like a mad dog. That kind of fight is part of Allen's impressive personality.

'So, you like my guys' record, eh?'

'Better than that, I'm on my way to making it a big hit at album rock radio.'

Bruce and I hit it off immediately, each of us appreciating the other's go-getter attitude.

Thanks to a lot of hard work by one of our local guys, Gene Denonovich, Loverboy were getting played a lot on KSHE-FM in St. Louis and becoming well-known in the city. I called Rick Balis, the station's program director, to thank him for his support and ask him if he'd like the band to come and play a free show for KSHE and its listeners. He was thrilled with the idea, so I called Allen, who made it happen.

I thought Rick would go for a club or a small theater, but just like the folks at KNAC who'd booked the Long Beach Arena for Blue Öyster Cult, he decided to throw the concert at Kiel Auditorium, which held over nine thousand people. A few of us flew in for the concert, and some very exceptional things happened that evening.

First, it was the first time we'd ever seen the band perform live. We knew they had written some catchy tunes, but we weren't ready for how good they were as musicians. These guys had real talent, and they were going to go far. There was the charismatic frontman Mike Reno on vocals and Paul Dean on guitar, but the secret sauce was the driving rhythm section, Scott

Smith on bass and Matt Frenette on drums. Rounding it all out was Doug Johnson on keyboards. They were something much more special than just another pop group.

The other enlightening element was how many girls were in the audience. We all thought we were launching a guy rock band, à la AC/DC, but with half the audience comprised of screaming girls, our eyes popped. When you have a band that appeals equally to men and women, you start to envision millions and millions of records being sold.

I went to use the bathroom before the show began and a kid who'd had one too many beers sauntered up to the stall next to me. His head began to weave in a circular motion, and with his eyes closed, he started singing.

'Turn me loose, turn me loose.'

It was a profound moment for me. Here it was, the whole record business in a nutshell, from the band making the record, to the excited Mason Munoz, to me and my promotion team, to Gloria Johnson leading the way, to the music being played on KSHE, and now the music was in this kid's head!

We met the guys after the show. They were good people—no outsized egos, no demands, just very thrilled to be there working on building a career.

Rick had successfully packed the Kiel Auditorium, and the band gave an over-the-top performance, blowing the place apart. We were on the verge of breaking what would become one of the biggest bands of the 80s.

I flew back to New York and called a meeting with Mason and Hope Antman, the head of publicity at Columbia.

'These guys are great,' I told them, 'but we have no image to work with. Only the album cover, which doesn't convey a band. I need a photo that, when they see it, *everyone* will know it's Loverboy.'

Hope understood and immediately put together a photo shoot. No more than two weeks later, she walked into my office and threw down a photo that was to become Loverboy's first big publicity shot. In the middle of some rockin' tough-looking guys, there was Mike Reno, wearing what would become his signature look, the red headband—perfect. We had the music, we had a great live band, we had momentum on the charts, and now we had a focused image. Even though Jimi Hendrix and Mark Knopfler of Dire Straits had previously donned red headbands (Knopfler's being the more athletic kind), I credit Mike Reno with the look that many 80s rockers would follow. Hell, even Springsteen would wear one!

Things were getting hot. Now all we needed to do was ship more records.

In a company the size of CBS, there was room for plenty of egos, and none bigger than some of the sales guys who continually felt their oats after selling shitloads of records and raking in gazillions of dollars for the company. At the end of the year, all of the branch managers from around the country would be flown in for meetings, and I was called in to one.

'Why is *Lover*boy a priority?' one of the main sales managers asked, snidely mocking the band's name.

'It's a priority because the record is breaking big at rock radio. We need to ship more records—and fast—so kids can find them in the stores.'

'Oh yeah? What proof do you have?'

'Okay, here's my marketing report. This may not be the fanciest marketing report you're ever gonna hear, but it's real. I just came back from a concert in St. Louis. While I was taking a piss in the bathroom, the kid in the stall next to me was singing "Turn Me Loose" at the top of his lungs.'

They looked at me, ready to laugh.

'That means that this music is getting through to this kid—not to mention the other nine thousand kids in the audience who were screaming their heads off, singing along with the band. It's gone full circle. The track is now #12 with a bullet on the rock airplay charts and is poised to go Top 10. We have a hit act on our hands. But I think the bigger question is, why isn't it a priority for you guys?'

They didn't like that one bit. I was told in so many words that *they* were the ones who decided who makes 'em and who breaks 'em. I should say here that the CBS sales force was the best in the world, and this interaction wasn't indicative of their everyday approach, but there comes a time when each of us in our business turns into an asshole, and this just happened to be their turn.

I always considered myself a good and loyal soldier for Columbia, but I've also always tried to do the right thing for any band I worked with. So, I called Bruce Allen.

'We've got a problem.'

The next day, I was called in to see Al Teller, the president of Columbia. He was about to get on a conference call with Bruce. He asked me for the lay of the land, then put the phone on speaker.

'Hi, Bruce, what can I do for you?'

'You can start to fucking ship more Loverboy albums into the stores, that's what!'

'Well, I know we've got a buzz going, but my sales team isn't quite convinced.'

'The record is becoming a big hit on rock radio, and the guys are on the road playing to enthusiastic audiences. I'm sure Rap told you what went on in St. Louis. This band is breaking, the demand is there. You want convincing? Here's what's gonna happen. If you don't ship forty thousand records into the stores immediately, I'm gonna trans-ship them in from Canada, and you guys are going to look like big assholes.'

This was probably not the best way to approach a record company president, especially one like Al Teller. But it worked. Bruce was lucky that Al was just as tough as him, if not tougher, and he probably detected a kindred spirit, or at least appreciated Bruce's bravado. Al was very smart, and he had an incredible head for numbers. He did the right thing—he shipped the records, right at the most difficult time in the year to place new albums into stores.

Those forty thousand records were instantly gobbled up, and by the end of the next year, we'd sold over two million albums. The band's follow-up—*Get Lucky*, featuring 'Working For The Weekend'—sold over four million copies. And the rest is history.

100 PERCENT ROCK'N'ROLL

'MICK JAGGER'S ON THE PHONE! Mick Jagger's on the phone!'

The words echoed from two out-of-breath secretaries, running into my office to let me know. My personal assistant Robin Solomon, who was with me going over some promotional plans, looked up incredulously.

'I don't believe it! The one time I'm not out there to answer the phone and Mick calls!'

Even though we were all used to working closely with superstar artists, our passion for the music kept us in a perpetual state of fandom. You might think that sounds unprofessional, but I always considered it a wonderful blessing—one that helped maintain the magic that the artists and record company personnel made together.

Mick was calling to thank me for helping him achieve something that no other artist had ever managed before (or since).

Having been promoted to Vice President of Album Rock Promotion, I set myself the goal of becoming the very best in the business, and by 1985, many artists, managers, and radio and record company personnel saw me as such. The VP stripes meant that I was also now an officer of the company (a big fucking deal).

Like most successful music business people, I had a sizable ego back then, but that comes with the territory if you're making big things happen. You've got to believe in yourself and believe you can achieve anything. Even so, I tried not to get carried away with myself. I would begin each project by asking myself, *What do I want to accomplish?* Besides the obvious, the answer usually included something that had never been done before, not only for the artist's sake but also to keep a spotlight on my own career.

One of the most valuable lessons Steve Popovich gave me was this:

'Rap, promote the artist as hard as you can, but also save an extra five percent to promote yourself. It's important that people always see and revere you as someone who can make special things happen—that you are the best.'

In a fickle business where personnel changes frequently, this can also guarantee job security. I have a natural competitive spirit, and I'm a bit of a show-off—when I win, I have to win big, bigger than anyone else. So, promoting myself came easy for me.

Columbia president Walter Yetnikoff had signed The Rolling Stones in 1983, but because Mick and Keith were on the outs at the time, the first new album we promoted was Mick's solo debut, *She's The Boss*, an excellent record full of in-the-pocket grooves and great songs like 'Just Another Night,' 'Lucky In Love,' and '1/2 A Loaf.' Because The Rolling Stones were my guys, I was out to do something so special for Mick that the world would have to take notice.

I was shocked that the Stones had left Atlantic Records, which had been their home for well over a decade. Some of the band's biggest releases ever were on Atlantic, including *Sticky Fingers* (with the working zipper album cover and songs like 'Brown Sugar,' 'Wild Horses,' 'Can't You Hear Me Knocking,' and Bitch'), *Some Girls* (featuring the Stones classics 'Miss You,' 'Beast Of Burden,' and 'Shattered'), and my all-time favorite, *Exile On Main St.* (the many highlights of which include 'Tumbling Dice,' 'Sweet Virginia', 'Rip This Joint,' 'All Down The Line,' and 'Happy,' with Keith on lead vocals). The Stones were synonymous with Atlantic president Ahmet Ertegun, and the label itself was rich with R&B history. Why on earth would they want to leave?

Well, because Walter had given them twenty-five million dollars, that's why. I would soon learn that with the Stones, it was all about the money. I guess it is with most bands, in truth. Just like in Neil Young's classic 'Heart Of Gold,' I am forever looking through rose-colored glasses, thinking there's got to be loyalty somewhere in this business, but it's rare. Not only did the Stones *look* like pirates, they *were* pirates. Every decision they made was based on how much money they could make. But I came to learn that the band had been through so much, and had been ripped off so many times, in so many ways, that now they felt this was their time—they didn't know how much longer it was going to last, so they were out to grab all the loot they could plunder.

When I heard the news, I immediately called Tunc Erim, Ahmet's right-hand man at Atlantic. Tunc (pronounced *Tunge* with a soft *g*) was a big man with an ample amount of thick curly dark-brown hair, known for being a party guy but also a great person with a big heart. Often, when I visited an FM radio station, the folks there would excitedly say, 'Guess who was here last week? Tunc Erim!' He was known and loved by all in a way that I admired—I wanted to be like him. He would invite me to the Atlantic Records parties at radio conventions and made me feel comfortable hanging out with the Atlantic family.

'Hey, Tunc,' I began, 'first of all I want to say how sorry I am that you lost the Stones—I know how much they meant to you. But I also wanted to call to get some pointers—any inside information you can help me with on how to deal with them.'

'Rap, you've got The Rolling Stones: you've got *big* fun ... and you've got *big* problems!'

I could hear the devilish smile in his thick Turkish accent.

'Well, Tunc, I've pretty much seen it all, and I've been able to handle it all, so how big could the problems be?'

'You've never seen *anything* like this!'

I'd handled difficult artists, I'd patched up frayed relationships, I'd gone toe-to-toe with some of the most notorious managers, promoters, and agents in the business, and I'd already been through the whole drug movie with Keith and Woody, so what could be so different?

Tunc told me about traveling with the Stones to somewhere in the Middle East. Mick had evidently hit it off with the daughter of a Saudi prince, and the prince was none too happy about it. Mick wanted the girl to travel with him and the band for a while, and Tunc was in charge of secreting them out of the country together, which meant being chased down by the prince's men wielding big guns and long curved swords as they ran for the Stones' private jet across the airport tarmac.

'Uh-huh,' I said. 'Got it.'

My mind froze as I wondered what I might be in for.

• • •

In 1985, when you released a record by a rock superstar, you were guaranteed that 80 percent of rock radio was going to add the record to their playlists during the first week. The next week, maybe you'd be up to 95 percent, and by the third week, you just had to clean up the stragglers. The object, of course, was to reach 100 percent, meaning all 150 or so rock stations across the country playing the record. Back then, a hotly anticipated new release by a superstar act could find itself debuting in the Top 15 on the charts. The next week it would go Top 10, maybe Top 5, and finally, in its third week, it could reach #1.

But what if you could get every single rock station in America—and the one in Nova Scotia, which for some reason was included in our charts—to add the record on the *very first day* of release? What if we could debut at #1, with one hundred percent of radio all playing the record on the same day?

This would be nearly impossible, due to the inconsistent programming styles at each station. Some elected to give new releases a few quick spins but would only officially add a record to their playlists later, when they had time to make room for it. Others could add a record but simply forget to report it to the trade magazines. And a few might have had a tiff with the artist or manager and would hold off just to prove a point.

Undeterred, I decided to make this near impossibility a reality for Mick and *She's The Boss*. I conferred with my main man, Mac, who had been instrumental in helping break Loverboy, and who was always up for a history-making adventure himself. We hunkered down and hatched our ambitious plan. On a conference call with our local promotion staff and then another with the independent guys, we explained our idea and what it would take to pull it off. Each one of them would have to make sure that the stations they were responsible for 'officially added' the record on the day of release, and they'd have to double-check to make sure that each and every station reported that add to the trades—most significantly to *Radio & Records*, whose charts were the benchmark for airplay. If only one station failed to comply, we'd debut at ninety-nine percent—still an amazing feat, to be sure, but not a history-making one.

Achieving this required us to have the best relationships with all the program and music directors at rock radio. My long-term view on doing business with radio was to give, give, give, and give some more. I enjoyed helping program directors build their stations' reputations by giving away blocks of concert tickets from superstars like the Stones, Bruce Springsteen, Billy Joel, Pink Floyd, and more, and by offering creative promotions like flying the Pink Floyd inflatable pig over their studios and creating massive attention for them in their local towns. Backstage meet-and-greets with bands were common. My style was to only ask for something special in return every once in a while. If you don't ask for too much too often, people usually come through for you in a pinch.

Tuesday is the day that all the radio stations report their playlist adds to the trades. This being Mick's first solo effort, the excitement was contagious, and most everyone was on board to help us out. Even radio stations whose playlists were packed figured out a way to scooch us in. Mac was calling *R&R* every hour to check in, and he had to double back to a few stations who hadn't reported yet or who just forgot to declare they'd added *She's The Boss*.

My biggest challenge was the station in Nova Scotia. I didn't usually talk to this particular PD, as the station was so far away, so I called to introduce myself and explain what we were trying to do. I ended my pitch by saying, 'So for all the great music and joy Mick and The Rolling Stones have given us, I want to ask you this as a favor for Mick. Will you please help?'

'I'd love to,' he replied, 'but there is one problem. I'm in Nova Scotia, and we receive all of our albums by mail a day later than everyone else in the United States. I physically won't have the record until Wednesday.'

'But when you get the record, you will probably add it immediately, right?'

'Yes, we like to be as current as possible for our listeners.'

'So, can you *please* add the record today . . . and just *play it* tomorrow?'

'Well, *theoretically* I could add it to our playlist, yes. I could make it an official add today, and play it as soon as it arrives.'

'That'd be great!' I replied. 'I was a philosophy major, and I love the word *theoretically*.'

When you're dealing with people of like minds—people whose lives have been changed by the music and artists they've loved for years—the impossible can come true. And it did. The station in Nova Scotia added the record. The next morning, we saw it in print:

MICK JAGGER DEBUTS #1 AT 100%!

Nothing like this had ever happened before. The folks at Columbia were going nuts. I got a congratulatory call from Al Teller, and then Mick called. This would be my first time speaking to him, and my heart was racing.

'Hello, is this Paul?' he began.

I told him how much The Rolling Stones meant to me personally, and that this was just the beginning of the kind of effort he would see me deliver for him and the band. Then he surprised me.

'I can't thank you enough for what you've done,' he continued, in that charming cockney voice that sounded just like Mick Jagger. 'I know about promotion and what an effort it must have taken to accomplish this. It's pretty impossible. I don't know how you did it, but thanks very much.'

I knew Mick was a student of the business, but I never expected that he would follow the intricacies of such things. And the fact that he would call me personally spoke volumes. Mick was the ultimate professional—he was on a mission to get things done, but he was also a class act. I would enjoy many more meetings with him and The Rolling Stones in the years to come.

The promotion force celebrated. We made bold red *She's The Boss* jackets with cream-colored sleeves featuring the Rolling Stones tongue logo on the side. Inside the jacket was embroidered, 'The 100% Club. No one else belongs.' We gave them to every promotion person who helped pull off this bit of rock'n'roll history, and we sent one to Mick. My assistant, Robin, and the other gals in the office presented me with a beret, a long white boa, some big shades, and a long cigarette holder. For that week, I was a star.

• ● •

I remember having dinner with Mick one night around the time of *She's The Boss*. Mick is very much about the business, so it was easy to just dive right in and discuss all. But the challenge for me, when it came to artists like The Rolling Stones or Bob Dylan who had made such an impact on me during my teenage years, well before I got into the music business, was that I couldn't help but be somewhat overwhelmed at first.

Of course, as I sat across from Mick, I saw a working professional who had orchestrated an incredible career for himself and the Stones. But well beyond that, my mind immediately flooded with all the Rolling Stones history embedded in my DNA, in particular the *Ed Sullivan* appearances, and especially the one where Mick was forced to sing '*Let's spend some time together*' instead of '*Let's spend the night together.*' I visualized the band's album covers, posters, and film footage. 'Gimme Shelter,' 'Street Fighting Man,' 'Paint It Black,' 'Mona,' 'Satisfaction,' 'Tumbling Dice,' 'Get Off My Cloud,' 'Ruby Tuesday,' and all the rest reverberated in my head. I flashed back to all the concerts I'd seen and my high school band playing all those Stones covers. And, yes, back to having to have the good version of 'Everybody Needs Somebody To Love' and making out with Sharon while listening to that song. It all hit me like a ton of bricks.

I found myself staring at one of the most recognizable faces in the world. That face and that familiar accent had lived inside of me and been a part of me for years. I had to shake my head and refocus, bring myself back to the present—back to being a professional record man.

On the other side of the table was a man who, like most artists, viewed fans from a distance, insulating himself and the Stones in a bubble far away from the fray. He probably had no idea that his music had played such an important role in shaping my life—or in shaping so many other lives, for that matter. But he was impressed when I told him I'd spent the eight dollars and waited a whole summer just to get my import of *The Rolling Stones No. 2,* kind of shocked that I knew about the two versions of 'Everybody Needs Somebody To Love,' and genuinely touched by the story of me driving right over to Sharon's to dance to our song.

Mick Jagger can certainly be all about the business, but that evening I saw a side of him that was vulnerable. I got a glimpse of his heart, and it was a beautiful moment.

BEASTS IN THE BIBLE

BOB DYLAN WAS my biggest hero in music when I was a teenager. As times were changing in the 60s, he brought to life the thoughts many of us were feeling but had trouble expressing. The poetry, emotion, and images he created were astonishing. *'You don't need a weatherman to know which way the wind blows'* is probably my favorite line of any song.

And Bob was authentic. He stood for something. When asked by worried censors to play a different song on *The Ed Sullivan Show* instead of 'Talkin' John Birch Paranoid Blues,' which poked fun at the ultra-conservative John Birch Society and its members' insistence that communists were lurking behind every tree, Bob walked off the set. The television appearance was an enormous opportunity, but keeping his integrity was more important.

On August 28, 1963, at the height of the protest movement, Martin Luther King, Jr. led the March On Washington at the National Mall. It was where he would give his 'I Have A Dream' speech. There was also a musical element at the gathering that day before King spoke. Along with Mahalia Jackson, Marian Anderson, Joan Baez, and Peter Paul & Mary, there was Bob Dylan, singing songs that spoke truth to power like no other.

Between his songs and his actions, Dylan became the spokesman of a generation. Bob wanted neither that mantel nor that pressure, but it came with the territory. For young people who weren't quite sure where they fit in the world, Dylan showed up right on time. I, like many, questioned the square box that most Americans lived in at the time. I hated the war in Vietnam—war in general, I couldn't understand racism, and I couldn't understand why women had to fight to play larger roles in the workplace. I felt smothered in the conformist society of the day, repressed in a world with an overload of social mores. If Lenny Bruce was taking good swings at these issues, Bob Dylan was hitting the ball out of the park. I wanted to bust out and help create a new world—one where the human race evolved into something better. With his words and music, Dylan was leading the charge. I know it sounds cliché, but he changed my life—somehow gave me permission to think and have a vision beyond what current society dictated. In short, he let me know that it was okay to be me and to be proud of it.

When I first met Bob, I was flat-out overwhelmed.

'The problem is,' he once told me, 'when people meet me, they think they're meeting the lyrics. I know how heavy the songs are—I wrote them—but they're the songs, I'm me.'

I was certainly guilty of being in that group. And I think it's the same for most people who meet him, which makes me often wonder what it must be like to *be* Bob Dylan, where no one quite knows how to talk to you at first. With his songs having helped shape my life, the way I thought about things, and how I wanted to carry myself in the world, it took me at least five conversations with the guy before I could calm down and be somewhat normal. Even then, I'd start out okay, then look up, mid-conversation, and suddenly it would hit me like a ton of bricks.

Fuck, it's Bob Dylan!

After talking with him on numerous occasions, however, I finally settled down and we formed a nice relationship. It was a highlight for me during my tenure at Columbia. And who would have thought that after all he had meant to me growing up, that one day I would be able to give something back, to help him achieve some of his goals, and be there to protect him when the wolves were at the door.

I have a lot of Bob Dylan stories, but this is my favorite. One day, Bob showed up unannounced at the acclaimed producer Chuck Plotkin's recording studio in Hollywood. He told Chuck he had some ideas for an album and asked if Chuck could put up some tape to lay down a few tracks. Of course, Chuck excitedly obliged, and they recorded a few things.

'Hey, this sounds good,' Bob told him. 'I think I want to make an album. Can we do that here?'

'Of course,' Chuck replied. 'Let me just call Columbia in New York, so we can complete the proper paperwork.'

'Okay, I'll come back once that's done,' Bob said, sounding quite pleased at the prospect.

Not wanting to miss an opportunity, Chuck suggested, 'Hey, Bob, as long as you're here, why don't we re-record those three tracks? They're not in perfect time.'

Already on his way to the door, Bob glanced back at Chuck and shook his head.

'Chuck, people aren't in perfect time.'

And that's a little glimpse into Bob's process. It's all about the feel and journey of making the music, not about total perfection. Once the story is told, if it resonates, it's good to go. Bob doesn't like to over-paint a picture. Many musicians have complained that they could have achieved a better performance if they'd had another pass at playing on a track. But like Picasso, Bob works quickly. I believe Michael Bloomfield, in particular, was frustrated by this, because although his guitar work is renowned on some of Bob's greatest recordings, he knew after getting a good feel for the music and getting into a groove that he could play his parts much better the second time around. But he never got the chance. To Bob's ears, what Michael played captured the essence of the song, and that was the goal. Listening to how powerful Bob's records are, it's hard to argue his process.

I first met Bob at the time of the *Blood On The Tracks* album while I was still the western region album rock promotion man. I told him how easy it had been to promote the album, that it just 'flew onto the radio.'

'Okay,' he replied, looking back at me. 'I guess we'll call ya when we need ya.'

This being my very first encounter with Bob, I walked away thinking, *Wow, what heavy significance did those words carry?*

It turned out the answer was: nothing special. After getting to know him, I realized it was just typical Bob small talk.

· ● ·

When I first took over the rock department in 1980, one of my first projects was to put together a comprehensive promotion plan for Bob's new album, *Saved*. I was excited, but who knew the wolves would show up so fast? With the release of his previous work, *Slow Train Coming*, word was that Jewish-born Robert Allen Zimmerman had become attracted to Christianity. Indeed, the album cover depicted a man wielding a pickaxe that clearly emphasized a cross, and some of the songs had unmistakable religious overtones.

By the time *Saved* showed up, there was no more guessing. The album cover depicted the hand of Jesus reaching down to touch the hands of his believers. The latest scoop was that Bob had now converted to Christianity. Whether I wanted to believe that or not, I had to promote an album of songs that expanded on the religious themes of *Slow Train*.

As fans and the media began freaking out, always ready to criticize, I chose to believe that this was just a phase that Bob was going through. And, even if it wasn't, I've always felt that when promoting music, we should concentrate on the art and worry less about an artist's personal life. Bob Dylan was free to believe whatever he wished. As it turned out, I would be proven right. Bob is on record as saying he gets his religious messages from songs and music, as opposed to any organized religion. But at the time I had to deal with radio programmers who were having a hard time with an artist who they felt was losing focus.

I was adamant that rock radio concentrate on the music and not get hung up with Bob's personal feelings or life choices. My trade advertisements utilized performance shots of Bob and focused on the album's songs. I felt it was my job to protect him and keep the wolves at bay until the tide changed. We did the best we could and got some decent airplay. The album did okay, but not that great, falling just shy of reaching gold status.

Soon after *Saved*, Bob started recording new songs in his home studio, and Naomi Saltzman, his business associate at the time, sent a trusted friend, Debbie Gold, to California to check in on the recording. Debbie had cut her teeth working with Jerry Garcia and the Grateful Dead, followed by some years working in the Bruce Springsteen camp. When she saw Bob puttering around in his home studio, she suggested that perhaps he might try hooking up with the producer Chuck Plotkin, who had been called in to save Springsteen's album *Darkness On The Edge Of Town* when Jimmy Iovine had trouble getting the mix right. I guess Bob took her up on the idea, and that's when he showed up at Chuck's place.

While on a business trip to Los Angeles, I was invited to the studio to hear the finished album, which was titled *Shot Of Love*. That was the first time I met Chuck, who recounted the story of the day Bob first showed up. Plotkin is one of the coolest people you'll ever meet. Even after working with some of the world's greatest talent, he has no false airs, and he is happy to tell it like it is without any superfluous drama.

As I listened, I was pleased to hear that the arrangements on *Shot Of Love* were rooted more in rock and less in the gospel sound of Bob's previous two albums. It would certainly make it easier to get airplay. After I heard the album, I was supposed to call Bob in New York and discuss my promotion plans with him. By this time, I was at ease talking with him, and I was looking forward to the conversation.

Chuck, wanting to be hospitable, pulled out some beautiful marijuana buds and other goodies and urged me to help myself to anything I'd like. I remember looking forlornly at these offerings and telling myself, *If I'm going to talk to Bob, I'm definitely staying away from all this stuff.* Truth was, by this point in my life I was shying away from drugs in general—they just got in the way of everything I was trying to accomplish.

Knowing how particular Bob is, I wrote down twenty separate promotional ideas, hoping he'd go for at least a few of them. I called and told him I thought the album was really good and that we'd do well with it at rock radio. I started to go down my list, but Bob seemed very reticent.

'No . . . no . . . no . . . no . . . nope, not that one,' he'd say. 'I just don't like to push myself that way.'

I could see he just wanted to let the music do the talking.

'What would happen if you showed up one evening at WNEW, unannounced,' I suggested, 'maybe on Scott Muni's show? No pre-hype— you just appear.' But he didn't like that idea either. We got through all twenty suggestions, and then I said, 'You haven't done an interview for radio in so many years. Would you at least consider that? Just one that we tape and can send out to all the rock stations across the country.'

'Yeah, I could do that.'

'Is there anyone you'd prefer to do the interview?'

'Yeah, I would do it with Dave Herman from WNEW.'

I was thrilled. Finally, Bob had agreed to do *something*. I thanked him and told him I'd be in touch with his office to put it together.

How easy is this? I figured. Dave Herman is in New York. Bob is in New York. But I couldn't get a date from his management. Finally, Jeff Rosen from Bob's office called and told me that Bob was off to England to do a concert there, and he wanted to do the interview in London. Really? Once again, logic never gets in the way of the record business.

Fine, I thought. Now I had to get the money from Columbia to fly Dave, Debbie (now officially working for Bob), and myself to London, first class, plus hotel and ground transportation. And get tickets and backstage passes to the show. We'd also now be using remote gear when we could have just knocked it off so easily at a proper recording studio in New York in half a day. Oh well.

On the morning of the trip, I got a surprise call from British Airways. Our flight had been canceled. My heart sank. But then they asked, 'Would you mind if we transferred you to the Concorde?'

'You mean, the supersonic airplane with afterburners that push it to twice the speed of sound and fly twice as high as any other passenger aircraft? Uh . . . yeah, that'll be okay.'

The Concorde was slender and tube-shaped. It had giant wings and massive engines, but the actual fuselage was small, with two rows of seats, two abreast, on either side of a slim aisle—about one hundred seats in all. Dave and I, both being tall, had to crouch to get into the thing.

Debbie looked over at me.

'Hey, do we have to behave ourselves when the guy punches this thing into supersonic mode, or can we yell and cheer?'

'I say, let's go for yell and cheer!'

Debbie became a close friend of mine. Totally switched on and friends with many notable rock stars, she was a beautiful brunette and a major character to boot. She is one of those folks who broke the mold, broke the mold, and then broke the mold yet one more time.

Debbie was the only person I knew who talked more than me. When we were together in a car, it was hysterical—a constant war of word barrages. She talked so fast that she could hardly get out all the words she was trying to say. One sentence wouldn't be complete before she'd lunge right into a new one. It made for a lovable and unique speech pattern.

Debbie confided in me that she and Bob had been an item at one time and that one of Bob's songs had been written about their relationship. She kept this a secret from most, but she's gone now, and hopefully, she wouldn't mind me mentioning it. Another note of interest is, that around 2008, she corralled me and a few other friends to help her create a board game, *Grateful Dead-Opoly*. If you can find one, buy it immediately—it's the most well-thought-out and entertaining rock'n'roll board game ever created, and it's even sanctioned by the band. If you're into the Dead, it's a must-have.

Flying on Concorde was an amazing experience. Even though the pilots and crew must have flown it many times, none of them had become jaded in the least. After takeoff, clear of residential areas and well over the Atlantic Ocean, the pilot delighted in making his announcements.

'In just a minute, we will be going supersonic. If you have a drink on your tray table, please hold on to it so it won't be shoved into your lap.'

We obeyed the command, and the pilot accelerated. There was a jolt, and you could feel your back being pushed against the seat the same way as when you punch a car into overdrive.

'Congratulations,' the pilot continued, 'you are now going faster than the speed of sound.'

We couldn't help but cheer.

Not too long after, the pilot made another announcement.

'Please hold on to your drinks again, we will be going to Mach 2 shortly.' Again, the same feeling. Then he added, a little more seriously, 'You are now going faster than a speeding bullet.'

There was a hush among the passengers, even those who had previously flown by Concorde—all of us trying to wrap our heads around such an idea. The first thing I could think of was Superman, *Faster than a speeding bullet*. We were flying as fast as Superman.

I looked out of the window. Usually, when you fly over cities, just above the clouds, you can look down and see the tiny buildings below. When you looked down from the Concorde, the *clouds* were tiny. When you looked up, you could see the beginning of space, darkness. And if you looked across the earth's horizon, you could begin to see the curvature of the earth. It was unreal.

There was no distinction in class on Concorde. Everyone was in first class. We were served lobster thermidor for lunch, and after that I was given a cigar, and a flight attendant asked me if I wanted a light.

'Oh,' I replied, surprised. 'I thought I was supposed to save this for later, and not smoke on the plane.'

'Sir, we expect you to smoke it.'

I did.

To make the experience even more illusory, we arrived in London in just about three hours, much faster than a trip from New York to Dallas on a conventional airplane. As we disembarked, we couldn't believe we were actually in England—it didn't seem possible.

That evening, we went to see Bob's show at the Earls Court arena. He was phenomenal, full of energy, and wielding extreme performance power. If he was popular in the States, he was God in England. The crowd went wild, and all of rock royalty had turned out to see him.

The backstage area at Earls Court was huge, so they were using trailers as dressing rooms. After the show, I went to see Bob in his. We had a nice conversation and confirmed we'd do the interview with Dave in his hotel room the next day.

As I walked to the back of the trailer to grab a snack from the catering table, Eric Clapton came to the door.

'Hi, Bob. Great show. You know, you and I should get together and do something. We've been talking about it for years.'

OMG—this was music to my ears! Here we go, just what we need to get Bob back into traditional form. I was already imagining the album, with Clapton firing off hot lead guitar phrases to punctuate Bob's powerful verses. It would play just like a great blues album, except it would be Bob Dylan songs!

Never mind the record company's perspective, I was getting excited as a fan. But as Clapton spoke, Bob started to blow him off.

'Oh, man, I don't know. I'm really into doing my own thing now.'

By now I'm thinking I should leave and not be hearing these guys' private conversation. But it's too late—I'm trapped at the back of the trailer, and they don't know I'm there. In my head, I'm screaming, *No! No! Bob! Don't blow off Eric fucking Clapton! This will be great!* And Clapton is really pushing, but Bob keeps backing away . . .

At the time, I was stunned, but as the years went by and I understood a bit more about Bob, I got it. His approach is organic—never forced—and it's worked well for him. It's who he is, and his art wouldn't be honest if he tried to do something in the name of attracting clever headlines. I even remember him being skeptical about Live Aid at first. Neil Young's acclaimed manager, Elliot Roberts, was handling Bob at the time, and he asked if he could use my office to call Bob. He had just finalized the deal for Bob to close the show—the most coveted spot on the bill, which would be watched by millions of people the world over. It was a really big deal.

I handed Elliot my phone and got up to leave the office to give him some privacy, but he motioned for me to sit back down in my seat and was fine about me hearing him give the good news to Bob. The conversation didn't go anything like he thought it would, though. I only heard Elliot's side of it, but I remember it almost word for word.

'Bob! I've got GREAT news! I just got you the closing slot on the Live Aid Concert! . . . What? How does it work? You mean, how does the money get to the people in Africa? Well, I'm not sure. No, I don't know how they will receive the aid . . . why should you do it? Because it's a great cause. No, Bob, I don't think it's a scam. You want me to make sure it's not a scam? Bob, the show is being put on by reputable people. No, I can't guarantee you that all the money will get to the people. It probably will, it should . . . I just don't know right now. I don't have all the details. So, you're saying you don't want to do it? Bob, it's the most coveted spot in the whole event! *Everyone* wants that closing spot. Bob, it's the brainchild of Bob Geldof, the promoters are Harvey Goldsmith and Bill Graham—these are good people. It's for a great cause.'

Elliot was always very cool, quiet, and buttoned up, but now, totally exasperated, he finally blew his cork and screamed at the top of his lungs into the phone.

'How's this, Bob? Why should you do it?! Why should you do it?!

BECAUSE IT'S FUCKING GREAT FOR YOUR FUCKING CAREER, BOB! HOW'S THAT FOR A FUCKING REASON!'

I'd never seen Elliot break a sweat, much less come unglued like that. And I'd never heard anyone yell at Bob like that. As we know, Bob did the show, but in true Bob fashion, he changed the songs he'd rehearsed with Keith Richards and Ronnie Wood at the last moment, which threw off the performance a bit. All of us watching had a hard time figuring out what some of the songs were, and Woody and Keith looked a bit nervous.

'Rap,' Woody later told to me, 'he didn't even mention a change five minutes before showtime, which at least would have given me and Keith time to adjust. He told us as we were walking up the steps to the stage!'

Wowzers. I guess Woody and Keith would never make it in Bob's band.

• ● •

Back to London. The next day, it was time for the interview. I gave Dave explicit directions: *Do not get into any religious stuff. Keep the focus on the music.* This would be Bob's first interview in years, and I had worked very hard to keep rock radio's focus on the music.

'Yeah, I get it,' Dave nodded.

I brought Dave to Bob's room and decided it might be best for me not to stay, just to let them have an intimate conversation. That turned out to be a mistake. The next morning, Dave gave me the tape, and I flew back to the States by myself because we were all on different schedules. I'd forgotten until that moment that I had a first-class ticket. I was ushered up the circular stairway into the little private cabin on the 747. I'd always wondered what that experience would be like. Flying first-class on British Airways makes you feel like a king—the pampering service, the nonstop delicious food and wine. But I also remember thinking, *God, this flight is taking f-o-r-e-v-e-r.* I had been so spoiled by the Concorde that now, reduced to flying only first-class on British Airways had become a drag. Haha.

When we got back to the States, Dave, Debbie, and I went into CBS Studios to edit the interview. We were surprised to learn a couple of extraordinary things. First, one of the older engineers there was delighted to tell us that he was the same guy who had edited the single version of 'Like A Rolling Stone' in 1965. He'd remained a CBS Studio engineer his whole life, and here he was once again working on a Bob Dylan project. Back then, some of the hipper Top 40 stations had played the entire six-minute version, but others elected to play the edit, which to many of our ears had made little musical sense. All of a sudden, without warning, the song seemed to quickly fade out in the middle of a verse. Lo and behold, that was exactly the engineer's plan. He told us that when the song hit three and a half minutes, he simply faded it out ... and then faded it back in again at the same spot for side two. Mystery revealed. So much for art.

The other amazing discovery was that Bob had elected to play his acoustic guitar in the background throughout the interview. You could hear some very choice chords underneath all the talking. It added a cool ambiance to the experience, but for the life of me I couldn't figure out why he did it, so I decided to call and ask him. What he told me blew my mind.

'I learned that trick from Mary Travers,' he said. 'Back when the government was after us for the protest movements, she told me if I play guitar underneath an interview, no one can edit what I've said to make it sound like I said something different.'

Indeed, the music would stop and jolt into a different chord and everyone would know immediately that the tape had been altered. Old-school street smarts.

It was a great idea, but now I was hamstrung when it came to editing this interview. And it was in dire need of editing because my buddy Dave Herman had done the complete opposite of what I'd asked! His opening question was about Bob becoming a born-again Christian. Dave was a legendary DJ, but I swear I wanted to strangle him right there on the spot.

You could also hear that Dave was intimidated by Bob, which is not uncommon. But when Bob sensed that—back then, at least—he was known to run interviewers around the block, offering nonsensical answers. The absolute kicker was when Dave asked for Bob's advice about his upcoming marriage—how the hell did *that* get into my interview? And if that wasn't enough, they went on to discuss the 'beasts in the Bible' for twenty fucking minutes. Help!

'Dave, remember the sticking to the music part?! Is there any discussion *at all* about the new album on here?!'

Thankfully, Dave was a good sport, and he sat with Debbie and me for three days straight while we edited that interview. Because of the music underneath and the conversation weaving around so many different subjects, placing complete thoughts in an order that made sense, and sounded coherent and meaningful, was hell. But in the end, we did it. Whew! What a job.

We pressed the finished interview onto vinyl and sent it out to radio to use with the *Shot Of Love* release. Although it was not as insightful as it could have been, the stations were chuffed to be able to air a current Bob Dylan interview after waiting so many years.

• ● •

Another time, Bob and I were sitting around a table in a backstage catering area somewhere when he asked me a most interesting question.

'How does Fleetwood Mac sell six million albums, and no matter what I do, I can only sell a million?'

I was taken aback. *Why would Bob even care about that? If you're Bob Dylan, what more could you want?*

I answered him honestly, but lightheartedly.

'Bob, Fleetwood Mac goes into a studio for six months, writes catchy tunes designed to be radio hits, takes the time to do many overdubs, and then works on polishing up the sound of the whole thing for another couple of weeks. You go into a dentist's office, pull up a sound truck, and in two weeks you've completed your album. But here's the thing, no matter what Fleetwood Mac does, no matter how many records they sell, they'll never be Bob Dylan.'

I thought this might make him feel better, but what I was beginning to understand was that he was thinking, *If I'm so great, my audience should be growing.* He pointed out that one would think that at least some records might sell 1.5 million copies, but they all seemed to top out at about a million. Interestingly, Bruce Springsteen's albums without a hit single on them would also stop at a million. The only thing I could offer was to tell Bob that his music was a specific art form that many people dearly loved, but it was also pretty intellectual stuff, and it required an audience that was deep into art and poetry. A lot of people love Van Gogh, but not everyone—his paintings are an acquired taste. But I kept going back to the point that he was *Bob Dylan*—how important his work was, how he had changed the world.

'Name one Fleetwood Mac song that's as good as or means as much as "Blowin' In The Wind." Name one that speaks to the culture as deep and cutting as "The Times They Are A-Changing" or "Subterranean Homesick Blues." Every artist I know wishes they wrote just one song nearly as magnificent. And you've written lots of those. As good as any of these artists are—and I'm a big Fleetwood Mac fan—there's only one Bob Dylan.'

I guess that made him feel a little better, but I knew he wasn't satisfied.

My fondest memory of Bob is of when he visited me in my office in April of 1984. We'd had quite a successful run with his *Infidels* album, which had been lauded as a mainstream comeback on its release the previous October. I enjoyed our relationship, and I always looked forward to our conversations. Sometimes, I'd need to talk to him about making a video or something, but he'd be more intent on turning me on to some great Russian poets.

On this particular day, we had no business to discuss. Bob just happened to have been in the building, and he'd stopped by to say hi.

So, he walks into my office and spies a large Bruce Springsteen poster. At the time, Bob thought Bruce had completely ripped off his persona and songwriting style. It didn't help that Bruce had been heralded as 'the new Bob Dylan.' One Bob Dylan was enough, as far as Bob was concerned. He was always asking me, 'What's that guy doing now?' I used to tell him that Bruce was certainly influenced by him, but he wasn't flat-out copying him, and that Bob should feel proud that he'd influenced another gifted artist so greatly. But Bob was having none of it.

So, he looks at the poster, turns around, looks at me sitting behind my desk, cocks his head, and in that very recognizable Dylan timbre, he asks, 'Is this guy still driving that stolen car?'

Only Bob Dylan could come up with that line.

'Bob, I swear, you gotta get over this. Bob Dylan means to Bruce Springsteen what Woody Guthrie means to Bob Dylan. A powerful influence that helps create a next-generation artist capable of extraordinary words and music. But just an influence—not a copy. No Woody Guthrie, no Bob Dylan. No Bob Dylan, no Bruce Springsteen. It's how the passing down of music works. Come on, man, you know that.'

Then we had a long talk about kids—just two dads talking. I told him about my first son, Adam, who was born in 1981, and about how Sharon and I were working on another. But I was concerned about what to tell them when they got older about the wild times of the 60s—the drugs, the free love, and so on.

'Well, at least you have a choice about what to tell them,' he chuckled. 'All my life has been laid bare in the press—the drugs, the women, all of it. I'm busted.' Then he gave me some good advice. 'Just tell them some of it. You don't have to tell them about all of it.'

It had been such a lovely meeting that I asked Bob if he'd sign one of his posters for me. Signing autographs has never been one of his favorite things to do, but he smiled and said he would.

'Thanks for everything,' the note read. 'Best wishes Bob Dylan.'

He dated it, too, which is very unusual for him. It meant so much.

• ● •

A year or two after Live Aid, I got a call from Bob. His last couple of albums hadn't done so well, and he was clearly down.

'I don't think people want to hear my shit anymore,' he told me. 'I think I'm gonna quit.'

I was stunned. Admittedly, I've always viewed the world through rose-colored glasses, and I thought that great artists like Bob were invincible—that they had some sort of inner strength beyond what most people possessed. As life went on, I would learn differently. Even the greatest artists in the world have down times and can get very depressed. Word on the street was that Bob had writer's block.

I could feel his pain. The man meant so much to me that it hurt me inside too. I reflected for a moment before I spoke.

'Bob, first off, you can't quit. This is not a job for you. You're Bob Dylan. It's who you are, it's what you are, you just *are*. You don't have much of a choice. And you know better than anyone that being Bob Dylan comes with a lot of gifts but also with a lot of ups and downs.

'Do you think after all these years and all the great songs you've written you can just stop on a dime? You're just having writer's block, and you're not the first. Did you ever consider that maybe your mind just needs a rest—a vacation, a pause, a regroup? Hell, if anybody's mind deserves a rest, it's yours. You've written hundreds of songs, many of the greatest ever written. You've changed people's lives, helped change the world—give yourself a break, man. I can only imagine how scary this is for you, but believe me, Bob, this is only temporary. A mind like yours just doesn't all of a sudden shut off. You are Bob Dylan, you'll always be Bob Dylan, and you just need to weather the storm.'

I spent an hour on the phone with him. I hoped that at least part of what I said had sunk in. But I was disconsolate for the rest of the day. If Bob Dylan was out of focus, the whole world was out of focus. Bob soldiered on, and you have to hand it to him to have the courage to do so. Indeed, he couldn't stop. In 1997, he released *Time Out Of Mind*, hailed as one of his best albums ever. It won three Grammy Awards, including 'Album Of The Year,' sold well over a million copies, and made *Rolling Stone*'s list of the 500 Greatest Albums Of All Time. Bob was back, with a vengeance.

Unlike any other artist I've ever known, Bob has always had the ability to somehow uncork a truly phenomenal piece of work, even in his later years. In June 2020, he released *Rough & Rowdy Ways*—a tour de force, right up there with some of his best work. Like a fighter going the distance, Bob Dylan is forever.

MEET THE BEATLE

PAUL MCCARTNEY IS the classiest, most gracious artist I've ever worked with.

One of the questions that is always asked of my generation is, *Are you a Stones guy or a Beatles guy?* Even though I'm a Stones guy all the way, I love The Beatles. How can you not? They evolved musically to exceptional heights and grew from being the most popular pop band in the history of recorded music to lifting a generation into a higher mindset. They made such an extraordinary impact on us all and embodied the 60s dream of the world living together in harmony and peace. They were seen as the leaders of the movement, guides to a new utopian existence. I'm not sure they understood how important they were in that regard. When they broke up, we could hardly stand it. If *The Beatles* couldn't keep it together, chances were, our collective dream was just that—a dream that could never evolve to fruition.

Even so, we followed their solo careers, which kept moving us forward. McCartney's band Wings was sensational, John Lennon urged us to 'Give Peace A Chance,' George Harrison took us to even higher spiritual places, and Ringo offered some fun songs that kept us smiling. Individually, The Beatles remained the greatest stars on the planet, more important than any other artists, and with a higher celebrity caliber than most famous actors or sports figures of their time. In short, they meant more to us than anyone.

When Columbia signed Paul, we at the label felt we were in rarified air. We had already benefited by having so many top-notch superstars on the roster, but we'd never had a Beatle. We enjoyed tremendous success with his album *Tug Of War*, featuring his hit duet with Stevie Wonder, 'Ebony And Ivory,' arguably one of Paul's best songs, aligning the black and white keys on a piano sitting side by side with the theme of racial harmony.

The next album did quite well for us, too, but the rest of the songs weren't quite as magical. Then came the movie and soundtrack *Give My Regards To Broad Street*. Both the film and the music were somehow lacking. When you're Paul McCartney, the bar has been set so high that anything less than brilliant seems, well, lackluster. Parts of the movie didn't work, and there were even a few sections that might be considered embarrassing for an artist on his level. The soundtrack faired a bit better, going gold, but only made it to #21 on the charts.

It seemed like Paul had lost his way for the moment. Fair enough, it can happen to anyone. Even a Beatle.

One reason may have been that Paul seemed to be surrounded by yes-men—people so enamored with him that he received no negative feedback, even if some constructive criticism was genuinely called for. I got a glimpse of this when Debbie Gold and I were in England to do the Dave Herman interview with Bob. We had a day off, so we went to visit AIR Studios, which had been founded by famed Beatles producer George Martin. Debbie wanted to suss out the place for future projects, perhaps with Bob. When we arrived, we were greeted by a bubbly young brunette dressed in a cute short skirt, looking very 'English pop.'

'Oh, you just missed Paul!'

'Really?'

We were surprised, since neither Debbie nor I had any clue that he'd be there. We were just there to take a look a look around the studios.

'That's too bad, we would have liked to say hello. I run the album rock department for his label in the States, Columbia Records.'

'Well, come with me. I'll take you somewhere special.'

She led us into one of the record rooms.

'Not more than ten minutes ago, Paul McCartney was *standing right here!*'

I looked over at Debbie. This was all beginning to sound a bit too starstruck.

'Yes,' the girl replied, 'you are standing in the same spot where Paul was standing just a few minutes ago.'

Okay . . .

'You are now *breathing the air* that Paul McCartney was just breathing.'

I looked over at Debbie, cocked my head, rolled my eyes, and bit my lip to stop me from laughing like crazy. If McCartney was surrounded by these kinds of people, there was little chance of him being in any sort of reality.

The girl then said that George Martin was there if we wanted to meet him.

'Abso-fucking-lutley!' I replied. 'Please, lead on.'

Debbie and I were extremely excited to have the chance to meet one of the greatest producers of all time—the man often referred to as the 'Fifth Beatle,' who had helped create those remarkable records and by extension helped shape the culture of the day.

George was very gracious and even played us a few tracks he was working on with Paul. While we were listening, I kept thinking about all those incredible sounds and string arrangements on the Beatles albums that Martin was responsible for.

• ● •

It was when we worked on the *Broad Street* project that I got a close-up view of the man himself. Paul McCartney's popularity was so enormous, his person so globally in demand, that 20th Century Fox had rented out an entire floor of the Plaza Hotel and placed different countries' press, radio, and television media into individual hotel rooms. Paul was able to travel around the world and visit each country by going from room to room, all the way around the building. It was fascinating to watch.

In our suite for American rock radio, we decided the best use of our time would be if we could avoid each radio station having to bring their own recording devices and then have to spend time setting them up, getting levels, and so on. Instead, we organized having one big reel-to-reel tape recorder, a couple of engineers, and two mics facing each other across a small table. All the interviewers had to do was come in, meet Paul, sit down, and talk with him. Then, as they left, we handed them their tape. Very cool, very slick, easy-peasy.

We always allowed extra time for introductions, as meeting Paul can be overwhelming, and most folks have some things they just have to say to him before they get started. In a most touching scene, Helen Leicht, who was working at WIOQ-FM in Philadelphia at the time, sat down in front of Paul and gave him a present—a Wallace Nutting painting of a farm with sheep. It reminded her of Paul and Linda's farm and their love for animals.

The Beatles meant everything to Helen, and McCartney in particular had held a most precious place deep in her heart ever since she'd been a teenager. The mics were opened, and Helen looked up across the table at Paul, but she couldn't speak. Everything that Paul and The Beatles had meant in her lifetime came rushing into her mind. She flashed back to when she was a teen and realized there was Beatle Paul, sitting right in front of her. Completely overcome by the moment, she wobbled a bit, then burst into tears.

Paul got up from his seat, came over to Helen, lifted her up, and hugged her. He let her cry in his arms—he knew what this was about. He had experienced it many times before, and he accepted the fact that he had a much larger role to play than simply being the artist, Paul McCartney. He was a world ambassador for some of the greatest music and cultural shifts ever. He was a Beatle, and arguably the most universally loved of them. He understood what it meant for people when they met him. And he also knew that countless girls had fallen in love with him at very young ages, and that love remained deep within.

The most captivating thing to watch was how he wanted to help someone get through this experience, not out of ego but out of love, understanding, and genuine caring. He took the time to connect with Helen, to hug her, to thank her, to calm her, to give back.

Helen finally composed herself, sat down, took a drink of water, cleared her throat, and adopted a most professional manner. She looked up with a smile to start the interview, but as soon as soon as their eyes met, she lost it all over again. It was an endearing moment. Through Helen's tears, we'd all thought back to being teenagers and our own emotions seeing The Beatles for the first time on *The Ed Sullivan Show* on February 9, 1964. Re-watching that moment while writing this, I'm not too proud to say I cried myself. Never before or since have we been so moved by the music, the performance, and the charming personalities of the Fab Four.

Eventually, Helen got it together and did a wonderful, heartwarming interview with Paul.

Our hotel suite was Paul's last stop of the day, and when we finished it was 7pm. He looked over at me and asked, 'Are we going to visit the troops at the office?' A visit to Columbia's twelfth floor was on our schedule, but it was getting late. I explained that yes, many people were there waiting to meet him, including all the secretaries and assistants, but I knew he'd been working non-stop since 9am, and I could see a tired look in his eyes. I felt the need to ask if he just wanted to call it a day.

'No, it's important,' he replied. 'We really should go. I want to go.'

I was so impressed by his willingness to give the extra time, to push himself on the brink of exhaustion, and for the work-a-day folks at his record company. These people were not the big execs, but in McCartney's view they were just as important—in fact, maybe even more so.

Black Rock was only six blocks away, and in a normal world, we'd have made that walk in six minutes. But we were in Paul McCartney World, with one of the most loved and recognizable faces on the planet. You can't walk Paul McCartney down six blocks in New York City. You can't even walk him half a block without a challenging crowd scene ensuing.

So, we traveled the six blocks in a limousine. It was funny—we were in the middle of rush-hour traffic, and we spent thirty-five minutes alone, turning the car around the block and edging our way down Fifth Avenue. Add ten minutes more to get to 53rd and 6th. It took forty-five minutes to go six and a half blocks! We were laughing, but there was no other way.

Paul's appearance at our offices was something no one will ever forget. He was upbeat throughout his entire stay. He graciously stopped at every single desk, all the way around the entire twelfth floor, hugged and kissed all the gals, took pictures, signed autographs, and did not leave until well after 9pm.

I witnessed Paul playing the bigger role—one that he was grateful for, and one he knew he owed his fans around the world. And I saw him do this for reasons that went beyond a sense of duty. His actions were heartfelt and genuine. He believed in what he and John Lennon had once written, '*In the end, the love you take is equal to the love you make.*' It was an honor to work with him.

• ● •

Not too soon afterward, I found myself in one of the most bewildering meetings I would ever attend. McCartney's contract was coming due, and Columbia president Al Teller called VP of promotion Ray Anderson, VP of marketing Bob Sherwood, and me into his office to discuss it. He recounted what we already knew. Every time Paul McCartney released an album on Columbia, the whole company went into overdrive in such a way that there wasn't much time or energy left for the other artists we were working. There were so many extra meetings, extra plans and events that we had to create, and so much extra money spent for a celebrity of this caliber, that we could easily lose valuable momentum on three or four other upcoming artists that might one day define the future of the label.

At a label as big as Columbia, with so many artists to take care of, established and new, we could ill afford to become a specialized boutique operation with over-dedication to Paul, even though he carried more gravitas than any other artist on the planet.

'As hard as this is to think about,' Al said, 'does anyone in this room need Paul McCartney on this label? If you do, raise your hand.'

We all looked at each other, anxiously waiting to see who would raise their hand first, but no one did. I kept looking down at my right hand, talking to it in my head, *Why aren't you lifting? It's freaking Paul McCartney! Come on, lift up!* But it just wouldn't. All the Beatles and Wings music rushed into my head. The Ed Sullivan appearances projected like mini-movies in my mind, and I was thinking about all the times I got high listening to the second side of *Abbey Road*. I didn't want to be one of the people to make this decision, I didn't want this responsibility. And then I thought, *If we do let him go, who tells him that? I'd feel just terrible hurting the guy—who wants to hurt Paul McCartney?!*

But I realized the question wasn't, *Do I need Paul McCartney?* It was, *Do we need him on our label?* That's two different questions. Of course, I *needed* Paul McCartney in my life—we all do—but the truth was, he'd probably be better off somewhere else. And there were three reasons for this truth.

First, Paul's album sales had begun to slide. While we still garnered a gold record with *Give My Regards To Broad Street*, for all the time and attention it took, business-wise, it didn't make sense. Second, Paul seemed to be losing his way a bit musically. This happens to all artists, even if you're a Beatle. Third, with a fresh start on a new label, McCartney might get a jolt of new artistic energy—and have a home where he could be treated with kid gloves 24/7.

So, this was a business decision. Sometimes I got so emotionally wrapped up in the music and art that business was harder for me than most. Sometimes business sucked. Sometimes business could break your heart.

Paul moved on, and he did great. But when he left, I felt a hole a mile wide.

MOMENTARY KAOS

I FIRST MET the members of Pink Floyd in our West Coast offices back in the 70s, when I was still in charge of rock promotion in the region. I had been heavily into the band since a DJ friend of mine, Barbara Birdfeather, had taken me to see them at the Hollywood Bowl in September of 1972. So, when Clive Davis signed the band to Columbia in 1975, I was ecstatic.

The band's manager, Steve O'Rourke, thought they'd been getting short shrift from their previous US label, Capitol Records, who he felt saw them solely as an experimental progressive-rock band incapable of achieving gold album status. Their contract had expired just as they released what would eventually become one of the biggest-selling and most important albums of all time, *The Dark Side Of The Moon*. As the record began to climb the charts and Capitol finally realized what they had on their hands, they called O'Rourke to quickly negotiate a new contract.

'Sorry, too late. We're on Columbia Records now.'

Can you imagine how these guys must have felt? All record companies make mistakes, but this oversight would account for many millions of lost album sales, as Pink Floyd's career would now be played out on the Columbia label. It wasn't a total loss for Capitol, however. *The Dark Side Of The Moon* would go on to set the record as *Billboard* magazine's longest-charting album—over eighteen years! It would sell more than fifteen million copies in the US alone, and, as of this writing, more than forty-five million copies worldwide.

When I first met the band, they seemed like a bunch of very unassuming young men. Their music was so powerful and had made such an impact on me over the years that it was hard for me to believe that *these* guys were the people who'd made it. They had no false airs about them, and no particular band member possessed any powerful charisma that overtook the room. Even when you saw them live, they just stood motionless, staring out into the audience, playing their incredible music while out-of-this-world stage production and quadraphonic sound filled your eyes and ears at every moment. This could include alluring psychedelic movies projected on the giant round screen that hung above the stage, an over-the-top light show, or never-before-seen props like inflatable floating pigs, flying-saucer lighting pods, thirty-foot marionettes, along with multicolored laser beams, giant metallic flowers that blossomed right before your eyes and then turned into rotating mirror balls, and much, much more. But there was no real frontman who pranced around onstage. Lead guitarist and co-lead vocalist David Gilmour displayed no fancy guitar moves—but he didn't have to. The music, played in time with the production, would hypnotize you.

And this is a very important point that should never be forgotten about seeing Pink Floyd in concert. All of the production was timed to the music. Whether it was an animated movie playing behind the band, an all-encompassing display of lights and lasers, or the building of a wall from floor to ceiling in an arena—all of it was done in sync with the music. Add to that the quadraphonic sound systems they used, and seeing Pink Floyd was a total sensory experience. The beauty of it was, you didn't have to take any drugs to appreciate it. The music and the show brought you to that psychedelic place.

I remember finding the bands' surnames very intriguing. Waters, Gilmour, Wright, and Mason all sounded so British. It made them all the more interesting to me, the idea of them coming from a country afar and having different lives and perspectives of the world.

Another interesting thing I soon discovered about them was that they seemed to be focused only on making their music. They had no interest in giving interviews, meeting radio folks, or promoting themselves in any way. They were also very suspicious of record company personnel, though this shouldn't have been surprising, given the lyrics to 'Have A Cigar' from their first Columbia release, *Wish You Were Here*, in which a record company man asks, '*By the way, which one's Pink?*'

Though the band members were quiet and almost introverted, I found them very approachable. So, when I met them, I just sort of blurted out, 'Do you guys not do any interviews on purpose to keep your mystique? Because, right now, a lot of us think you're aliens from another planet disguised as humans who have landed on Earth just to make this far-out, unbelievable music.'

'No,' said Waters. 'We don't do them because no one knows how to talk to us. All they want to know is what shirts and underwear we're wearing.'

'So, if I brought you to someone who was a big fan, who totally understands you and could talk intelligently about your music, would you talk to him?'

'Sure.'

'Great. I want to take you to my friend Jim Ladd's house. He's an exceptionally cool music guy and a disc jockey at KMET-FM here in Los Angeles. He's also got a nationwide interview show called *INNERVIEW*, which is all about the music and the artists who create it. He could care less about what you're wearing.'

I got excited. I was going to be able to generate the first nationally syndicated Pink Floyd interview in the United States. Fans would finally be able to hear the band members speak, discover that indeed they were not aliens, and get a glimpse into their artistic process.

Jim Ladd is one of the greatest FM disc jockeys there's ever been. The song 'The Last DJ' by Tom Petty was written about him, and he has a most deserving star on Hollywood Boulevard. If Steven Clean was the king of social commentary, Jim was the king of sound paintings. He would pick a theme and tell an entertaining and meaningful story through the most incredible song sequences and segues. And you never knew when he was about to surprise you. One evening, I was driving around Los Angeles listening as Ladd did a show themed around western gunfighters. Of course, you heard all the greatest deep cuts from the albums Ladd kept as treasures in his mind. But following 'Me And My Uncle' by the Grateful Dead, out of nowhere, he segued into Marty Robbins's 1959 hit 'Big Iron.' A flat-out country song on rock radio? I almost drove off the road. But it was a stroke of musical genius, and it fit right in.

Back to 1975. The next day, the band and I drove up Laurel Canyon Boulevard, made a left at Kirkwood Drive where the famed Canyon

Country Store and little Italian restaurant are located, and worked our way
up the Canyon to 8522 Oak Court. We parked up at the end of a dead-end
street.

'Is this it?'

The band did not see any houses in front of them, just a bunch of rocks
and trees. I motioned to a tram on our right, with tracks leading up to a
house on top of a hill. The tram was a six-foot-square basket shape that
you stood in as it was pulled up the hill by a cable. We got into the basket.
Without any sight of Ladd, all of a sudden there was a whirring sound,
the basket jolted, and we slowly began moving up the hill. The Floyd were
wide-eyed—they'd never seen anything like this.

'Whoa, this guy must be cool.'

Jim met us at the top of the elevation, and we entered the house, which
was like something out of a fairy tale. Long-haired, lanky Ladd immediately
hit it off with the guys, and I sat out on the porch overlooking the canyon
while he conducted the interview. This first meeting would lead to a long,
close relationship with Roger in particular.

That interview gave me insight into the band's work ethic. Once, while
we were driving around doing some promotional work, David told me, 'You
know, people think we sit around, smoke a big joint, trip out, and just start
playing. But that's not how it is at all. Every day I go to the office, just like
you do with your briefcase. I go to the Pink Floyd office, and my briefcase
is my guitar. I know what Pink Floyd is, how it should sound, what it needs
to move forward, and how it can be the very best it can be. And we work
very hard on that.'

I also got a glimpse into Roger Water's psyche. Early on, he confided
in me, 'My dad died in the war, and I never knew him. It left this giant hole
inside me. All my work—the songs, the lyrics, the live performances—is me
just trying to fill up that hole. But no matter what I do, I can never fill it.'

Hearing that made me shudder, and I felt hurt inside for him. I knew
how much my own dad meant to me, and I'd never thought about how it
might be to not have a father at all. Leonard Cohen once told me that he
had terrible luck with women, but it made for great songs. I think Roger
was in a similar situation. His life is on display in much of his music—*The*

Wall and *The Final Cut* in particular are highly autobiographical. It's not always pretty, but it's always powerful.

• ● •

The Final Cut would be the band's last album together. After sixteen years and a dozen albums, creative differences were prying the band apart, and Roger felt he'd be better off pursuing a solo career. Because he had taken on such a strong leadership role in the band, especially with *The Wall* being so much about himself, he thought his departure would mark the end. But Gilmour and Mason wanted to continue as Pink Floyd. To their minds, the band had continued after the departure of Syd Barrett, so why couldn't they carry on now?

This was the final blow to what had become an already frayed relationship. Waters sued Gilmour and Mason in an attempt to prevent them from using the name. He felt he had contributed so much as a songwriter and creator of their live productions that, without him, the band was somehow inauthentic. It got ugly. Very harsh words between Roger and David exploded all over the press. And I was caught right in the middle.

Back in the spring of 1984, I had promoted Roger's first solo album, *The Pros And Cons Of Hitch Hiking*. Now it was 1987, and he was going to release his first official solo album since leaving the band, *Radio KAOS*. The album came out in June. Just three months later, in September, Pink Floyd were set to release *A Momentary Lapse Of Reason*, and for approximately four months, from the late summer into the fall, both artists would be mounting tours at the same time.

Like much of Roger's work, *Radio KAOS* is a concept album with a complex story covering an array of important topics, one of which is the future of communications technology as a way to bring people together (mind you, he wrote this in 1987). In the story, a boy named Billy, who is mentally and physically challenged and confined to a wheelchair, discovers he has superhuman powers and can hear radio waves in his head. He learns how to communicate through a cordless phone, accesses computers and speech synthesizers, and calls a DJ at a radio station in Los Angeles known as Radio KAOS. He tells the DJ his story, part of which is how his family has been affected by greed and monetarism. On the album, that DJ is played by Jim Ladd.

At the time, Roger had also been affected by the changes to free-form rock radio, which had bent to the will of the almighty dollar to create a more hit-driven format largely run by consultants. It seemed to be pushing creative disc jockeys like his friend Jim off to the side. These events coincided with other agendas around the world that made making money a major priority over everything else. Waters was successfully able to tie these different themes together. At the end of the story, Billy hacks into a military satellite and fools the world into thinking nuclear missiles are about to be launched around the world. With everyone thinking they are about to die, they come to realize that competitiveness and putting the dollar above everything else is much less important than love for family and the overall health of the community at large.

Anxious to do the best I could for Roger and this groundbreaking album, I suggested that he needed to let us market the record as being by 'Roger Waters of Pink Floyd' or words to that effect. I told him that as big as Pink Floyd had been, they were pretty much a faceless band. While I and perhaps another three hundred thousand mega-fans might know him and the other members, more casual fans just knew the name of the band. But Roger was trying to distance himself from Pink Floyd, and he wanted nothing to do with the name. He was hurting, and I could feel it.

Nonetheless, the show he mounted was in the typical Floyd/Waters vein: a huge production with triple projectors, computer graphics, newsreel footage of the end of the world in the making, and a radio station control room stage left, where Jim would reside, playing the role he had taken on the album. Across the top of the stage was a giant ticker-tape device that displayed Billy's communications with Ladd, as well as Jim's communications with the audience, in large green type.

As a kick-off promotion the day before the tour's debut in Providence, Rhode Island, we had the local FM station invite a large group of fans to the dress rehearsal. I flew up to see it myself, and it was lucky I did. The show was great and was filled with Waters' dark sarcasm and heavy-handed messages. To someone like me who had always been a fan, the show did not disappoint, but there was one big problem that smacked me right across the face as I watched the production. Many of us had become disillusioned by what was happening to our once very artful FM radio format, and the new Top 40-esque version playing mostly popular hits rather than deep album cuts and exposing little new music. Jim Ladd, however, was way past disillusionment. He was downright incensed.

Ladd had been fighting the good fight to keep free-form rock radio alive. It was not only about the freedom to play whatever music you wanted but was also about being able to express your opinions about that music and the culture of the day. While most of us moved forward with the times, slowly watching our 60s dreams fade away, Ladd refused to budge. For Jim, being a rock jock wasn't just a cool job, it was an artform. His radio shows were works of art, and the radio consultants and money men were fucking with that art. He refused to read prewritten cue cards or perform an on-air shift with music from a preplanned playlist by a PD or radio consultant. Here's where you should stop reading and listen to 'The Last DJ.'

> *Well, you can't turn him into a company man*
> *You can't turn him into a whore . . .*
> *And there goes your freedom of choice*
> *There goes the last human voice . . .'*

With Ladd refusing to work as an everyday jock under these circumstances, *INNERVIEW* was the only thing currently paying the rent, so going on tour with Roger Waters came at a most auspicious time. Waters had always used his platform to import meaningful messages to fans. Now Ladd was onstage with him, sharing that powerful platform and in charge of the messages rolling across the ticker tape. And aside from recreating the *Radio KAOS* communication segments, Ladd was using that ticker tape to pour his heart out regarding the current state of rock radio.

The problem was that all the anger that Jim had built up inside came spewing across without a filter. A slew of incendiary, anti-radio-establishment messages were dispersed throughout the show. While the intent was pure, the messages themselves damned to hell the majority of

FM stations across the country. Those messages were bound to turn rock fans against their local stations, and seeing those messages play out in front of their hometown crowds, all the radio folks in attendance were bound to get extremely pissed off.

It was as biting as anything Roger Waters ever wrote himself, which of course was why Roger loved it. But it could spell disaster for him as an artist. Sure, it's okay to nibble at the hand that feeds you to make a point, but taking a chunk this big—telling audiences that their local rock stations suck—was going to cause every program and music director across the country to drop *Radio KAOS* from their playlists. I wouldn't blame them if they never wanted to hear from Roger again.

I've always fought to change the world myself, and I didn't want to upset Roger, much less my old friend Jim, but I wasn't seeing a yellow flag here. Instead, huge red stop lights were flashing a mile a minute in my head. *Danger! Danger! Danger!* I usually try to handle artists with kid gloves, but this time there was no time for niceties. I ran up to Roger as soon as he got offstage and blurted out everything that was on my mind. It needed to change, and it needed to change fast, before the show's official debut the very next day.

I couldn't believe I had summoned the courage to come on so strong, and to Roger of all people. It was never my place to mess with any musician's art—my job was only to promote what the artists wanted to communicate to the rest of the world. But this was going to be a disaster, and I'd never forgive myself if I didn't tell Roger the truth about what I knew would be a huge mistake for him. He could see the anxiety in my eyes.

'Okay,' he said. 'Meet me backstage in about fifteen minutes to discuss this with Jim.'

When I got to the designated room, which was where the catering facilities were kept, I was shocked to see not only Roger and Jim but the entire band sitting in chairs waiting for me. This was going to be a trial, and it was going to pit me against Roger, Jim, and the band, who were going to be the jury. The hardest part was, I was on their side. I knew what they were trying to say, and I wanted to see those salient points made myself. The issue was how to say them.

I stood before everyone and made my speech, which went something like this . . .

'A lot of you don't know me, but Roger and Jim do, and they know I'm not your typical record company suit. I am a part of *our* generation, with similar beliefs on how things could and should be. I grew up listening to Pink Floyd, which helped shape the way I think. But I also have a foot in the commercial side of the music business, and I want you all to succeed. I want the audience and the industry people to understand and internalize the messages you are trying to put across. But if we just piss people off, we will not open their minds to possible change.

'I am hoping you guys will come up with more reasonable language to make your point. The messages about the current state of radio are so incendiary that when all the stations who are currently playing the hell out of Roger's new album see them, they're gonna leave the concert mad as hell at Roger, and most likely will drop the record from their playlists. But *Radio KAOS* is an important work, and I don't want it stifled.'

Roger stood up, and his first salvo was to show leadership and be a hero to all his crew.

'But we're artists,' he declared, 'and it's our job to tell the truth!'

Roger got a big applause. That fact was going to be hard to refute. Luckily for me, there was a comedic interruption. The sax player, who was three sheets to the wind, stood up, very wobbly, and blurted out in slurred tongue, '*Yeah*, we're artists!' At which point he jumped up and grabbed the chandelier that hung over our heads, swung himself past me, and landed on a large table of food behind me. *SPLAT!* He immediately passed out. Everyone couldn't help but laugh, and this lightened the mood in the room. But I had to stand my ground.

'I know you are artists, and I know the job of an artist is to say things that us every-day folk can't always articulate for ourselves or have a platform to do so. You don't have to change the tenor of the show, I'm just asking you to work on *how* we say certain things so that the people you want to impress will think about what you are saying, instead of just getting mad.'

Roger Waters can be tough, and he sometimes finds himself in awkward positions. It's hard to preach what your heart tells you when you also find yourself caught up in the monetarism of the star-maker machinery, earning millions of dollars as part of the media world you sometimes despise. It's tricky business, and it will fuck with your mind. Just ask Bob Dylan and so many others who've had to deal with the trappings that huge success can bring. But I also found Roger to be very smart and not beyond compromise, if that's what was needed to save the day.

Roger dismissed the meeting and came over to speak to me.

'Okay, I get it. But *you're* the one that has to explain it to Ladd and work on those messages.'

Jeez. Thanks, Rog. Honestly, I don't think he had the heart to do it himself.

I knew this was going to be extremely difficult. Jim Ladd was one hell of a strong personality, with convictions twice as strong. He could even be more stubborn than Roger, which is saying something. This meeting was going to be painful for two reasons. First, because I loved Jim and was very sympathetic to his causes. Second, because Jim was an artist in his own right, and now I was asking him to change his art. How do you tell Van Gogh that the red in a particular painting is too red, and could you please tone it down?

Jim and I went back to his room to talk it over. It took an hour just to get him to understand that we had to make changes at all.

'Look, Ladd, I love you like a brother, but if the show goes up untouched, we're going to hurt your friend. Let's find a way for you to remain Jim Ladd without doing that.'

Jim pulled out the script, and we began to go over it line by line. If it wasn't so serious, the scene would have resembled the movie *A Night At The Opera*, where Groucho and Chico Marx are ripping up parts of a deal in the funniest of ways until there's only a tiny piece of paper left in each of their hands. But this time it wasn't funny. It was two friends at loggerheads trying for some common ground. We fought over every sentence, and there were many that Jim felt so strongly about that I just had to give in. I just needed to take the edge off a bit, so that Jim could still go out on tour and make his points with his head held high but at the same time not hurt himself or Roger. We worked all night until the sun came up. I hoped that by the end Jim would understand and that this painful, exhausting evening we'd spent together wouldn't ruin our friendship. (Thankfully, it didn't. We remained close right up until his passing in 2023.)

Roger and Jim went on to tour to adoring fans, but the concerts weren't selling out. Not because the show wasn't great, but because what I had told Roger was the truth—without the name 'Pink Floyd,' not enough people knew he was. In some cities, the venues were only half full or even a little less. At the same time, Gilmour, Mason, and Wright were touring as Pink Floyd and selling out multiple stadium dates. Roger was distraught. I tried to make him see that he should be proud—that he was a big part of selling out those stadiums even if he wasn't physically there. He'd been such a major force in Pink Floyd, and his work was a large part of why those stadiums were selling out. On top of that, he was selling a sizable bunch of tickets for his own shows.

Roger didn't see it that way, but about halfway through the project, he began to realize that it would be good for him to let us start referring to him as a major force behind Pink Floyd. It was a little too late by then, but in the long run it would prove helpful in building his solo career. Album by album, tour by tour, Roger built up his fan base again until he was able to fill arenas. It was a struggle, and it took time and a lot of courage. Not having the money to create as big a production as he was used to, he played some shows where I know he wished he was able to bring more to the table. But he finally got there, eventually bringing back *The Wall* with new messages about the senselessness of war and the state of politics (especially in the United States) and using state-of-the-art technology to once again take audiences on an incredible multi-dimensional ride. I don't agree with all of his politics, but I take my hat off to him for reinventing himself and clawing his way back to the top.

The Jim Ladd story would have a happy ending too. Eventually, a program director at KLOS who recognized Ladd's genius hired him to do evenings, *his* way, and Jim mopped the floor with over-the-top ratings in Los Angeles. From there he became a hit coast to coast, broadcasting nationally on SiriusXM. There will never be another like him.

• ● •

Just three months after the release of *Radio KAOS*, David Gilmour, Nick Mason, and Richard Wright were preparing to release the first Pink Floyd album without Roger Waters on it, and to mount a tour without him for the first time. Would fans accept this new version of Pink Floyd? Would they turn out in the numbers needed to make *A Momentary Lapse Of Reason* the success it needed to be?

Making an album is one thing, and the cost of it is fronted by the record label. Back then, before the modern '360' deal was born, labels made money solely on record sales; the touring business was completely separate and run by the bands, who retained all the money made from live shows but also had to put up their own money in advance to mount a tour, including costs for the stage production, road crew, transportation, hotels, and more.

Mounting a Pink Floyd spectacular, with all the people needed to make it work, was a gargantuan task. It took upward of two hundred people to accomplish, and it cost millions and millions of dollars. Steve O'Rourke once confided in me that the tour for *A Momentary Lapse Of Reason* cost $55 million to set up, which meant the band only broke even halfway through the run. There was a large pot of gold at the end, to be sure, but the upfront investment required was scary. You could feel the tension in the air—everything was on the line. The band and Steve had pushed all their chips into the middle of the table—they were all in.

When I first heard *Momentary Lapse*, I felt it had its own Floydian quality, even if it lacked a bit of the bite Roger would have added. When bands split up or lose key members, it can never be the same, and to expect such will only lead to disappointment. *A Momentary Lapse Of Reason* sounded different from the usual Floyd fare, but in some ways, it was like a breath of fresh air. Unlike earlier Pink Floyd records, it was not a concept album, yet it contained some great, radio-friendly songs, like 'Learning To Fly' and 'On The Turning Away.' The album was recorded on David's houseboat studio, the *Astoria*, which lent its own magical vibe to the project. It also marked the return of Richard Wright, who had left the band during the making of *The Wall*. As great as *The Wall* is, any Pink Floyd album without Richard Wright is missing a key ingredient, as far as this fan is concerned. His musical landscapes and wonderful artistry are essential to the overall Pink Floyd experience.

With this new approach, sans Roger, I wanted to talk to Steve about doing extra-large event promotions as well as something the band had never done before: making an effort to finally meet all the FM radio people across the country who had been playing their music for years.

As I was working with Roger on his *Radio KAOS* project and simultaneously with the Floyd guys on their new offering, I was forever caught in the middle, with both sides asking me what the other was up to. I told them I had huge respect for all of them and was not going to get in the middle of their fight. I would work just as hard for each of them, and whatever anyone told me would be kept to myself. This worked pretty well in terms of maintaining their trust, but it didn't stop either side from burning my ears off with their opinions about the other.

It was during this time that I began to build a real friendship with Nick and David. When I traveled to London on business, I always made a point of visiting each of them. Nick would always invite me over to see the large car collection he was building.

'Hi, Rap,' he'd say, 'feel free to go down the garage, walk around, sit in the cars, and take pictures, if you like.'

The collection included various period race cars. Two of my favorites were a very old Indy 500 car from 1956 known as a Dayton Steel Foundry Special, and a very rare 1962 Ferrari 250 GTO (of which only thirty-six were built). Nick rented out some of his collection for movies and commercials and also competed in some of these cars in period race events.

David was equally gracious, but his passion was for vintage airplanes. He, Nick, and Steve O'Rourke had all learned how to fly. Sometimes, if they needed to have a meeting, they'd all get into their respective planes and fly to Paris, where they'd have a nice long lunch together. But in keeping with his reserved personality, David never tried to impress. It wasn't like, 'Hey Rap, come down to our airport and see my airplanes,' it was more like, 'Hey, you wanna go flying tomorrow?'

I met David at his London home and off we went. When we arrived at the small airport where he housed the planes, I got the tour. At the time, the highlights included a gorgeous yellow biplane, a beautiful dark blue trainer that I believe was a T-6 Harvard, a shiny metal P-51 Mustang, and a freaking jet. I think the jet was a British fighter called a Folland Gnat. It was painted bright yellow, and it looked fierce.

O'Rourke pulled me aside at the airport.

'Rap,' he said, 'whatever you do, don't get in the jet.'

'Why not?'

'Because David likes to . . .' He motioned his fingers like a corkscrew.

'Well, I'll just ask him not to do that part.'

'He's gonna do that part. Just don't get in the jet.'

I opted for the trainer.

Also with us that day were Pink Floyd's music publisher, Peter Barnes, and his wife.

'Ladies first,' David said, putting Peter's wife in the trainer, and off they went. While we watched them in the air, Peter, a very funny man, gave me a concise explanation of music publishing.

'An artist is busking in the street. He puts a hat down and people throw money into his hat. The music publisher puts a hat down right next to the artist's hat and does nothing at all. Then people throw money into his hat too.'

I watched as David performed an expert landing, and then it was my turn to fly. I sat in the biplane first, as it had always been a dream of mine to fly in one of those. But the weather was dicey, and the plane had a wooden propeller. He explained to me that if it rained while we were flying, the raindrops would pellet the prop and chew it up pretty badly.

Moving to the trainer, I asked the flight crew if they had a parachute, just in case. They laughed and said that yes, they had them, but I wouldn't need one.

'But if you have them,' I asked, 'would it be okay if I sort of wore one? I mean, I trust David and all, but I only know him as a member of Pink Floyd. *First in space* and all that, you know?'

They gave me a period parachute—the kind that has very long straps that go down your back, and you sit on the main bag.

'Does this thing still work?'

'Oh yeah.'

'Okay, just show me what to pull, in case . . .'

I sat down in the cockpit of the two-seater. It was an old World War II plane with a single propeller and a big stick in the middle of your legs. I guess that because it was a trainer, both the front seat and the seat behind the pilot had similar equipment. I was given a headset so that I could communicate with David, and then the Plexiglas cockpit was closed over our heads. We sat on a slight angle, facing upward, as the plane had two large wheels beneath the wings and the fuselage angled down toward the tail, where there was one smaller wheel.

As we taxied down the runway, I flashed back to what it might have felt like flying one of these during the war. The stick was wiggling all over the place, and the gauges were turning this way and that. Then I heard David's voice over the radio.

'You okay, Rap? Over.'

'Yes, over.'

You could feel the vibration of the motor as we made our way toward the takeoff point. When we got there, David turned the plane onto the runway and stopped. There was a giant dark cloud right in front of us. As is typical of English weather, it had drizzled all day, and the cloud looked ominous.

'You see that big dark cloud in front of us? Over.'

'Yes, over.'

'Well, we have two choices. We can take off and die, or we can return to the hangar and have another spot of tea. What would you like to do?'

'Uh, tea sounds good.'

'I think that's the right answer.'

As David turned back toward the main part of the airport, I was chuckling inside. Because I was wearing headphones while hearing all of the different sounds—the airplane engine, the radio calls, and mostly Gilmour's voice—I felt like I was in a Pink Floyd record.

The airport itself was in keeping with the planes that were kept there. Everything felt like it was from the 1940s. We went back to the waiting room, where there was a small café, and had bacon sandwiches with our tea. As we watched the weather, I felt like we were flying aces waiting for the rain to clear to fly our mission. As luck would have it, a front moved in, and we never got off the ground. Even so, it had been a really fun day.

• ● •

Before the *Momentary Lapse Of Reason* tour started, I had a follow-up meeting with Steve, Nick, and Dave about how important it would be for them to finally meet some radio people. Because of the huge successes they had achieved, they had never had to press the flesh or put themselves out promotionally in any way. Even so, I explained, if they made themselves more available, it would go a long way in terms of how much exposure their music would get on the FM airwaves. When artists meet the people who help them along the way to say thanks, a genuine bond is created, and those folks feeling a kinship want to support the artists even more.

They agreed, and in every city, before each concert began, we invited key radio and retail personnel backstage to meet the band. It was a big thrill for so many of them, but especially for the folks who had played Pink Floyd records their whole careers and who were now finally getting to meet and talk with the guys.

We borrowed some of the band's inflatable pigs to fly over the major radio stations across the country. I talked the general manager of KLOS in Los Angeles into letting me paint the radio station pink, fly the pig overhead, and have Dave and Nick do a live interview on their roof. It stopped the traffic.

The guys weren't used to any of this, but they were good sports about it all, even if they enjoyed giving me a hard time about it. Once, after three margaritas, Nick declared, 'Rap, we're far too old, far too tired, and frankly, far too rich to have to put up with this bullshit!'

We laughed our heads off. But at the end of the day, *A Momentary Lapse Of Reason* remained in heavy rotation at rock radio for at least three more months than usual. We sold four million albums. And the answer to whether or not the fans would accept the legitimacy of this version of Pink Floyd was in. It was a resounding yes.

• ● •

In November of 1988, a little over a year after the album's release, I got another call from Steve O'Rourke.

'Rap,' he began, 'the band wants to thank you for all you've done to make this project a success, and for all you've done for us over the years. We want to get you a Christmas present. What do you want?'

'Steve, I love you guys. But you can't call someone up and ask them what they want for a Christmas present. It feels too weird. Besides, I don't want things. A thank-you will suffice.'

He thanked me again on behalf of the guys, and we hung up.

The holidays came and went, and then, in the first week of January, I got another call.

'We figured out what to get you for your present. The band wants you to come and play one song live with them.'

'Really? Wow. That's very sweet. So, like at a rehearsal, yes?'

'No, one song, live onstage with the band, at a show.'

'What?' I was having trouble taking this in. 'You mean one song live with them in front of an audience?'

'Yes, at a proper gig.'

I had once mentioned to my current assistant, Cathy Thiele, how much fun it would be for me to one day plug into a giant sound system and experience what it would feel like to play on an arena-sized stage. 'You know,' I'd told her, 'like, get to play side by side with Keith or someone on that level, and really let it rip.'

Cathy also had a nice relationship with O'Rourke and had actually called to put the idea in his head. (Thanks, Cath!)

Needless to say, I was blown away. My head was swimming.

'Yeah, wow, that would be pretty amazing,' I told Steve.

He went on to tell me that since the American leg of the tour was over, I'd have to come to London, Paris, or Russia to play.

'Okay,' I replied, 'I'll think about that.' Then I thanked him very much and told him to thank the guys. I thought it was a kind gesture, and I left it at that. But then, two months later, Steve called again.

'Hi, Rap. We haven't heard from you, are you coming?'

'Are you *serious*? I thought that invite was just a nice gesture.'

'No, they want you to come and play.'

'Steve, you know, I'm a real player. I don't want to get up there and just pose and try to look cool.'

'Gilmour knows that. That's why it's a real present.'

Now, I was stunned. Come and play in our band for a song. Really? Who does that?

At the time, I was making a video of my close-up magic act to submit to the Magic Castle in Hollywood, to see if I could get booked for a proper run of performances. I had to make a decision. I only had time to put all my extra energy into one extracurricular activity. Either play live onstage with Pink Floyd or play live for a week's engagement at the Magic Castle.

As I've mentioned already, I'm a classic overthinker. But this one was a no-brainer.

I called England to find out the details. David told me that the best song for me to play on would be the encore, 'Run Like Hell.' It would save having to get me on and off the stage in between songs, it's a lot of fun to play, and the encore is when all the production buttons were pushed at once—all the lights swirling, the lasers going off, images projecting on the big screen, robots coming out of the stage, lots of pyro exploding overhead . . . you name it. He told me I could learn the song from the live album that had recently been released, *Delicate Sound Of Thunder*. They play 'Run Like Hell' and most of their other songs the same way each evening to keep in sync with the production. Playing with Pink Floyd, I would feel like I was part of a larger orchestrated performance.

I got hold of a guitar player from a Pink Floyd cover band to make sure I knew the song perfectly. Sure enough, there are some subtle chords in there. I practiced 'Run Like Hell' for three freaking months. I chose to go to London, worrying that if I was backstage in France, let's say, where I couldn't speak the language, I might have trouble trying to tell some security guy that I really *was* supposed to be onstage with the band and miss my big chance. So, the first week in July of 1989, Sharon and I flew over with my Fender Telecaster, which would be perfect, as it was the type of guitar David was mostly using on this tour.

When we arrived, I immediately called O'Rourke.

'Where should I meet you guys? What should I do?'

'Sorry, Rap, I can't talk to you now, I'm in the middle of trying to figure out how to get the band and production to fit onto two giant barges, so we can play Venice.'

Of course you are, I thought. Typical Pink Floyd—the more grandeur the better. Knowing my playing with the band wasn't quite on the same level as a groundbreaking (or water-breaking) concert in Venice, I began to worry. But Steve finally got back to me about where to meet David.

The evening of the show, I was treated just like a real band member from the get-go. Sharon and I met David at a hotel and took a small minibus with his family and guests to the London Arena. When we arrived, David had the promoter hold the doors for a few minutes so that I could have a proper soundcheck. He wanted to make sure I would be comfortable with how everything would sound at showtime, which was very kind and thoughtful.

For 'Run Like Hell,' I would take the place of Scott Page, who doubled on guitar and sax. David showed me the riser where I would stand behind him and asked if I wanted to use one of his Telecasters. I tried one, but David uses heavier strings than I'm used to, and his string action is high off the frets, so you really have to bear down to play. I opted to make it easier on myself and use the one I'd brought from the States.

'You wuss,' he laughed.

I slung my guitar over my shoulder and David plugged me into his rig, which towered over my head. It appeared to be a stack of high-fidelity amplifier heads along with other gadgets that could easily pass as the knobs, dials, and switches on an alien spacecraft. All I know is that when I played a few licks, I magically possessed that David Gilmour signature sound—big and bold, with echo, delay, and all. It was the greatest sound I'd ever gotten out of a guitar.

I thanked him and handed my Tele to Phil Taylor, David's legendary guitar tech, who put it in the rack next to all of David's guitars as we went backstage.

July in England can be very warm, and this night was especially hot and muggy. We walked backstage to find Harvey Goldsmith, the famous promoter, looking very unhappy. Marc Brickman, the band's lighting designer, wouldn't let Harvey turn on the air conditioning system in the building until the first half of the show was over, for fear that the moving air would blow away the smoke effects required to show off the band's laser lights. Harvey was hot and sweaty, as we all were. It was pretty funny to hear Harvey grumbling away.

'Goddamn Brickman and his goddamn smoke machines! Won't let me turn on the bloody air!'

I was hanging with David and Nick, who were both being very kind to me and trying to take the edge off.

'Just go out and have a good time,' David offered.

Nick, who can be a very funny man, told me not to worry—they didn't even know the song that well themselves. Yeah, right.

I explained to David that I had studied all their exotic chords and asked rhetorically if he wanted me to just play soft chords behind him. His answer surprised me.

'No, those chords are just for the record. This is live. Just hit a power chord—that's what I do! And I want you to have a good time, so you can play some leads if you like. Just make sure you sound like Pink Floyd.'

I assured him that I had been working on the song for three months and had made sure I sounded like Pink Floyd. Did he just say I could play some lead guitar?

I went outside to try to chill for a bit. There was my old friend Marc Brickman, lighting designer extraordinaire, who I'd known since my Springsteen days, smoking a cigarette, trying to do the same. This particular stage production featured big robots that came out of trap doors from under the stage, as well as lighting pods that looked like flying saucers. Each flying saucer had a man in it, controlling a very powerful spotlight. When a band member did a solo, the saucer would hover very low over their head and shine a white-hot spotlight down on them.

So, here I am trying to chill and get my mind off the big event, and Brickman says, 'Hey, Rap, when you do your lead part, I'm going to have one of those flying saucers swing down low and try and knock you off your riser!'

As if I didn't have enough to think about already! Marc's a great guy, but he's also a tough kid from New York, so you never know with him. Forget chilling out, now I had even more shit to worry about!

That evening was kind of strange. For the first half of the show, Sharon and I watched from the audience, but for the second half, I was going to be *in* the show—quite surreal.

Sharon and I went backstage again during intermission and listened to the second half of the concert through the concrete walls of the arena. I was getting more anxious as the minutes ticked by. Finally, the moment of truth arrived. The band had finished their last song and had come off the stage waiting for the encore. I was escorted to the back of the stage, and I could hear the audience clapping and screaming for more.

I'm not sure if this was a nightly ritual, but right before the band went back on, a well-dressed man appeared with a big silver tray holding a bottle of port and some glasses. David told me that port is good for soothing the throat and that certain opera singers even gargle with it. I was asked if I'd like a glass.

'Sure.'

Forget the savoring part, I gulped it down like a shot of whiskey, hoping they'd offer another to help calm me down. But no chance. David walked up the stairs to the stage and began playing some riffs to wind up the crowd as a few laser beams began to swirl around the auditorium. I quickly followed and met Phil at stage right. I stood there as he draped my guitar around my neck and hooked me up. I felt like I was being knighted.

'Hi, Rap, how are you feeling?' Phil asked. 'Would you like a cloth to wipe your hands? Some water? A pick?'

And all I have to do is play? I remember thinking. *I could get used to this.*

The stage was still dark, except for the odd laser light or two shooting about the arena. David kept hammering out some very trippy guitar sounds. The crowd was starting to roar. All of a sudden, Phil looked wildly in my direction and yelled at me.

'Duck!'

He put his hand on the top of my head and shoved me down to my haunches. I'm a bit over six feet tall but Phil is even taller than me, so my head felt like a basketball being slam-dunked. He crouched down beside me as a hot green laser beam shot just inches over our heads.

'Careful,' he laughed, 'you could get killed up here!'

My heart was going a mile a minute. I was remembering the time I saw the *Animals* tour at Anaheim Stadium in California back in 1977. Everything was so big—the stage, the quadraphonic sound system, the white sparks flying off the magnesium flares attached to two giant cranes rising slowly on each side of the stage—as the band opened with the throbbing, echoing bass line from 'Sheep.' When the whole band kicked in and the stage exploded in light, I saw Snowy White, an excellent guitarist, playing his Goldtop Les Paul as backup to Gilmour.

Wow, I remember thinking, *I wonder what it would be like to be Snowy White, playing backup to Dave Gilmour in Pink Floyd on such a grand stage?*

Never in a million years did I think I'd be standing here, but now I was about to find out.

'Go now,' Phil said, pointing to the riser where I'd stood at sound check, 'because in a second a robot is going to come up out of the stage, right where you're going to walk. Stay on the riser and don't leave that spot until the end of the show.'

I quickly moved to the riser, which was about ten feet behind David and Tim Renwick, who was playing second guitar downstage, slightly to my right. Tim is a wonderful guitarist I had known years before when he was on Columbia with the band Sutherland Brothers & Quiver. Both guys looked back and smiled. They looked genuinely happy for me, knowing what a thrill ride this was going to be.

The stage was dimly lit but I could still see all the rest of the Pink Floyd band around me—Nick Mason on drums to my left, Gary Wallis to his left on percussion, then Richard Wright and Jon Carin on keyboards, and Guy Pratt far left on bass. The backing singers were to my right, and over my head loomed the gigantic round screen that all those fabled psychedelic movies were projected on. It was dark in the arena, and I couldn't see much past the end of the stage—just a few kids in the front. The others I just heard as a mass audience, clapping and hooting every time David made sounds on the guitar. It's a weird sensation, being surrounded by darkness yet hearing the clapping and cheering of fifteen thousand people who are right in front of you. You can feel them, but you can't see them. The air feels thick.

I looked down at my guitar and hit my strings in a kind of muffled way to echo what David was doing, just to make sure it was on. David started playing notes in a rhythmic pattern, and the crowd started clapping in time. Multicolored lasers were flashing all over the arena, increasing the anticipation. I wiped my left hand on my pant leg to get the sweat off. The drums started beating in time with the crowd, and suddenly everything got really loud. The soundmen must have slid all the faders up to show volume. The stage lights exploded in my eyes, from dim to instant white hot. It was so bright I had to blink to adjust my vision. The crowd started screaming, and I turned up the volume on my guitar. I felt adrenaline rush through my veins. Here we go . . . holy shit!

The introduction to 'Run Like Hell' has chords that cascade down the neck of the guitar, and with three guitarists playing the same phrases, the sound was full and majestic. I drank it all in—the bigness of it all, the huge stage, all the musicians, the incredible music, the roar of the crowd. The sound coming out of the monitor speakers onstage was perfection. Loud but not too loud—as if you'd turned up the hi-fi sound system in your home living room. I could hear everyone in the band clear as a bell.

The adrenalin was kicking in now, and David kept walking back my way, laughing and yelling in my ear.

'Let 'em have it, Rapper! Drill 'em!'

He was clearly having a lot of fun watching me grin from ear to ear. I was shaking my head and smiling back.

'Stop,' I yelled, 'you're gonna mess me up!'

I thought I'd see more of the production, but it was all happening behind us and over our heads. The audience was clapping for things I couldn't see, and there was so much going on that everyone was looking in different directions, almost cross-eyed. Some were looking at David, Nick, and Richard, while others were captivated by the lasers, robots, flying saucers, fireworks, and so on.

I was already in a euphoric state and then things got even better. In the middle of the song, after a trippy Richard Wright keyboard solo, there is a breakdown for a few lead guitar bits. David played a lick, then turned around and motioned with his finger for me to answer. Instinctively, I did, and the next thing I knew we were trading licks. All of a sudden it hit me like a ton of bricks.

Let me get this straight: I am in London Arena, playing live onstage with Pink Floyd, and I'm trading licks with David Gilmour. Is that what the fuck's happening?!

I allowed that thought to last no more than a nanosecond, because more than pleasing the crowd, who wouldn't know if I'd made a mistake or not, caught up in the giant echo loop we were all in, I wanted to concentrate on playing well for David, Nick, and all the other great musicians in the band. I didn't want them to think I was a poser. I needed to hold my own.

I'd nailed all my parts, and the song was finally coming to a close. 'Run Like Hell' has a reprise ending. Tim looked back, wanting to help me, and mouthed the words 'one more time.'

'I know,' I mouthed back and gave him a big smile.

The song came to an end with a resounding crescendo. I saw huge pyro sparks shoot from the end of the stage to the ceiling and felt the heat of the same as the screen behind us exploded in fireworks glitter. The crowd went bonkers.

It was the end of the show, and David motioned to me to walk to the edge of the stage with the rest of the band. I felt like I'd played well, and now I could finally take in all the applause and hoopla happening around me. I took a bow standing next to David and Nick, threw my pick into the audience, and waved my hand. *See ya next time!* What a fucking blast. The band's other keyboardist, Jon Carin, walked by and gave me a thumbs-up and a smile. That meant so much to me—like I was on par with the gang. And, for just a little over seven minutes, I was. I was in Pink Floyd—for real.

I remained a band member throughout the evening as Sharon and I cruised in a boat with the rest of the players up the River Thames to an after-party thrown by their UK label, EMI. Another Pink Floyd perk—why take a typical limousine when you can cruise in a boat up the Thames? If nothing else, these guys knew how to have fun. It felt like a fairytale.

What was kind of funny was that none of the invitees from the label, the British press, or radio, knew me as a record exec, only as a guest guitarist they'd seen play with the band. So, I got the royal treatment along with the rest of the guys, including a lot of overdone compliments about my playing and such.

Record company executives can be a bit overbearing, but you really don't know how much until you're on the other side. People were coming up to me giving me triple sincerity.

'Wow man, you played so great!'

'Jeez,' I asked David, 'are we all really like that?'

'Yeah, kinda,' he winced.

'Whoa. I'll remember that and try and tone it down in the future.'

I came back to the States a hero. A picture of me playing with the band appeared in *Billboard* and all the rest of the trade magazines. A good friend of mine, Luanne Nast from the *Album Network*, even designed a faux cover shot for me.

I remember coming off the stage that hot July night thinking that if someone told me now that I couldn't be in the record business anymore, for whatever reason, that it would be just fine, because nothing I do would ever top this. Of course, there was much more adventure to come, but for a blue-collar surfer kid from Bellflower, California, yeah, nothing's better than being in Pink Floyd. Even if it's just for seven minutes.

'You know, David,' I would kid Gilmour later, 'the band just doesn't sound quite the same without me in it.'

STEEL WHEELS &
GUITAR LESSONS

'LADIES AND GENTLEMEN...The Rolling Stones!'

I had already gotten to work closely with Mick on both of his solo albums, and so far there hadn't been any Arabian princesses to deal with. I'd met Woody and Keith during the New Barbarians tour in 1979, but my first meeting with the rest of the band came during our first official Rolling Stones release, *Dirty Work*, in 1986.

We had a big hit at rock radio with the song 'One Hit (To The Body),' and next up was a cover of 'Harlem Shuffle.' I was invited to the video shoot at a giant soundstage in Midtown Manhattan. It was just me, the band, and their wives and girlfriends. It was cool to feel like part of the gang. When I was introduced to Bill Wyman and Charlie Watts, the song 'Paint It Black' immediately ran through my head, the drums and bass being such iconic parts of that track. The song had lived inside of me since I was a teenager, and all of a sudden, the all-important rhythm section of The Rolling Stones was standing right in front of me.

As far as Keith was concerned, I was hoping he would be more lucid than I'd found him on the New Barbarians tour. Besides Dylan, Keith had been such an influence on my life that I felt I needed to connect with him in some way. He did not disappoint.

The dressing rooms were upstairs, above the soundstage. I found Keith in one of them, sitting in a plush, high-back chair dressed in his typical style: black jeans, a white pirate-type shirt, a big scarf hanging down. He appeared to be just a little lit. This was his usual demeanor during the times I spent with him in the 80s. He always seemed to be swaying just a little this way and that, and he had a glow and a glint in his eyes that danced to and fro as he spoke. And, of course, he always spoke in that deep, slurred timbre—another part of that irresistible Keith Richards charm.

I walked over and introduced myself, wondering if he'd even remember me from the New Barbarians episode.

'I'm gonna gush on you for about a minute,' I blurted out, 'just to finally get it out of my system after all these years, and then I'll be good to go.'

Keith looked up and smiled as everything I'd ever wanted to tell my hero came tumbling out in one long, run-on sentence. It was embarrassing, but I couldn't help myself. So, I'm rambling away about how the Stones are my all-time favorite band, how I learned to play by copying his riffs, how I still owned my brown corduroy coat with epaulets, like the one he wore on the *December's Children* album cover, blah blah blah blah, and all of a sudden, he cocks his head and furrows his brow as if he's trying to remember something.

'Haven't we met before?'

'Yeah, I spent a week with you guys on the New Barbarians tour.'

'Oh my, I was *so bad* on that tour. I offended so many people. Did I do anything to offend *you*?'

'Yeah, kinda,' I admitted, hemming and hawing. 'You accused me of stealing your bottle of Rebel Yell when we were on the plane.'

'Oh, I am so sorry,' he replied. Then he got up from his chair, smiled, and gave me a very sincere hug. I was touched.

'Well, you're making my day,' he continued. 'I'm so proud of the Stones, but as a musician, as a guitar player, it's my job to pass it on to people like you, Dave Edmunds, and others'—how the hell I got put on the same pedestal as Dave Edmunds, I don't know, but it was great to hear. 'It was passed down to me from guys like Chuck Berry and Muddy Waters. I am a disciple of Chuck Berry. When I am buried, on my gravestone, all I want them to put is, *He passed it on.* That's what will make me happy.'

In an instant, all the trappings of rock stardom disappeared. We were now just two guys talking guitar. We both smiled that knowing smile. I guess I shouldn't have been surprised, having had similar experiences with other famous musicians, but this was Keith, and he was part of my DNA. I *needed* to have this conversation with my all-time guitar hero. I'd gone full circle from being in my bedroom at age seventeen, guitar in my lap, listening intently to those early Stones albums, trying to figure out what he was doing. Now I was standing right in front of the man and having a real conversation about it.

And then it got even better. When we started talking about my high school band, The Jades, covering Stones songs, Keith stopped me cold.

'But the songs didn't sound entirely correct, did they?' he asked.

How could he know that?

'Yeah,' I admitted, 'no matter how hard we tried, there was something just a little bit off, and we could never figure it out.'

'It's because you weren't in G tuning!' he bellowed, eyes beaming. 'It's my secret.'

Keith went on to explain the open-G tuning that he'd learned from Don Everly when the Stones were on tour with The Everly Brothers years ago. It's an old slide-guitar blues tuning that Bo Diddley had shown Don, in keeping with the *pass-it-on*, guitar secrets thing. Keith said that when he watched Don onstage, he could hear all kinds of great chords coming from the guitar, but Don was barely moving his fingers. Keith fell in love with the simplicity of the whole thing, but instead of using a slide, he experimented with different chord changes he could make by barring across a fret and adding one or two fingers in front to make different chord shapes. And because of all the open notes, the guitar really rang out with a heavy rhythmic jangle.

'Paul, go home and take the bottom E string off the guitar. It just gets in the way. Then tune the A string to G, leave the rest, and tune the top E string to D. Then bar any fret you like, play an open chord, and add your second finger one fret up on the B string, your third two frets up on the D, hammer on and off, then report back.'

'Yes sir!' I saluted.

But . . . what? Take the bottom E string off the guitar completely? He's gotta be pulling my leg! Or maybe he's just a bit too lit.

I go home, say a quick hi to Sharon and the kids, run up to our bedroom, pull out a guitar from under the bed, and do as the master suggests. Then I start to play bar chords, adding two fingers, and just like Keith said, all of those Rolling Stones hits start falling effortlessly out of the guitar—'Brown Sugar,' 'Tumbling Dice,' 'Honky Tonk Women,' 'Start Me Up,' 'Can't You Hear Me Knocking,' and on and on.

Whoa! I'd just opened a new door in my guitar world, and it was a big one. I ran downstairs, animated, yelling at Sharon and the kids.

'G TUNING! G TUNING!'

They thought I was nuts—I give them reason to think that every now and then.

When I came back to the video shoot the next day, I don't know who had the bigger smile on his face, me or Keith.

• ● •

Another life-changing moment happened on the second day of that video shoot. After about three hours, I began to feel like I'd rather be home, playing with our young sons, Adam and Sam, than hanging out with The Rolling Stones. Adam had been born in 1981, and Sam exactly three and a half years later in '85. I had so much fun with those two, giving them bucking bronco rides on my back, playing football on our front lawn, and introducing them to the more fun things in life, like midnight snacks. It was hard to find anything more satisfying. Having said that, this feeling caught me by surprise. Maybe it was a gift from above, maybe it was just me growing up. But it was a revelation. Here I was, in the greatest place I could be, hanging out with my all-time favorite band, the greatest rock'n'roll band in the world. And yet, as good as it was, I realized that hanging out with Mick and Keith wasn't nearly as fun as hanging out with Adam and Sam. If I left early, I'd make it home just in time to see them before bedtime. I couldn't believe what I was about to say.

'Hey, guys, it's been a blast, but I gotta get going.'

'Okay, thanks for everything. We'll see ya soon.'

I closed the heavy metal soundstage door behind me. It made a loud reverberating bang as the bright sunlight outside blinded my eyes. I walked out into Midtown Manhattan, just east of the theater district, into a typical New York Street scene, people hustling and bustling in every direction. *How weird*, I thought to myself. *These guys are rehearsing right in the middle of town, and no one knows they're in there.* If they did, there'd be a riot to get into the place. It was like a giant secret. And I'd just left a situation that anyone would give their eye teeth for.

But something huge had just changed inside of me. My priorities were being rearranged, right before my eyes. I had always tried to walk the fine line between family and work. I didn't want to become one of those dads whose children hardly knew them. And I didn't want to lose that all-important bond that Sharon and I had. As I left the video shoot, I felt like I was losing something, but somehow, I was okay with it. What I was gaining felt much bigger and much brighter. I smiled, looked up, and thanked God and the universe for showing me what was really important. I'd known too many people who'd elected to let the music business take them over. When their run was done, they were shocked at how many 'friends' didn't pick up their phone calls. By that time, many of them had distanced themselves from their wives and families, and now they found themselves in limbo, no longer having a foundation to come back to.

I'd always known how important it was to preserve my home life. I was clear that home was reality and work was Disneyland. But this was the first time that it hit me over the head that being with my wife and kids made me much happier than *anything* the record business could ever provide.

· ● ·

The Stones didn't tour *Dirty Work*. Word was that Mick and Keith were feuding, and it was rare that all the five principal members of the band were together in the studio at the same time. The record was fun, but it didn't live up to their previous albums on Atlantic. Mick and Keith's solo albums did okay, but it was clear they weren't nearly as strong separately as when they partnered together to fuel The Rolling Stones.

I guess they'd both gotten it all out of their systems by now, though, because when their next album, *Steel Wheels*, was delivered, you knew that most everything had been put back together again—or at least patched up well enough for them to make a terrific record and put on a historic tour. And I wanted to do something historic to go with it. When I listened to *Steel Wheels*, I heard three songs that I knew could be big rock radio hits. I wanted to ensure that each one would reach #1 on the charts, but, as usual, I had a larger plan in mind. I wanted not only for the Stones to have three #1 rock singles in a row but for each single to debut at #1—another first.

A fair number of new groups had emerged in the 1980s and received a lot of fanfare while The Rolling Stones remained in the background due to in-fighting, solo projects, and so on. But now they were once again thrusting their elbows out. Move over, everyone—Mick, Keith, and the boys were here to set the record straight. They were on a mission to prove that they were, indeed, the world's greatest rock'n'roll band. And I, in turn, was going to make history at rock radio on their behalf. As a team, we would harness the focus of the music industry and the entire country, uncontested, for at least three solid months. In short, the plan was *all Rolling Stones, all the time!*

During the 70s, record companies serviced radio with full albums, and the programmers and disc jockeys at each station decided which tracks they wanted to play and in what kind of rotation. By communication through tip sheets and word of mouth, a consensus emerged as to which track would be the lead single, which meant it would be played at least four or five times a day. For a popular album, a second or even a third track would be played in a medium or lighter rotation.

In the fall of 1980, after Gloria Johnson chose to play 'Turn Me Loose' by Loverboy, making it the first consensus track from that album to spread across the country, I began to think about having some kind of control over the destiny of an album's airplay. Instead of just delivering full albums to radio and letting them decide which tracks to play, I wondered if we could send them one track at a time—one that we chose to focus on, followed up by a second and then a third track, just like the Top 40 guys did. This idea seemed to go hand in hand with the direction that rock radio was going in—more and more, it meant playing the best songs from the best rock records in a preplanned rotation.

But rock stations weren't set up to play singles. Their turntables played 33 1/3rpm twelve-inch album discs. How could we send them one song as a single without disrupting their system, making them have to put on a plastic singles adapter and then change their turntable speed to 45rpm, just to play one song?

I called Mac with an idea and asked how best to implement it. Then I called one of our major pressing plants in Carrollton, Georgia, and asked them to send me an LP pressing of a single Loverboy track and to create a groove so that, at the end of the song, the turntable needle would remain caught in a continuous loop until someone stopped it and lifted the tone arm from the disc. When I got the pressing, it looked weird. I thought they'd use an entire side and let the grooves stretch out. But instead, the song appeared as it would on a traditional album, about an inch in width, and the rest was just flat shiny vinyl. It worked great, but it seemed like a waste of vinyl. But then I thought, *Who cares? We've got tons of money, and this is a great answer—a twelve-inch single!*

The twelve-inch single quickly became an industry standard. We could now send one key track off a new album to rock radio, and even a couple of weeks before an album's release. This created anticipation in the marketplace and ensured a crowd of people at record stores the day the album arrived for sale. Not only that, but our album projects lasted longer, because instead of having radio play three tracks at once, thereby more quickly exhausting an album's life on the air, we were able to extend the airplay on any given project for a much longer period by releasing one track at a time. Extended radio exposure meant more albums sold. As a bonus, we also created twelve-inch single cover art that included important information about a forthcoming album that disc jockeys could talk about, and sometimes we were able to list upcoming tour dates as well.

If there was a time that the twelve-inch single was used (and even overused) most effectively, it was for *Steel Wheels*. With an album so good, and with the band's first tour in eight years looming, excitement was reaching fever pitch. I knew rock radio would want to make these songs staples on their playlists.

When we released the first single, 'Mixed Emotions,' it was immediately added in super-hot rotation at every rock radio station across the country, so it naturally debuted at #1. But after a few weeks, instead of following our usual game plan of releasing a second single and working it up the charts as the first single was working its way down, I held back the release of the next track, 'Rock And A Hard Place,' for much longer than I should have. In fact, I held it back for so long that radio stations were long past the point of burnout with 'Mixed Emotions.' Programmers were dying to replace it with a fresh track. When we finally released 'Rock,' it took only three or four days for every FM rock station across America to immediately swap out the first single for the new one, placing it in the super-heavy-rotation slot that had just been vacated by 'Mixed Emotions.' Voi-fucking-la! On the next week's airplay charts, 'Rock And A Hard Place' debuted at #1.

This caused some of my competitors to be perturbed, as by replacing one #1 single with another, I had frozen out the band that had been waiting patiently at #2 for their chance at finally reaching Mecca. To complicate matters even more, because 'Mixed Emotions' was still in decent rotation, it gave us two singles in the Top 10, monopolizing that section of the chart. Other songs would have trouble moving up and into this coveted space. This prompted some heated phone calls.

'What the fuck was that?'

'Did you really need to pull that stunt?'

What could I say? First off, this was The Rolling Stones, and they deserved every historical moment they could get. Second, I finally felt like part of the gang I'd wanted to join since I was seventeen years old. Now I was a pirate too, and our ship was flying the flag of the legendary tongue-and-lips logo.

From August through September, 'Rock In A Hard Place' remained at #1 on album rock radio. The tour was going through the roof, and we were selling albums like hotcakes. I had one last mission to perform, one last card to play, one last town to plunder. I needed to debut our third single, the beautiful ballad 'Almost Hear You Sigh,' at #1 as well.

I repeated my first move, letting 'Rock' hang out in the top slot forever. I felt like an archer pulling back an arrow on his bow, farther and farther, almost to breaking point. Programmers were more than ready to play another track from *Steel Wheels* in heavy rotation. And then . . . *whoosh!* I finally let the arrow fly. And just like that, I got the same result. Everyone switched out 'Rock In A Hard Place' for 'Almost Hear You Sigh.' When the next week's airplay charts were published, there sat our third single, debuting, once again, at #1.

Mission accomplished—rock'n'roll history written. No artist had ever achieved anything close to this.

It hadn't been my intention to hurt other artists by my actions, but there was collateral damage. I had successfully frozen out every other artist from reaching the coveted #1 slot for three months. And that's when things got ugly. The phone calls were blistering. Warner Bros, Elektra, Atlantic, RCA, A&M—everyone wanted my head on a stick. The heads of album promotion at other labels were calling their presidents, asking them to reach out to ours to have me fired. It got so bad I had to leave the office for a day to hide out.

• ● •

On October 29, 1989, I took an eight-year-old Adam Rappaport to see The Rolling Stones play at Shea Stadium. Before the show, I wanted to go backstage and tell the guys the great news about their three #1s in a row.

To get backstage at a Rolling Stones concert, you need more credentials than people carry in a nuclear facility. First, there is the coveted 'All Access' laminate worn around the neck, which for most bands lets you into the backstage area within walking distance to the dressing rooms. With the Stones, it only gets you to a large room that's a kind of holding tank for industry guests. From there, you need a series of stickers that denote the specific areas you're allowed into. The stickers come in different shapes, sizes, and color patterns, and give you stage access, catering access, entry to the press box, entry to another holding station near the band's dressing rooms, and so on. The most coveted sticker gets you into the Stones' dressing room area. The security is unmatched by any other act in the business. By the time Adam and I reached the real inner sanctum, we looked like decorated four-star generals.

The first band member I ran into was Ronnie Wood, who immediately gave me a big hug. I quickly introduced him to Adam, who out of the corner of his eye saw hot dogs being served, along with a pinball machine and a pool table. Asking if he could wander a bit, I let him go as I began to tell Woody the news.

'Woody,' I began, 'I've been able to keep you guys at #1 on both the album and singles charts for a solid three months! And each of your three rock singles debuted at #1. It's totally historical.'

'Holy shit, Rap, that's amazing! I gotta get Keith—you need to tell him this!'

So, Woody goes into Keith's dressing room and brings him out. But in the less than three minutes that have passed, Woody has forgotten what I've told him. He knows it's something great, but he just can't bring it forth to the top of his probably altered brain state.

'Hey Keith, Rap just told me . . . he told me . . . Rap, tell Keith what you just told me!'

I chuckled, shook my head, and repeated the news to Keith. His eyes lit up and he smiled a huge smile. Then he turned me around, kicked me in the butt, spun me around again, gave me a big hug, and looked me in the eye.

'Can you do it again?'

'Keith, if I do this one more time, I'll be killed.'

'Well,' he replied, flashing a bigger, more devilish smile, 'it *is* the Stones, man.'

He gave me a wink that I think meant *just kidding* . . . kind of. I wished he was kidding. But if I had to take one on the chin for The Rolling Stones, I don't think he would have minded.

'Thanks, mate,' he added, with another smile. 'Means a lot.'

I went across the room to talk to Mick and spied Adam playing pool with Bill Wyman. Talk about an out-of-body experience. All those years ago as a teenager, watching television shows like *Shindig!* and *Ed Sullivan* featuring the Stones and Bill, with his well-known, stony-faced demeanor, staring straight out into the audience, hardly moving anything except his jaw, chewing gum, his fingers walking up and down the neck of the bass while he slid into the famous bass lines of songs like '19th Nervous Breakdown.' I'd had two sons, which was mind-blowing enough, and now the oldest was playing pool with Bill Wyman. Yeah, right, I'm dreaming.

I approached Mick to tell him the good news. I was pumped. Mick Jagger has a pretty even personality, and you can tell that the wheels are constantly spinning in his head.

'You know,' he said, not missing a beat, 'I think we were just a bit early with that third twelve-inch. Maybe by a week or so.'

'Mick, stop. Who cares? You've been #1 on the rock album and singles charts for three fucking months! It's historical—it's never happened before, and it will never happen again. Come on, man, give me just *a little* smile.' I pressed my fingers on either side of my mouth pushing up my lips to feign a smile. 'Stop analyzing for just one minute and be happy.'

Mick let down his guard for a moment, the wheels stopped spinning, and he thought about it. Then he looked up with a glint in his eye, cocked his head, and smiled that charming Mick Jagger smile.

'Yeah, I know, I know, it's just—,' he began, and then he started thinking again.

Christ, I thought, *does this guy think about stuff even more deeply than Bruce Springsteen?*

'No, no, it's good,' he finally added. 'It's *really good*. Thanks.'

Before we left, I brought Adam over to meet Keith. Obviously, this was a big deal for me.

'Adam, this is Keith Richards, the greatest rock'n'roll guitar player in the world.'

'Aw,' Keith replied, looking down at Adam, 'don't believe everything your old man tells you.'

I asked if we could get a photo.

'Of course,' Keith said, before suggesting, 'maybe we should kneel down, you know, because he's so little.'

It was great to see a sensitive side of the man.

On our way out of the dressing room, I asked Adam what he thought the best thing was about Keith.

'His skull ring!' he replied. 'That thing is awesome.' Then he added, 'Thanks, Dad, that was great—I got a hot dog, played pinball, and I played a game of pool with this really cool guy.'

'Yeah, I know that guy.'

'Let's go home. I gotta tell mom all about this!'

'Hey, Ad, these aren't just a bunch of fun guys you hang out with, it's a band—they play. They're gonna play a show, and we have to stay and watch it.'

'Oh,' he replied.

I could see him trying to put two and three together. Adam could have cared less about the show—he'd had a blast, and now it was time to split. But we stayed and watched, of course, and because the show had a lot of impressive stage production—big lights, big pyro, and Jagger running around all over the place—it kept his interest.

Years later, I would take Adam to see the Stones again at Madison Square Garden, hoping he'd get what it all meant to me. I wanted so much for him to be impressed. As we walked out, I asked him what he thought.

'Honestly dad, they're just a really good rock'n'roll band.'

Wow, I thought. I was disappointed. But then it dawned on me. Without all the memories my generation had in our heads of the early British Invasion, Altamont, the movies, the drug busts, the many years of concerts, famous album covers, and songs that helped shape the culture of the day . . . if you just took the Stones at face value, seeing their performance for the first time, yeah, that's what you see: a really good rock'n'roll band. I could feel the wheels turning, the world changing. What had meant so much to me would eventually fade into history.

'But what about the rock'n'roll? The backbeat? *Ah, wah ah wah, ah wah ah wah*—doesn't that make you want to move your leg and tap your foot?'

'Dad, I grew up with rap music, so the beat that makes me move is *boof, bada-boof*. But don't worry about it—all the beats come from Africa anyway.'

Talk about learning stuff from your kids.

• ● •

In 1992, The Rolling Stones left Columbia for Virgin Records. Why? For the same reason they'd left Atlantic Records to come to us—more money. Forty-five million bucks, to be exact.

Before they left, I asked Keith if he'd sign an autograph for me.

'Sure,' he said, 'just send me something to sign.'

I had a great photo that the legendary photographer Henry Diltz (The Doors' *Morrison Hotel*, *Crosby, Stills & Nash*'s debut album) had taken of Keith backstage at the Denver New Barbarians show in 1978. Henry had given me a few photos as a keepsake from the time he and I were on the tour.

One of my favorites was of Keith in his dressing room, warming up with a Strat in G tuning plugged into a small Mesa/Boogie amp, oblivious to the camera. Not playing the rock star, just a guitar player getting in tune with his instrument. I sent it to Keith.

What I got back was the photo with a caption denoting the secret tuning that he'd been so eager to teach me.

To Paul, 5 strings, 3 notes, 2 fingers, 1 asshole ... Love, Keith

That photo and caption says everything you need to know about rock'n'roll and Keith Richards. Of all my gold and platinum records and the many autographed photos and guitars I've collected over the years, this little seven-by-ten-inch picture with those words means more to me than any of it. It hangs on the wall right in front of me in my office, and I get a smile out of looking at it every day.

Yes, it's only rock'n'roll, but I like it.

THE MAGIC TRICK

WITHOUT A DOUBT, the most important part of successful music promotion is preparation. I equate it to sports. Tom Brady and Michael Jordan are the greatest in their fields because of how much time they spent preparing before games. Brady was the first on the football field to warm up and the last to leave the building, watching film to learn how he could consistently improve. Jordan's similar work ethic is well known and revered.

Sports figures often talk about how they imagine a game before it's played—how they envision their success, how they see the win and work toward it. Similarly, for me, each project had a specific plan behind it, and each would follow its own particular arc to fruition. I believe my approach to record promotion was more cerebral than that of a lot of my competitors. I've always viewed promotion as an art form itself, and I thought deeply about the psychology of the human mind and how to influence someone's thought process.

I would write a mini-play or movie in my head of how I wanted things to play out, scene by scene, a bit like the movie *The Sting*. Here, I want to tell any of my radio friends who might be reading this that I love you more than you'll ever know. I loved all of your unique personalities, your visions, and your talents. But I also had a job to do, which meant I had to figure out ways to get you on my side. And if the first approach didn't work, I could come up with some pretty cunning schemes to get the job done.

The most important part of any promotion plan is the setup. This initial phase is the same as making a garden ready for planting. In a garden, you must first till the soil, add nutrients, and make sure there will be plenty of water and sunshine to give seeds a chance to grow. With new music, you want to fertilize the programmer's mind so that the music has a chance to survive and grow, eventually to be heard by the public.

As a promotion person, you have the luxury of deciding how you want to present the music to a programmer. And how you present the music can help form their opinion of it. That's what you're after: a way to guide them to a positive point of view.

Most music programmers have an innate *prove it to me* attitude. And to be fair, they need to choose their music wisely, to ensure that listeners don't tune out. They are looking for songs that will resonate with their audiences. And in that regard, most music programmers are ultra-conservative.

In radio, where competition for ratings is ever-present, there used to be a favorite saying among rock programmers: 'What you don't play won't hurt you.' Meaning, it's much easier to say no than to risk audiences tuning out over some new unfamiliar music that might take listeners too long to get used to. And that is the age-old battle of a promotion person fighting for their artist's new music to be heard: to get past the gatekeepers so that the public can decide for themselves who they want to embrace.

I found that the very worst thing you could do is visit someone's office without any preparation, play them some music (or, in our modern era, send them a digital file), and then ask for their opinion. This may sound a bit Machiavellian, but the fact is, you don't want *their* opinion. You want the opinion that you help create. But without any setup or guidance, if they give you a base opinion that's not what you want to hear, you and that record are dead in the water—usually forever.

If you're playing new music to a programmer in their office, there is a good chance that they will be distracted at some point, perhaps by a call from their boss or a salesperson, or by a disc jockey bounding in, right in the middle of your presentation, needing an immediate answer to a timely question. The programmer might see something flash across their computer screen. Their spouse might call right in the middle of the most important part of a song.

One of my favorite strategies was to ask a PD or MD to lunch and to make sure that lunch was at least a twenty-minute drive away. In the office, they might still be thinking about a fight they had with their significant other before they left for work, or whether the kids made it to school okay, or any of life's myriad daily bothers. But go cruising with them in a car, roll down the windows on a beautiful spring day, let them take in the sunshine and the scenery, crank up the radio (tuned to their station), and all of a sudden, they feel like they've escaped—they're on a mini-vacation! Their mood lightens perceivably. In this environment, they listen differently, their ears open to enjoy the music for its own sake, without any preconceived notions. And then I'd say something like this.

'Hey, let me play you some advance music I have. No pressure—this isn't coming out for months—but I'm really excited about it.'

Now, not only is the programmer's mind in a positive place but they can just sit back and enjoy the music and the ride and not worry about me asking for an immediate add on their radio station.

There is also something magical about listening to music while driving in a car. Maybe it's the motion, I'm not sure, but a lot of us industry folks would always want to give our music the 'car test' before giving it our total stamp of approval. If you want to make sure you've got a hit on your hands, listen to it in the car. It's striking how it shows itself.

Once a PD or MD has let a song flow into their minds, that song will become a good memory. And then, months later, when a project is due for release and it's time to ask for the song to be added to their playlist, I'd give that person a heads up and let them know that the record was coming out in a couple of weeks. Nine times out of ten, I would get a response like, 'Oh yeah, I loved that song—we'll find room for it, for sure.'

It's also very helpful to know the psychological makeup of the person you are trying to convince. Another strong rule of mine is that there always needs to be a reason beyond the music itself that gives it added weight, signals extra importance, and places it ahead of the pack. For instance, there was a very important radio consultant in the South who absolutely lived for the blues. If I told him a new artist that I was working with was heavily blues-influenced, his ears would perk right up. He already wanted to like the song before he'd even heard a lick of music because he was interested in furthering the blues genre. Similarly, if I knew what bands a programmer held close to their heart, I would draw a thread from any of those to the new music I was promoting, perhaps even citing them as an influence, prompting the programmer to listen with a more attentive ear. I also found it very effective to invite industry folks to the recording studio while a record was being made, so that they felt like they were a part of the process or at the least got in on the ground floor.

In the late 80s, Columbia signed a wonderful artist named Chris Whitley, who played authentic, blues-style music on Dobro steel resonator guitars and had a powerful, resonating voice to match. I invited a half-dozen key programmers down to the famed producer Daniel Lanois's recording studio in New Orleans to meet Chris and listen to some early tracks. This was especially important because, although Chris was an authentic artist, his music wasn't down-the-center rock. I would be asking programmers to creatively find a way to fit Chris's music into their rock mix.

Talk about being in a good mood to listen to music. As soon as we hit the French Quarter, we were transported to another world. Daniel's home studio was built in an old mansion and possessed some very trippy ambiance indeed. After a delicious Creole/Cajun meal and many handcrafted cocktails at a nearby restaurant, we went to the studio where Daniel's protégé, Malcolm Burn, played us some of the tracks that he and Chris were working on. The music was impressive. None of us had heard anything quite like it before, and everyone loved hanging out at that studio and meeting Chris, who was very humble, bordering on shy.

When we returned home, beyond having those programmers begin to spread the word about what they'd seen and heard to their radio friends, I took Chris on a road trip to some other cities, where he met and played a few songs in person for key radio personnel at stations known for setting the trends in new music. All were very impressed, not only with how genuine he was but also with the vintage Dobro guitars he was playing. At a big station in Denver, the program director had blown us off, sending word through his music director that he was too busy to see us. But when Chris opened his guitar case, the music director's eyes bugged out and he picked up the phone right away to call the PD.

'You're gonna want to come out and take the time to see this.'

All of these efforts took place before the big game, so to speak—before Chris's album was even released. By the time it came out, the garden had been tilled, watered, and given nutrients, and the sun was shining. Because we took the time to introduce Chris and his music to the industry's gatekeepers and let them feel involved with his artistry, they were willing to open their gates and bend their own rules and allow his style of music on their airwaves.

We garnered a lot of early support from the rock format, as well as from some of the stations that were beginning to lean in a singer/songwriter direction. The word spread that Chris Whitley was the real deal and worthy of attention. We had created built-in momentum. As the weeks went by, his music was added to many radio stations' playlists in an even flow across the country. Imagine how different it would have been if we had released his album cold and had to talk programmers into playing something this unique, one at a time, from scratch. Preparation, preparation, preparation.

Another key part of the puzzle was getting Chris on tour, ideally as an opening act with a headliner of substantial credibility. As luck would have it, Tom Petty was getting ready to go out on the road. Tom and his band, The Heartbreakers, were an elite bunch, and the list of artists who craved that opening slot was long. I knew all of their managers would be heavily lobbying Tom's manager, Tony Dimitriades, for that coveted position. The usual move is to bring someone on tour who is popular enough in their own right to help sell more concert tickets, but I knew Tom was a musician's musician, and if I could just get him to hear Chris's record, I was sure he'd be seriously moved—perhaps even moved enough to consider Chris as his opening act. I knew someone who knew someone, and I made sure Chris's album, *Living With The Law*, was put in Tom's hands. Sure enough, Chris's music won the day, and he went out on a coast-to-coast tour with Tom Petty.

I guess the successful end result of this entire play could be called *The Sting*, but I always felt it was more like *The Smile*. Another new artist launched.

Unfortunately, Chris Whitley isn't with us anymore—too many demons got the best of him. But we were friends, and I miss him to this day. One of his hobbies was sculpting with metal. I got excited when I'd find an old stovepipe or a cool tire rim in the street that I could present to him for his work. I loved watching his eyes light up and seeing that big grin as he thought, *Oh, I know what I can do with this thing!* Be sure to check out *Living With The Law*—in particular the title track, 'Big Sky Country,' and 'Poison Girl.' You will hear some of the best music ever made.

• ● •

Sometimes I had to resort to flat-out trickery when the organic approach to promotion wasn't possible.

I have loved the art of magic since watching my uncle Alvin Goodman blow minds in and around Miami when I was a kid. Uncle Alvin had taught me the basics, and I dabbled in magic until middle school. Right before Sharon and I left for New York, we visited the Magic Castle, a private club for magicians and their guests located at the base of the Hollywood Hills in a beautiful old Disney-like mansion.

That night, we witnessed a fabulous magician performing close-up magic on a table just a few feet from us using three coffee cups and three cherries he'd borrowed from the Castle's kitchen. The cups were turned upside-down, and the audience was amazed at how the cherries disappeared from the magician's hand one at a time, then wound up under the cups in different configurations. Everyone chuckled at the whimsical rhythm of the cherries disappearing and reappearing when, all of a sudden, the cups were lifted to reveal three large lemons, which had come out of nowhere. Right there and then, I decided I wanted to learn close-up magic.

One day, while I was visiting Harvey Leeds, whose office was on the floor above mine at Black Rock, I spied a magic wand. As I was leaving, I grabbed it.

'Hey, you can't take that!' he said, stopping me cold.

'Why? Are you into magic or somethin'?'

'As a matter of fact, I am. Big time.'

And thus began a wonderful friendship based around the magical arts. Harvey and I would visit and hang out with other magicians in two of the most famous magic stores in New York, Tannen's and Flosso's, buying diabolical tricks and sharing the secrets of magic. And then one day, Harvey announced, 'I'm going to take you to see the greatest close-up magician in the world.'

That Friday evening, we went down to a small club in the Village called Mostly Magic, where we and around fifty other audience members completely lost our minds watching the most unbelievable magic we'd ever seen. Large silver dollars seemingly melted through the magician's tabletop from one hand while being retrieved beneath the table with the other. An audience member tied two large white silks tightly together with multiple knots, one on top of another. With a simple wave of the hand, the knots vanished in the blink of an eye as the silks separated and fell to the table. A cigarette was ripped apart and magically restored. There was an invisible small purse—just a purse frame—from which the magician continually produced a run of beautiful red sponge balls. There were amazing card sleights and a wonderful illusion set to music where four white paper napkins were rolled into individual balls that disappeared elegantly in the magician's hands and then magically reappeared inside a once-empty box. Impossible! With the musical accompaniment, the trick played like a symphony.

The most amazing part of it all was that this magician had invented all of his own magic. His name was Tony Slydini, and he had taken his stage name in homage to the most famous magician of his era, the great Houdini.

At eighty years young, Slydini was known as the Master of Misdirection. I once saw him remove a loose button from Dick Cavett's jacket at a party, then mime sewing it back on with invisible thread. Upon close inspection, the thread became visible again, the button now stitched firmly back on. Cavett and the rest of us were gobsmacked.

Slydini had become a living legend in the world of magic, inventing sleight-of-hand moves that are still practiced today. The overall allure of his legerdemain was that it didn't come off as clever tricks: it looked like real magic.

We asked Slydini out for coffee after the show. He accepted our invitation, so we walked a few blocks to the oldest coffee house in New York, Café Reggio. Tony was also known for his charming Italian accent. When we arrived, he issued his famous cordial welcome: 'I'm-a gonna show you something you not-a gonna believe.' There, while we sat in an old wooden booth beneath the original copper-paneled ceiling, sipping espressos, Slydini performed mind-boggling card effects right in front of our faces for four hours straight.

When I discovered Slydini gave lessons, I decided to give him a call.

'If-a you wanna come to just-a learn a few tricks,' he told me in that endearing accent, 'don't come-a to see me. But if-a you wanna learn the *art* of-a magic, the true secrets of the craft, then come see me.'

I studied magic with the master at his home studio on 45th Street every other week for two and a half years. I felt like a Jedi Knight being taught by Yoda. The secrets I learned allowed me to leapfrog to an elite level of magic. I practiced for endless hours, and eventually Tony sponsored my entry into the Society Of American Magicians—the oldest magic club in America, founded by Harry Houdini himself—and also the Magic Castle in Hollywood, where I remain a member to this day. In fact, I recently loaned a rare painting of Slydini to the Castle. You can now see the great magician, seemingly in action, on your left as you enter the Close-Up room.

Magic would become a big part of my life in general, and it also turned out to be much appreciated in my business. After dinner at a fine restaurant with a program director and his wife, it became quite natural for me to perform a half-hour of magic during dessert. Certain artists I worked with looked forward to my card sleights—Bob Dylan, in particular. We once got into a discussion about performance and mechanics, and how, no matter how you feel on any given night, it is the muscle memory of the mind and the body that sees you through to a great show. Bob said he'd learned that from watching Frank Sinatra.

'Paul,' he declared, 'you and I are doing the exact same thing!'

'I get where you're going with this, Bob,' I replied, 'but whatever we're doing, I assure you, we are not doing the exact same thing.'

He laughed.

One of the most valuable lessons Slydini taught was this:

'The audience believes what *you* believe. If you appear to place a coin from your right hand into your left, even if you secrete it somewhere else, your eyes must follow the make-believe coin into your left hand. You must stare at the closed fist, point to it, make magical gestures around it—you must *believe* the coin is in there. If you believe it, the audience will believe it too. When you open your hand with a little flourish and the audience sees that the coin has vanished, they will gasp.'

• ● •

This master's secret came in very handy when I was charged with promoting a live recording Columbia issued in 1989 of Dylan performing with the Grateful Dead.

As we've already established, I consider Bob Dylan to be the greatest music artist of my generation—of many generations. The sheer number of iconic songs this one man has written is staggering. Many compare him to Shakespeare, who is widely regarded as the greatest writer in the English language and the world's greatest dramatist. For my money, Bob Dylan might just be one better than Shakespeare.

The Grateful Dead, known for playing twenty-minute jams in between some of the most trippy and alluring songs ever written, were a band like no other. *There is nothing like a Grateful Dead concert*, so the bumper sticker goes, and indeed there wasn't. Their brand of rock, country-rock, blues, and a hint of bluegrass, fashioned through psychedelic LSD trips, took listeners to an almost spiritual place. Whether you were high or not (high preferred), you could dance all night with the biggest smile on your face during their jubilant four-hour (minimum) concerts. There was a magic that seemed to come from above and would shower over every Dead show. The long jams were musical journeys, the band communicating with each other, pushing the music to gleeful, euphoric heights, not unlike the Sufi music of the whirling dervishes. The exultant end of a lofty Jerry Garcia guitar solo, propelled by the driving forces of Bob Weir, Phil Lesh, Ron 'Pig Pen' McKernan, Bill Kreutzmann, and Micky Hart, would bring unbridled cheers from their audiences. A Grateful Dead concert could leave you grinning for a month. To get a glimpse of the magic from the many live recordings available, I recommend starting with *Grateful Dead (Skull & Roses)*, *Europe '72*, and *Dick's Picks* volumes 1–4.

When I heard there was going to be a collaboration between Bob Dylan and the Grateful Dead, I was ecstatic. The idea of hearing Dylan's songs backed up by the Dead, with Jerry Garcia's soaring lead guitar solos between Bob's verses, was almost too much to handle. The idea of Bob singing some Dead songs was just as intriguing. Their collaborative album was going to be recorded live during a stadium tour that featured both artists doing separate sets and then playing together and was set to feature seven Dylan songs backed by the Dead. I was over the moon, and I couldn't wait to hear it.

When I finally received an advance test pressing, I told my assistant to hold all my calls and put the record on. It didn't sound as good as I thought it would, and the more I heard it, the worse it got. My heart sank. The truth was that it wasn't very good at all. In fact, it was awful.

Maybe it's just me, I thought. *Let me listen to it again.*

But no. Whatever this experiment looked like on paper, it just didn't work in real life—at least not at the shows this album was culled from. I later heard that Bob hadn't wanted to rehearse much and preferred to do everything on the fly. That was plausible—he has always liked to keep things fresh and authentic, his backup bands having to learn to follow him through last-minute changes of tempo, key, and arrangement that can take place at any time during a live performance—but I don't know the real story. Maybe he and the Dead were just not on their game on the evenings these recordings were made.

Whatever the case, their collaboration just didn't click. But I was in charge of promoting the album, and I dearly loved both artists. Sometimes I would view my job as taking care of and protecting artists' careers while they were experiencing a rough patch or had strayed into some kind of controversy. And I would have to figure out a way to put a shine on this project.

If you read about this album on Wikipedia, you'll find that it was trashed by all the major music magazines of the time. You'll also read that, 'though ultimately poorly received, the album initially sold well . . . earning a gold certification.'

How did this happen? How could an album that missed the mark so badly go gold? The answer is: with a magic trick.

With a bit of luck, I had two incredible images that would help me better sell *Dylan & The Dead* to radio. First, someone had taken a striking photo of Bob surrounded by the members of the Grateful Dead. Everyone in the photo looks great; they're smiling and full of energy. It's a powerful image. Second, the album cover was fantastic. Art directed by Rick Griffin, it features a colorful illustration of an old Western-style train coming down the tracks, straight at you. It looked similar to the train on the cover of Bob's *Slow Train Coming*, and to the Deadheads it also connoted the song 'Casey Jones.' To the left of the train is the familiar Dead image of a skeleton head wrapped in a wreath of roses, and to the right there is the familiar image of Bob with his big curly hair and dark sunglasses. Across the top, in a bright red and yellow comic-book typeface, is the title, *DYLAN & THE DEAD*. The entire image bursts toward you as if exploding out of a fireworks display in the sky.

Usually, when I got an advance copy of a record, I would start playing it for programmers as soon as I could, to help set up the project. This extra time would give programmers a chance to sit and listen to the new music with ease and make up their minds about which tracks to play, long before the release date. But for *Dylan & The Dead*, I did the opposite.

Just as I had hoped, there was great anticipation and excitement from radio and fans about this collaboration—everyone was chomping at the bit to hear it. Even though I knew the truth, I started to hype the coming of this album like there was no tomorrow. I took out two large, full-page ads in the trades. Week one featured the compelling band photo, and week two presented the powerful album cover, both with huge headlines announcing, 'DYLAN & THE DEAD—COMING SOON!!'

When I spoke to the programmers, I had to tell a white lie, as sometimes we do in magic (yeah, the coin is really there).

'Man, I can't wait to hear this thing!' someone would say.

'Me too!' I would agree. 'My all-time favorite artist is Bob Dylan, and I'm a *huge* Deadhead. I think it's gonna be amazing!'

I stoked their imaginations, and they believed what I appeared to believe. I felt a tad guilty, but I was at least telling half of the truth—I really *had* been excited to hear it.

I explained the situation and the strategy during our weekly conference with all the local guys.

'You will receive your allotment of albums to take to radio the usual two weeks before release. But here's the plan. *Do not* bring this album to your stations until Tuesday, the 'add day' for this record. In fact, don't even bring it in the morning—bring it to them late in the afternoon and tell them it's hot off the presses!'

In my calls to programmers, I 'explained' that the producers were still mixing the album. It would be a rush release. 'God,' I'd add, 'I can't wait to hear this thing!'

On release day, the magic began. My guys rushed the records to their stations late in the afternoon, and the programmers were caught off guard.

'Wow, it's finally here!' the program directors would tell their music directors. 'Look, we don't have time to listen now, but I'm sure it must be great. Pick your three favorite songs and add those tracks to the playlist right away!'

Boom! Overnight, *Dylan & The Dead* was getting heavy airplay everywhere, coast to coast. Fans who also wanted to believe that this album was going to be something very special rushed into the record stores to buy it as soon as they heard it on the radio.

After a couple of weeks, I began to hear from some of the programmers who were hearing the record for the first time as it was being played over their airwaves.

'Rap, I gotta tell ya, this record isn't as good as I thought it was gonna be.'

Now I could take a breath and tell the truth.

'Yeah, I know. I'm disappointed myself. I don't know what happened, but if you want, you can start backing off it slowly. I won't ask you to hammer it any longer.'

But the job was done. There had been enough excitement and heavy airplay right out the gate that in just under a month, the album generated an instant gold record—five hundred thousand copies sold! The Dylan camp was happy, the Dead camp was happy, the record label was happy, and, needless to say, I was thrilled. And, like a good magician, I was able to keep my credibility without giving away the secret. Just as Slydini had taught me, everyone came to believe what I believed—and for just long enough to make the project a success.

● ● ●

The 'fastball' could also come under the heading of trickery. But this next scheme wasn't so much about psychology as about mathematics, once again, and having great relationships with radio. At any rate, it worked like a charm, although it also inadvertently shook up the rock world, discombobulated the album charts, and caused considerable consternation among our competitors.

Tommy Conwell and his band, The Young Rumblers, hailed from the great music city of Philadelphia. We'd already had really good luck with another Philly group, Scandal, fronted by Patty Smyth, and also with The Hooters. In fact, stop reading this and immediately go listen to 'All You Zombies' and 'And We Danced.' You'll become an instant fan. There's something in the water in Philly.

Tommy was an exciting, Springsteen-esque performer. During club performances, he'd jump off the stage and walk across the tables and up and down the entire stretch of the bar, all the while wailing on his guitar. He danced around everyone's drinks, never missing a beat, and never knocked over a single one.

By 1988, Jim McKeon had been tapped by RCA Records to become the label's head of rock promotion. We hated parting ways, but it was a great advancement for him, and I wished him all the best. To replace Mac, I brought back our very talented former New York promotion man, Jim 'Rocky' Del Balzo, following a brief stint at MTV. The nickname Rocky was given to him early on by a Little League baseball coach, long before Sylvester Stallone made it synonymous with his movies. He was small in stature but had such a big personality and was so funny. All the artists and everyone in radio loved him.

I also promoted Alan Oreman, affectionately known as 'AO,' from Atlanta to be the third member of our album rock team, moving him to Los Angeles to give us a presence there. There was great synergy between us. Rocky, AO, and I excelled at getting our records played and creating excitement for our new acts.

When Tommy Conwell & The Young Rumblers came along, we knew we had something special, and we couldn't wait to introduce them to the rock radio community. The lead track from their debut album, *Rumble*, was a song called 'I'm Not Your Man.' We invited a number of radio programmers from across the country to Philly to see Tommy and the band rip it up in their hometown. I remember it being a wild night. Once again my smart and thoughtful assistant, Cathy, made something wonderful happen. She arranged for everyone to be taken to the show on one of those big red double-decker buses from England. It turned into quite an adventure as there was a very heavy downpour of rain that evening and we had an untamed driver. People were hanging off the sides of the bus as the guy insisted on careening around corners at breakneck speeds to get us to and from the show. We all got soaking wet, but we made it back to our hotel unscathed, save for a bruise here and there.

Tommy and the band killed it that night, and 'I'm Not Your Man' took off like a shot. My good friends at Philadelphia's WMMR-FM, program director Ted Utz and music director Erin Riley, led the charge with heavy spins, and after a few good weeks of airplay across the country, the listener response was pretty good, but it wasn't quite over the top. 'I'm Not Your Man' didn't feel like a bona-fide hit, but it seemed destined to become what we call a 'mid-chart' record—one that won't garner enough heavy rotations to make it past #20 on the rock singles chart.

Our radio friends liked the way the song sounded on the air, and they were open to helping us out, giving Tommy more spins each week in hopes that momentum would build. We successfully worked the song into the teens, then the Top 10, and finally we got the record to #5 on the charts, which felt extraordinary. Everyone at Columbia was excited, and everyone else in the industry was taking notice, because 'I'm Not Your Man' wasn't an organic Top 5 record, and it looked out of place on the chart in the middle of superstars like Foreigner, Bon Jovi, ZZ Top, and The Rolling Stones. Getting this song by a brand-new artist to #5 was clearly the work of a great promotion team, calling in all their favors and asking for weekly increased rotations.

Rocky and I were ready to take a big bow in the weekly singles meeting, where the heads of all the different promotion departments—Top 40, rock, adult, urban, jazz, and so on—report to the president on how their records are faring across the country and explain their gameplans on how to move each project forward for the next week. Having done the virtually impossible in taking a record that usually would have died at #22 on the chart to the Top 5, Rocky and I were beaming with pride, ready for a big 'thank you' from Columbia's president at that time, Tommy Mottola.

'Great job guys, absolutely great,' Mottola began, but then he added, 'I want to cross this record over to the Top 40 format, and I need it to go #1 at rock radio.'

What?!

Rocky and I looked at each other, panic-stricken. Our jaws dropped. We didn't know what to say. Getting this record to the Top 5 was a miracle. To now leapfrog over four of the biggest superstar artists in the world with a brand-new band and a track that every single rock programmer in the country had already completely burnt out would require nothing short of divine intervention. But when the president of Columbia Records asks you to do something, you don't tell him why it can't happen—you figure out how to make it happen.

We went back to Rocky's office to discuss.

'Okay, genius,' I quipped. 'What the hell are we gonna do now? The freakin' record shouldn't even be Top 5, and everyone wants to drop it off their playlists this week.'

Rocky and I were well known for hatching creative plans to achieve our goals, but this one was a doozy. As I've already mentioned, the charts worked by simple math. The record that got the most reported heavy rotations in a week was the one that went to #1. We knew that with everyone being so fried on the track already, there was no way we could convince any more stations to put it in heavy rotation for a week. But what if we asked our friends at radio to take one last ride with us and play 'I'm Not Your Man' in heavy rotation for just one day? And what if that day was Tuesday, the day that all radio stations reported their airplay to the trade magazines? We called the idea 'Heavy For A Day.'

We started working the phones the very next morning—Rocky, AO, myself, and our local staff. A typical conversation with a programmer would go like this:

'Hi, it's Rap. Look I know you are totally burned out playing "I'm Not Your Man," but could you just do me one last little favor? I don't care what rotation the record is in now, but could you put the song into heavy rotation for just a single day? After that, you can completely drop the record off your playlist—you don't even have to back it down slowly if you don't want.'

'You mean all you want me to do is play it in heavy rotation for *one* day?

Sure, I can do that. Is there any particular day you want me to do it?'

'Yeah, can you do it this coming Tuesday?'

'Sure, no problem.'

I swear, 70 percent of the programmers we talked to didn't even know what we were doing, and they probably could have cared less if they did.

In the world of radio promotion, Monday is the most important day to make your last pitches before Tuesday's reports to the trades. As it turned out, that coming Monday was the beginning of the Jewish High Holidays, and I had to be in synagogue, talking to a much higher authority than Tommy Mottola, so Rocky and AO had to make the bulk of the calls to remind stations to please play Tommy Conwell's record in heavy rotation the next day. That's a ton of work and a ton of asking. All I could do was sit in the synagogue, having a private discussion with God.

'Hi, look, I know I'm only supposed to talk to you about family and pray for things like good health, but if you happen to have a #1 record up there and you're not using it, I sure could use it this week!'

I came back to work on Tuesday, and by the afternoon, after checking the radio stations' reports to *R&R*, it looked like we were going to pull off a miracle. Then Rocky looked at me, wild-eyed, like he'd just thought of something hugely important.

'Oh shit!' he exclaimed. 'I gotta call Bon Jovi!'

'Why?' I asked. Rocky and Jon Bon Jovi were good friends.

'Because he's sitting at #2 on the chart with his new hit song, and he thinks he's going to go #1 tomorrow!'

'Uh-oh. Do you think it's a good idea to call him?'

'Well, he's gonna be real upset either way, and I just think he'd appreciate a heads up.'

Then I heard one of the most amazing conversations ever.

'Hi Jon, Rocky here. Hey, listen, I know you think you're gonna go to #1 tomorrow, but Tommy asked me and Rap to do something, and we had to do it . . . so one of our records is going to *kind of* slide into that spot.'

I could hear screaming on the other end of the phone: 'WHAT?! Tommy told you to do WHAT?! What the hell are you talking about?! I'm going to be #1 tomorrow!'

'Well, Jon . . . you're kinda not.'

More screaming and now profane language blasting out of the phone.

'Yeah, yeah, I know. Look, it's just something we had to do.'

And then came the most amazing line of all.

'But it's okay, Jon. You can be #1 next week.'

I looked at Rocky.

'Did you just tell Jon Bon Jovi *when* he can be #1? I mean like, do we really have that much power?'

We both looked at each other in amazement, because yeah, for that one day, we kinda did.

As sure as you're born, on Wednesday morning, when the charts became available, Tommy Conwell & The Young Rumblers' 'I'm Not Your Man' had blown like a fastball right past four of the biggest rock stars in the world and rocketed to #1. We were jumping up and down in the office like little kids.

We did look like geniuses for that moment, but there was one thing we hadn't considered. When a record makes an abhorrent jump like that, it shoves every other artist on the chart *down*. Uh-oh. All the other labels and artists who'd figured Tommy's was the record that was going to slide that week and were looking forward to moving up on the chart had now all been pushed *backward*! Worse, when records move backward on the chart, radio programmers view them as over and start to drop them from their playlists. Uh-oh indeed.

All fucking hell broke loose. Our phones started ringing off the hook. Heads of promotion from Warner Bros, Elektra, Atlantic, A&M—you name it, they were all calling us up, screaming their guts out.

'What the hell did you guys do?! Who did you pay off? That's illegal! This can't be happening!'

The whole industry was going crazy. Every other promotion team had to scramble to call all the rock stations to assure them that their records weren't failing—it was just that the charts had gone screwy this week. Rival record company presidents were calling Mottola's office, and the managers of the artists affected were calling all of us as well. We took a lot of heat that day. But Mottola loved it. And Rocky, AO, and I felt like we'd accomplished the impossible. The truth is, we had.

DAMAGE
CONTROL

ONE OF THE THINGS I'm asked about most often is payola. Yes, it did exist, but thankfully not on my side of things. As I've mentioned, the unspoken quid pro quo was that we would give the rock stations plenty of albums, concert tickets, and extravagant promotions to help increase their listenership and, in return, they took a chance on playing some of our up-and-coming acts as well as our superstars.

Top 40 is where the cash flowed. But I want to make an important point. Not many disc jockeys or PDs were really on the take. Yeah, there were a handful of them, but really what happened was that local independent promotion men across the country sidled up to their local Top 40 stations and simply asked them to report what they were going to add to their stations before letting the labels know. This gave the indies some real power. Not only could they give our promotion execs early info on what records were being added, but they could also steer these stations into what to play next each week by giving them a fair assessment of how each label's records were building across the country.

We hired these independents more for insurance so that they would keep our records at the forefront of the conversation. If there was any funny business going on, we on the label side would be exempt from prosecution. We were only giving money to the independents. What they did with it afterward was none of our business. And every label hired them for the same reason. You can see the insanity of it all: if *every* label is paying these guys, who has any real advantage? The cost of a hit single in the 1980s was at least $150,000 per record. Now, think about how many singles were being worked at the same time by all the different record companies that existed during that heyday. We're talking millions and millions of dollars. It's the biggest scam I ever saw in my life.

There was one time when I thought a dirty deal was going down, and with one of my biggest heroes. As indicated previously, sometimes a band or manager would rub an important radio programmer the wrong way. This was obviously not helpful at a time of much-needed airplay for a new release, but such was the case during the mid-80s with our brand-new Judas Priest album, *Turbo*.

Judas Priest were on a huge roll at the time and had become a superstar act. Their music was prominent on rock radio, and they were selling out arenas. We had done so much good work with them over the years that now, when they released a new album, it just flew on to radio, with very little help needed. They had earned the right to an 'automatic add.'

'Turbo Lover,' a song that combined the band's love for Porsches with sexual innuendo (cars, speed, and sex—always a good combo for a great rock song) was flying high. I watched with glee as it took only two weeks for the entire rock panel of 152 radio stations to be playing the new record. Well, almost. Make that 151. For some reason, by the third week, WNEW-FM in New York still wasn't playing the record. Priest had always been popular on the station, so something seemed amiss. I decided to call mega-legend disc jockey and music director Scott Muni, who had become a good friend, to find out what was up. I discovered that indeed, they weren't playing the record, and worse, they had no intention of doing so.

'Fats,' he began in his deep gravelly voice, 'I'm not playing this record because Bill Curbishley threw me out of the backstage party after The Who's last concert here.' (Fats was a term of endearment Scott used for anyone who felt like family to him, and Curbishley was Judas Priest's storied manager.)

'Huh? I've never heard of a manager throwing out *any* radio person from backstage, especially if that person is named Scott Muni.'

'He said I was unruly,' Scott replied, becoming more upset as he relived the scene in his memory.

'Well, you must have been quite a handful, given the fact that Bill manages the king of unruly, Keith Moon!' Amongst a long list of insane behavior, Keith was famous for blowing up hotel toilets with cherry bombs. 'Look, we have to have a sit-down. This can't stand, and you two need to work it out for larger reasons than just this one record. You guys are supposed to be friends. Will you go to a lunch with Bill?

'Yeah, but only if you're there.'

'Of course, I'll be there.'

Then I called Bill in England.

'Everything is going great guns here,' I told him, 'except we have one problem. WNEW isn't playing the record because Scott says you threw him out of The Who's backstage party last time around. I'm having trouble believing that.'

'I threw him out, all right,' Bill replied. 'He was being unruly.'

'Come on, Bill, this is rock'n'roll. Rock'n'roll is unruly by nature—hell, Moonie *invented* unruly! And Scott Muni is the fucking king of New York rock radio. Of all the people to throw out!'

Now I was upset. But something really bad must have gone down between these two because Bill seemed even more upset than Scott. And Bill Curbishley is one tough cookie, not to be messed with. Nonetheless, I asked if he'd go to lunch with Scott.

'Sure, but only if you come too.'

Bill was flying to New York on business in a couple of weeks, so I set up a lunch at Scott's favorite watering hole, the Delegate. Scott was known as the king of rock radio in New York because WNEW-FM was the only place you could discover a new band or artist. Its competitor, WPLJ, enjoyed better ratings but was more like a jukebox, just playing the hits and adding new artists only after they were proven and well-established. Scott had quite an ear for music, and he would go out on a limb playing new bands and helping them break through. He singlehandedly launched the careers of our beloved Psychedelic Furs, for one, not only by playing their first album but by asking them to perform at the huge WNEW Christmas Show at Radio City Music Hall.

Scott was like a father to us record folks. A common salutation would include a built-in desire for our preservation: '*Hey, Fats, is everything okay for you at the label? If anyone gives you a hard time over there, let me know, and I'll straighten them out.*' I was constantly heaping free concert tickets and promotions his way to thank him. But God help you if you crossed him.

You became persona non grata. Once, I asked him why I hadn't heard Joni Mitchell's new album on the station.

'Warner Bros are really pissing me off,' he replied, again in that deep familiar growl. 'I'm waiting to see how long it takes for them to realize that nobody is buying her record in New York because nobody knows it's out.'

The lunch between heavyweights like Curbishley and Muni was going to need some kind of levity if it had a chance at succeeding. I knew I was going to have to be the referee, so I went out and bought an official NHL hockey referee's jersey, featuring black-and-white stripes and orange armbands, along with a referee's whistle. I hid the jersey under a large sports jacket and set out for the Delegate.

My plan was to arrive early, before any fireworks could start. Scott was already there at the bar, already working on his second drink. I kept my greeting light, and not too long after, Bill came walking through the front door. His eyes immediately met Scott's. Both men locked into each other's gaze, scowling with indignation. Bill walked briskly toward us, Scott got up off the bar stool, and it looked like they might throw punches. As soon as Bill got to within arm's length of Scott, I quickly threw off my sports coat to reveal the ref's jersey, stretched my arms out to hold each of them at bay, and blew my ref's whistle as loud as I could.

It was earsplitting. Everyone in the restaurant stopped what they were doing and looked up. There was total silence . . . then insane laughter. People at the bar and throughout the restaurant were cracking up. Bill and Scott's mouths dropped open. There was nothing left for them to do but shake their heads and have a laugh themselves. But although I'd broken the ice, when we sat down for lunch, things began to heat up again quickly.

'I can't believe you threw me out of backstage!' Scott seethed. 'ME!'

'Scott, you were really out of control,' Bill replied, looking a bit embarrassed but just as pissed off.

'Out of control?' I said, stepping in to try to lighten things up by reminding him of some of the things Keith Moon would get up to. 'Couldn't have been worse than blowing up toilets with sticks of dynamite, keeping piranha fish in his bathtub, or axing an entire hotel suite full of furniture to smithereens, could it?'

That got a bit of a snicker.

'Okay,' Bill said, 'what's it gonna take to fix this?'

'It's gonna cost you,' Scott replied.

'How much?'

'Ten thousand dollars.'

My heart sank. One of my all-time heroes—a man who fought for music and the people around him, a man who always did the right thing— was on the take? Oh, no. I was gonna be sick.

Then, Scott added, 'Make the check out to the T.J. Martell Foundation.'

The T.J. Martell Foundation was the music industry's leading charity, providing funding for innovative research for the cure of leukemia, cancer, and AIDS. It was founded by Tony Martell, a top executive at the Epic label, whose son, T.J., had died of leukemia when he was only twenty-one. He'd been a good friend of Scott's.

Without missing a beat, without even a thought, Bill looked Scott right in the eye.

'Done,' he said, putting out his hand, and that was when I witnessed the ten-thousand-dollar handshake. It was heavy.

I let out a long breath and smiled inside. My hero had become even more of a hero. And Bill Curbishley had been a class act. Emotions calmed, and we all settled down to a nice lunch. Scott played a new track from *Turbo* that afternoon. And, once again, everything was as it should be in the land of rock'n'roll.

• ● •

I had been working with Rob Halford and Judas Priest since they debuted their first album on Columbia Records in 1977. I used to tease Rob that he hit notes only a dog could hear. You couldn't find a nicer bunch of guys, though at one point, the idea of 'nice' metal bands always used to throw me. The first time I saw Priest in person was their Los Angeles debut at the Whisky A Go-Go. They looked like dangerous motherfuckers who could shove a shiv into your side when you weren't looking, just for fun. It was the same as with Blue Öyster Cult—they were tough guys in leather and spikes, but when you went backstage, you'd overhear Eric Bloom on the phone to his wife, asking if the kids had made it to Hebrew school okay. Huh?

The thing about Judas Priest is that although the music is heavy, there is always a strong melody attached which stays with you and is easy to sing along with. How many times have I caught myself singing, '*Breaking the law!*' or screaming, '*You don't know what it's like!*' at the top of my lungs while speeding on the expressway?

When I got to know the band, I realized that although they were genuine in their look and approach to the metal art form, they didn't live their everyday lives in leather and spikes. Some of their stage wear was reminiscent of the chainmail armor worn by knights of old, and sometimes, for fun, they'd give me pieces of their costumes to bring home to my kids, who wore them when playing as medieval soldiers. It was fascinatingly strange to see the same dark black, silver-grommeted vests, arm cuffs, and belts, first onstage in a heavy metal performance and then the very next day on my kids as they ran around with toy swords and bows and arrows.

During the band's early years, guitarist Glen Tipton was an able player but still learning. After I got to know him, he confided in me that he'd grown up in a working-class industrial community and was looking for a way out. I'll never forget his exact words: 'I'm trying *this* now to see if it works.' Like so many, Glen found his vocation by necessity. At first, K. K. Downing played all the leads and Glen played straight rhythm. Over time, and with a lot of practice, Glen got so good that he started taking over many of the lead solos. The result was a double whammy tour de force of guitar power onstage.

With their first five albums on Columbia, although they always had great tracks for album rock radio—gems like 'Exciter,' 'The Green Manalishi (With the Two-Pronged Crown),' 'Breaking The Law,' and 'Living After Midnight'—Priest couldn't sell much more than a gold album. By 1982, their stage show had been building nicely, they were on the cusp of headlining arenas, and they desperately wanted to break into platinum status. I told them I was of the same mind. We were about to release *Screaming For Vengeance*, which was at least three tracks deep with high-powered rock singles. I told them that one of them, 'You've Got

Another Thing Comin',' might even have a shot as a crossover Top 40 hit.

'Tell you what, man,' they replied excitedly, 'if you get us a platinum album, we'll buy you a top-of-the-line motorcycle jacket, just like the one Rob wears.'

I thanked them and told them it wasn't necessary. But if they *really* had their minds set, I added, though I wasn't the motorcycle jacket type, I had been promising myself a cool-looking bomber jacket.

We cranked up the promotion machine at Columbia with a vengeance (pun intended), and the music immediately blew up big time on rock radio. We rode that album all summer long. 'You've Got Another Thing Comin'' was released as a single in August of that year and helped propel the album far beyond one million copies sold.

The accompanying tour ran through February of 1983. That spring, a box showed up at my office. No phone call, no message, just a mysterious box. I opened it. Inside, there was a note:

We can't thank you enough. Cheers! Judas Priest.

Under the note was the most beautiful brown leather bomber jacket you could imagine. To even remember the conversation, much less go out and shop for a bomber jacket, told me all I needed to know about what kind of people these guys were.

As Judas Priest grew in popularity and began to make some real money, the band members decided to take up golf. Of course, this was not in keeping with their image. One evening, I went backstage to say hello before a show, and there they were, all dressed in full-on black leather and spikes, but also putting golf balls on a little makeshift green they carried with them on the road. It was a pretty funny sight.

'Shut the door!' they shouted. 'And don't you dare tell anyone!'

I never would, of course, but they made me swear to them that I wouldn't. I thought it was cute—and hey, Alice Cooper had been into golf and beer years before, when both were thought of as unconscionable for any authentic hard rock metal artist, and he did just fine.

Judas Priest were not the only ones having fun on the road. When you went backstage in any arena to visit them, the band's dressing room would be on one side of the hall, and directly opposite would be a large room for the roadies and technical crew. This was where the amplifiers, guitars, and sound and lighting equipment would be repaired when needed. That was if you looked to the right side of the tech room. But if you looked left, you would see an entire section cordoned off for the building and repairing of large-scale model rockets! After their band work was completed (hopefully), the road crew spent their off-hours building and launching these beautiful black-and-silver Estes missiles high into the sky, retrieving them via parachutes that popped out after a finished flight. Think about it: what better place is there to launch and retrieve rockets than an empty giant arena parking lot?

Back then, having fun was a job requirement, and Judas Priest and their road entourage were getting their share. The whole thing was rock like it ought to be. And every heavy metal band I've worked with cites Judas Priest as one of their two most major influences. As of this writing, they are still selling out arenas.

For the ultimate heavy metal experience, put on the first two tracks from *Screaming For Vengeance*, 'The Hellion' segueing into 'Electric Eye.' Crank up the volume—your head will explode. Then put on the title track and repeat—and, for any shredders out there, take note of the guitar solos.

• ● •

Along with Judas Priest, the other band always cited as a major influence by metal acts is Iron Maiden. In 1990, a year when the other members of Maiden were taking some time off, frontman Bruce Dickinson recorded his first solo album, *Tattooed Millionaire*. When he and I began talking about plans for this release, we found we had a surprising shared love: fencing.

I had learned to fence in the mid-1970s with a famous Hollywood master named Ralph Faulkner. Ralph had competed at the Olympics in 1928 and 1932 and went on to teach fencing to actors for the big movie studios. He choreographed countless fencing scenes for movies and television, doubled as a stuntman, and sometimes appeared as the lead actor himself when there was a requirement to show off the real thing.

The most intense person I've ever met, other than Bruce Springsteen, is Bruce Dickinson. No matter what he is attempting to do, whether it's being the energetic frontman for Iron Maiden, piloting the band's Boeing 757 jumbo jet, or fencing, he is out to kick ass and take names. When we decided to have a go, I believe he was rated as England's seventh-best foil fencer. He carried his gear with him on the road, and he kept in shape by practicing his footwork in the long hallways of the hotels where he and the band stayed. As for myself, I had become a competitive épée fencer (using a traditional rapier-style dueling blade). I wasn't the best, but I could hold my own. I finished in the top third during competitions and won bronze and silver medals.

Ever keen to push the WTF envelope, I suggested we suit up and have a bout down the hallway of the twelfth floor. I was sure we'd get some smiles and definitely some raised eyebrows. We looked quite regal in our fresh white uniforms, replete with white gloves and fencing masks. We fought our way down past the promotion and marketing offices, blades slashing and clashing all the way. People stopped working and looked up in amazement. As far out as the record business could get, it wasn't every day you saw a sword fight happening right outside your door. Folks ran out of their offices and began to take sides, cheering for their favorite swordsman.

I pushed Dickinson back into the corner office of our celebrated head of marketing, the self-proclaimed 'lovely and talented' Bob Sherwood. In a dazzling display of swordplay, Bruce let me drive him back further, before falling backward over Bob's desk to complete the effect. Our blades were now grinding against each other just a few feet from Sherwood's face, the sunlight shining through the large windows reflecting brightly off our swords. It was Errol Flynn all the way!

Bob was no stranger to off-the-wall antics himself. He was known for his outrageous entrances and presentations at our conventions, his most famous show-stopping moment being when he walked into a large ballroom in front of the entire company wearing nothing but a speedo, covered from head to toe in gold paint, to the sound of 'Goldfinger.' When the spotlight hit him, the entire convention audience rose and gave him a standing ovation.

Bob will love this, I thought. But he was on the phone at the time, looking none too happy, and our fencing frolic didn't seem to be changing his mood. Then it dawned on me: *He doesn't even know who we are, because we're wearing fencing masks! Hell, this could be just anybody randomly fencing their way into his office.* Not taking into account the fact that he might be on an important call, I figured that as soon as I revealed myself, Bob would crack up, for sure. I took off my mask, breathing heavily, matted hair, sweaty. But when he saw who I was, Bob looked even less pleased.

Uh-oh, I thought. *No help here.*

I'm not sure if it was the phone call or whether fencing in the hallways was just a bit too over-the-top in a world where bowling in the hallways was much more accepted.

'Rap?! What the fuck?!'

Then Bruce took his mask off and smiled at Bob.

'Dickinson!'

Sherwood looked back and forth at each of us.

'You guys are gonna kill somebody!'

Yep, I got it now—this was definitely worse than bowling.

'Get the fuck outta here! And get off the twelfth floor, NOW!'

Jeez, another great plan gone awry.

We were being forced off the twelfth floor, but we still wanted to fence. Someone told us there was an entire floor under construction that was not currently being used by anyone. We crammed ourselves into the elevator, along with a gaggle of new fencing fans, and pushed the button. Sure enough, when we reached our destination, we all tumbled out to find the floor was completely vacant. This was where the real fencing took place.

We elected to use épées first. Because I was much taller than Dickinson and it was my weapon of choice, I had the advantage. In épée, the taller person has the upper hand because of their reach. More of a dueling sword, it's easier to wait and keep your opponent at bay while you gauge his attack. But Dickinson was so fast it was hard for me to get a handle on his timing. He kept lurching inside quickly, flying past my blade—it drove me nuts. I adjusted giving myself more distance, but the guy had the legs of a boxer, and we were dead even at the end of the bout.

Then we switched to foils. The foil game, using a lighter blade, is even faster, and I was no match for England's #7 best. Bruce was bobbing, weaving, feinting, and then suddenly dashing forward at blinding speeds. He was twice as fast as anyone I'd ever encountered. Within minutes, I was Swiss cheese. My height no longer gave me any advantage, and it was hard to gauge his attacks with him moving back and forth so quickly. In less than three minutes, the score was something like 7 to 2—I was getting killed. To save face, I took off my mask, looked him in the eye, and said, 'You've made your point, pun intended, I'm done.'

We shook hands and exchanged the traditional fencer's reverence after a bout, 'Nice fencing.' Then we went back to work and figured out which track to release first from *Tattooed Millionaire*.

· ● ·

There's no doubt that I've had many varied interests in my life. I admit to being a hopeless romantic, and I was simply enamored during my formative years by these passions. The cool thing is that it felt quite natural when these extracurricular activities helped create more meaningful bonds with artists and industry people over the years. Who knew I'd share so much with so many? As well as Bruce Dickinson, I also became fencing pals with Canadian folk-rock icon Bruce Cockburn, and I turned Billy Joel's tour manager, Jeff Schock, onto the sport. I surfed with key radio execs and Journey's Steve Perry, exchanged card sleights with Rick Rubin and Dave Edmunds, produced a magic illusion with Will Smith in front of the Virgin Megastore on Broadway, and played guitar alongside some very top-notch musicians and rock stars. All of it felt like it was meant to happen.

One day, a good friend of mine, music executive Pam Edwards, remarked, 'You're the only painting, guitar playing, surfing, fencing, magician I know.'

I guess she was right!

50 CHOCOLATE SOUFFLES

IN A BUSINESS chock-full of eccentric personalities, none loomed larger than some of the artist managers I encountered. We've already met Loverboy's tough guy Bruce Allen and Judas Priest's even tougher guy Bill Curbishley. Here are a few more standouts.

In the mid-60s, Steve Paul owned a popular club in New York called the Scene. A music pioneer and entrepreneur, he also hosted a local television show by the same name. Each week, you were invited via your TV into the club and could watch performances and jam sessions with up-and-coming artists like Moby Grape, The Blues Project, The Doors, and Jimi Hendrix.

In 1973, Steve created Blue Sky Records, a custom label for Columbia, and started to manage artists. Two of the most notable were Johnny and Edgar Winter. A very eccentric fellow, Steve had a thing for the color blue. I remember visiting the Blue Sky offices. There were blue walls and blue note pads, and every day Steve wore a blue outfit from head to toe: blue jeans, a blue shirt, a dark blue blazer, and, to accentuate all, blue cowboy boots. On the TV show, he entered from behind a blue curtain wearing (what else) a blue top hat!

I was a huge fan of Johnny Winter, and I worked tirelessly to promote him. Every time I saw him, he'd exclaim, 'Paul Rappaport, my *favorite* promotion man!' I never knew if he said that to all the guys, but it made me feel special.

Johnny had a powerful voice and an incredible guitar style. He played with finger picks on his right hand and a slide on his left, and he also tossed in notes with the free fingers from his left hand. It sounded like the guy was playing with twenty fingers. A must-listen is 'Mean Town Blues' from *Live Johnny Winter And*—it will smoke your ears.

Steve made me feel like one of the family. He once invited me to an intimate party for Johnny and Edgar in one of the bungalows at the Beverly Hills Hotel. There were about forty people in attendance. If Johnny and Edgar didn't look outlandish enough—both being albino, tall, and thin, with long stark white hair—the rest of the party would have done P.T. Barnum proud. You've never seen such a diverse gathering of over-the-top, out-and-out freaks in your life. It truly looked like backstage at the circus.

The place was packed, and the marijuana smoke was so heavy that even if you chose not to partake, you got high anyway. Of course, about an hour into the gathering, everyone got the munchies, but instead of providing party food, Steve decided to call room service and order individual chocolate soufflés for everyone.

'Hi, I'd like to order fifty chocolate soufflés please. Yes, I realize that's a lot of soufflés.' Stammering and laughing uncontrollably from the weed, he continued, 'Yes . . . I know how long it takes to make them.' Bending over in tears and laughing so hard he could barely get the words out, he added, in a high, squeaky voice, 'And can we have fifty sides of whipped cream to go with those?'

Steve was a stickler for details.

I'll never forget the look in the eyes of the train of waiters—there had to be at least five of them, each holding a giant tray of chocolate soufflés and whipped cream—as they entered the bungalow. Their eyes bugged out as if they'd walked into a fantasy Federico Fellini movie. The truth is, they had—just minus Fellini and a few cameras. And it was the best chocolate soufflé I ever had!

· ● ·

Journey is one of the greatest bands I ever worked with. Sometimes they get slagged by the press as being somehow lightweight, but they are some of the finest musicians and songwriters in music, and Steve Perry, inspired by Sam Cooke, is one of the greatest lead vocalists of all time. Neal Schon is a guitar giant. 'Don't Stop Believin',' 'Faithfully,' 'Separate Ways,' and 'Wheel In The Sky' are just the tip of the iceberg of hits that we all love to sing along with.

The story of how the band came to be is a long one, but make no mistake, there would be no Journey if not for their manager, Walter James 'Herbie' Herbert II, one of the most outrageous characters I ever dealt with. He shepherded the band through three albums of progressive rock and then found Steve Perry, the proper frontman who would take them to the next level.

I promoted those first three albums, and we did okay with them, but the addition of Perry was the game changer. I saw him sing with the band for the first time at a show in Los Angeles, following his debut performance with the band at San Francisco's Old Waldorf in October of 1977.

Herbie grabbed me before the show.

'Here, sit next to me.'

The band came out and started to play. Not more than thirty seconds had gone by when Herbie, who had a beefy build, bumped me forcefully with his left shoulder, nearly knocking me out of my seat.

'Whaddya think? Whaddya think?!'

I took a breath. 'Herbie, they haven't even played for a full minute yet! Give me a second.'

By the end of the show, though, it was clear that Journey were on their way to becoming superstars.

For Perry's debut album with the band, *Infinity*, Herbie, ever the visionary, enlisted the talents of Queen's producer, Roy Thomas Baker. Roy's method of stacking harmonies became a Journey trademark. RTB (as he was known) was a major league character in his own right. I remember going to a recording session where Steve grabbed me, exasperated. 'I'm going to kill that guy! I've sung the same song twenty times in a row, and each time it's perfect!' I listened with Steve and Roy to a playback. Yes, perfect. He looked at Steve and smiled. Then, in his high-pitched trill voice, he exhorted Steve to 'do it one more time, dearie.'

Perry looked at me with daggers in his eyes. All I could do was shrug my shoulders. Perry went back in. Again . . . perfect.

Obviously, it all worked out—*Infinity* went triple platinum, selling over three million copies. Herbie and the band never looked back. At the height of their career, Journey had seventy people working in their offices. Herbie bragged that they could produce an album and design the cover artwork and point of purchase material all in-house, then provide a worldwide release within three days. Typical Herbie eccentricity found him opening a new San Francisco office in a building overlooking Tower Records just so he could look out the window during a new Journey release and watch all the kids leave the record store with the album tucked under their arms.

Herbie was a 'professional' marijuana smoker and also a notorious joint roller. Watching him roll joints using a gatefold album cover to catch all the miscellaneous seeds and twigs was almost as good as watching Dave Marsh play pinball. He sometimes found himself having to yell at people to make a point or to get a job done, as any manager can attest to. He would start his day by twisting up a joint and then hopping on the phone to do business, earning himself the nickname 'Twist And Shout.' We all got T-shirts.

Those were heady days. All of us were so young and making more money than we'd ever dreamed of. I remember Sharon and me having dinner in the turret room of San Francisco's famed Julius's Castle restaurant, hosted by Herbie along with famed road manager Pat 'Bubba' Morrow and a few other close Journey friends. From high atop the restaurant, looking out the surrounding turret windows, there's a view of the Golden Gate Bridge on one side and the Oakland Bay Bridge on the other—just stunning. We drank so much Dom Perignon that the restaurant ran out of the stuff. Undaunted, Herbie asked someone from Julius's to run to the liquor store to buy more. Nothing was allowed to fail under Herbie's watch—not even the champagne supply!

Of all the Herbie Herbert stories there are, this one is the all-time classic. Bubba grew up in Yonkers and had many Jewish girlfriends. He was fond of their jargon, and he became adept at imitating it. This rubbed off on Herbie, and at times he and Bubba would have meetings as two imaginary characters they created for themselves, Saul and Murray. This went on for some time, and Herbie became so enamored with it all that he got very into Yiddish. Bear in mind that neither Herbie nor Bubba were Jewish. Nevertheless, they were now on a Yiddish kick. They sent around copies of *The Complete Idiot's Guide To Learning Yiddish* to everyone in the industry, along with a note explaining they were now speaking Yiddish themselves, and if we wanted to communicate, we'd at least have to speak a sentence or two of the German/Hebrew dialect to start the conversation.

One day, Herbie called me to discuss the release of a new Journey single. We were in the middle of a hot Journey release, selling at least fifty thousand albums a week. The timing of a single was crucial to keep momentum going, and we were on a very tight deadline.

'*Vas makhstu*,' he begins ('how are you?').

I tell him I got the book, it's a cute joke, and then I go on to talk about the single. Herbie keeps talking in Yiddish before finally switching to English.

'Rap, what the fuck? A good Jewish boy like you can't even learn a couple lines of Yiddish?'

'Herbie, we're on a deadline!'

'I know.'

He tells me he will not discuss the single until I read the book and call him back and speak a few phrases.

How many millions of Journey albums were we looking to sell? How important was this timely conversation? It didn't matter. Welcome to rock'n'roll business in the 80s.

'Learn your Yiddish and call me back.'

I did.

$$\bullet \ \bullet \ \bullet$$

Bill Graham is mostly known as rock's greatest concert promoter and producer, but he took on management responsibilities as well. One evening, he met a very young Carlos Santana when he and a conga-playing friend were trying to sneak into the Fillmore West to see Cream and The Paul Butterfield Blues Band. Bill caught them crawling through a window, but rather than immediately throw them out, he elected to have a conversation with them.

It turned out that Carlos and his friend couldn't afford tickets but really wanted to see the show, being musicians themselves. Carlos told Bill that he was into Latin rhythms and wanted to fuse them with rock. Bill had a soft spot for Latin music, and he was intrigued by Carlos's ideas. He let the guys into the show and would go on not only to promote Santana concerts but also to manage Carlos, as well as Eddie Money and other notable rock artists.

Once there was a daytime listening party for one of Santana's albums at Bill's house in Marin County. Local folks from radio, retail, and the press were invited, along with some of us from the record company. Bill had a nice piece of land, and as you entered the grounds there were a few catering waiters and waitresses walking around, offering drinks and hors d'oeuvres. This was followed by a proper lunch, with a big spread of food served buffet-style under a tent. I started at one end of the buffet and worked my way down the long table to the end.

Bill, being Jewish, was also serving lox and bagels as part of the feast. It all looked great to me, so I got a bagel with some cream cheese, and when I got to the very end of the line, who should be there, slicing and personally serving you the smoked salmon, but Bill Graham himself.

It was so warm and fuzzy: *Welcome to my home*. Bill could have had any of the waiters perform this task, but he wanted to be a gracious host. That tells you a lot about the man. Indeed, the story goes he once handed out umbrellas outside one of his shows at Winterland to protect the crowd from the elements while waiting in the rain.

Bill was also famous for making every band he ever promoted feel at home in his venues. He built elaborate backstage environments that were guaranteed to put smiles on their faces. When The Who came to play, he brought in ping-pong tables painted like Union Jack flags. When Pink Floyd came, he built an English pub that you walked into and sat down to enjoy a beer and a steak and kidney pie. When Springsteen played, he built a New York-style bar that also featured a gelato stand on the side. I remember standing alongside Ronnie Wood, both of us eating gelato while watching Bruce perform. Bill's lavish backstage creations were a far cry from the usual crackers and cheese served by most other promoters. If you were an industry person going to a Bill Graham show, half the fun was wondering what surprise Bill was going to pull for the artist playing that night.

Being a consummate showman, when he put on his memorable New Year's Eve concerts at the Cow Palace—usually featuring the Grateful

Dead—Bill would dress up as Father Time, scythe and all, and make an appearance before all the balloons and confetti fell from the ceiling. I attended one show where he descended from the rafters dressed as 'Baby New Year' wearing only a diaper. On another occasion, he floated across the ceiling atop a Cheech & Chong-sized giant glowing joint.

Bill was about creating memorable experiences for both his audiences and the acts that played for him. He was a modern-day P.T. Barnum. The production he assembled for The Rolling Stones when they performed at Day On The Green in Oakland, California, personifies his vision. He built a stage so big that he was able to put the band inside their famous signature logo.

CHANGING OF THE GUARD

EVERY SO OFTEN in our business, a train comes rolling down the track so big and powerful nothing can stand in its way. It's just gonna happen. It's meant to happen. Such was the case with Alice In Chains and the Seattle sound that came barreling down the tracks soon after them. And just in time, I might add. In the mid-80s, MTV was at its height. The good news was that we were breaking bands faster because their videos gave them instant visibility. The bad news was that there was a chance their careers would burn out faster because of too much visibility. But the worst news was that kids watching MTV were saying to themselves, 'Hey, I could do that.' They figured all they needed to do was learn a few chords and just look great. It turned out they were right, and thus began the hair band era—more hair, less accomplished songwriting and musicianship.

I hated it. I had grown up with artists who aspired to make great music their raison d'être. The money would follow. Now, it appeared that money and fame took the front-row seat. The music business was becoming the money business.

At the time, Columbia was trying to plow new musical ground with bands like Fishbone and Poi Dog Pondering. They were great bands, but their music was so unique they didn't quite fit any particular form of radio. I was asked to try and establish them in the rock format, but it was a struggle. The only rock band we had at the time was Warrant. Their first album had done well at rock radio, but when they switched to more of a pop vein, my friends at the FM format began to shy away.

For the first time in my career, I was having a hard time trying to get something going. I was used to winning and winning big. Even though it was the music that just didn't fit the format, I began to take the mediocre performance of these bands on rock radio personally. It made me question myself. I thought I was losing my touch, and I went into a tailspin, down the rabbit hole to deep depression.

The fact that the rock genre itself seemed to be over, except for a handful of posers poisoning my former hallowed art form, only depressed me further. I was in a bad way.

Our new president, Don Ienner, a protégé of Clive Davis, could see it happening. Thankfully, he decided to do something about it.

'Meet me tonight for dinner.'

'What time, and where?'

With so much on his plate, Donnie's time was precious. If he was asking me to dinner, something big was up.

'Meet me in the Village at midnight.'

Midnight? The guy was known for not sleeping. Maybe that was his lunchtime.

It turned out Donnie was meeting not just me but also Mike Klenfner, now an independent consultant, to discuss a business deal with Bill Graham. Klenfner arrived on his small scooter. He was a big man, weighing in at over 250 pounds and built like a football linebacker. So, this was a sight to see, Klenf, nicknamed 'the original beef,' atop this tiny scooter. But it was just another part of his flamboyant persona that so many people loved.

After Mike left, Donnie turned his attention to me.

'Rap, you are one of the all-time promotion greats, the best rock guy out there. Not only do you play the game hard, you have vision. But just like any great player—let's say in baseball, for instance—you're in a slump. The problem is, you're trying to impress me. You're overswinging. Stop trying to hit home runs and just go out there and get your stroke back. Hit me a single, a double.'

I was shocked—in a good way. Donnie's sincerity, and the fact he cared enough to help straighten me out, spoke volumes. I'd worked for six previous Columbia Records presidents, but other than Clive Davis, who'd done me a solid when I first joined the company, I'd never been coached up like this. At 3am on the corner of MacDougal Street and somewhere, I went from feeling like a lowly worm to King Kong. I was out to take back the throne of rock's best. I didn't sleep all night. Refocused, I couldn't wait to get back to work.

As fate would have it, that's when Alice In Chains showed up. I had gotten a cassette tape from my friend Peter Fletcher, our West Coast product manager, who told me, 'Rap, this one is going all the way.' But because the music was so different from anything I'd ever heard, it took me a second to get a handle on them.

One day, I was driving with nine-year-old Adam Rappaport and playing some new music in the car. (Both my boys have great ears for music. I'll never forget when Sam, three years younger than Adam, played me some of his mixes and asked me if I'd heard this 'really great' song called 'Sweet Home Alabama.' Right after that, 'Breakfast At Tiffany's' blared out of the car speakers. 'Don't tell anyone this song is on there. But I really like it.')

At the time, we had a band called Love/Hate, and we were working their song 'Blackout In The Red Room.' I loved it and played it for Adam.

'Jeez, Dad, I don't get it.'

'What? We're about to drop a million bucks on these guys. We're putting them out on the road with AC/DC.'

'I don't care if you spend two million, I just don't hear it.'

'Okay,' I said. I was shaken. 'I have another band here that's kind of quirky...'

Then I played him 'Man In The Box,' and his eyes lit up.

'Whoa, Dad, this is amazing!'

'It is?'

'Yeah, play it again, and turn it up!'

And that was my first litmus test, letting me know that I had a possible tiger by the tail.

Alice In Chains came to play a club in New York. I went backstage to meet them before the show. I especially wanted to meet Jerry Cantrell, because I was fascinated with his groundbreaking guitar sounds. If memory serves, he had a couple of beat-up Stratocasters with colorful stickers plastered all over them. These were clearly workhorses designed to bring that ultra-heavy Alice In Chains sound to the fore. Jerry was no poser—he was the real deal. I also met drummer Sean Kinney, bassist Mike Starr, and lead singer Layne Staley, and they were all nice guys.

But nice ended as soon as they hit the stage. The immediate power and overwhelming sound of Jerry's guitar mixed with Layne's rip-your-face-off vocals, underpinned by the energy of Sean and Mike, was something to behold. It was a brand-new sound. It was as authentic as you could get—something as powerful as The Who or Led Zeppelin. A sound that reached deep into my gut and knocked me flat. I was totally consumed. My entire body began to move to their infectious groove. *Holy fucking shit!* Not only was I seeing the next big thing, I was seeing rock itself reborn. It was one of the greatest moments of my music business life. I had an ear-to-ear smile throughout that entire performance and well into the night. I had just witnessed one of the greatest rock bands of all time, and they were ours! I was saved! Fuck me, the whole world was saved! Hair bands goodbye, see you in my fucking rearview mirror . . .

To be clear, the Seattle sound that would eventually be known as grunge had been percolating for some years already, with bands like Screaming Trees, Soundgarden, and more. But Alice In Chains were destined to break down the doors on a wider, more universal level, blazing a trail on radio for the likes of Pearl Jam and Nirvana to follow.

I am proud to have played a significant role in the careers of many artists, and I would never say that they couldn't or wouldn't have broken through without my help. It might just have taken more time or happened differently. Having said that, I do know that in certain instances I made a huge difference—and Alice In Chains was one of them.

The metal department, run by Bridget Roy and Josh Sarubin, did a fantastic job, and through their efforts, we sold fifty thousand copies of Alice's debut, *Facelift*. Now it was my turn to see if I could break the band into the mainstream via radio.

Before I could break that wall down, however, I ran smack headlong into it. The problem was that just like me in the beginning, my friends at album rock couldn't wrap their heads around the music. It was so new and so different that they'd never heard anything like it, and for all my excited conversations with programmers, I would be deflated by their responses.

'You want me to play "Man In The Box"? Forget whether I like it or not, I don't even *understand* it.'

No one, and I mean no one, wanted to play Alice In Chains. They were fine playing bands like Judas Priest during the evenings, when audiences wanted to hear harder stuff, but as hard as that music is, the guitars and vocals have an easy, sing-along melody. The beginning of 'Man In The Box' has a guitar crunch so great yet so unique that it was unlike anything heard on the radio at the time. When you finally hit the chorus one minute into the song, it's powerful as hell, but again, the complex chords and parallel harmonies brought something new to their ears.

As with many other projects, sometimes a little bit of luck comes your way to start the action. At the time, DC101-FM in Washington was one of the most conservative rock stations going, and program director Dave Brown was a tough cookie to crack. He was also a huge baseball fan, and he and I bonded when I flew him to Boston to see one of our new bands but also took him beforehand to see a Red Sox game at the famed Fenway Park. We sat in field-level seats on the first base side, which was amazing. But it still didn't help much when it came to pioneering new music on DC101. Then, one evening, Dave's nighttime jock got hold of 'Man In The Box' and played it. Dave called me the following morning.

'Rap, my night guy played a record of yours called "Man In The Box" by Alice In Chains. He did this totally on his own, but I have to tell you, the phone lines have been melting down ever since with requests to hear it again. And I don't mean the usual *hot phones* lighting up for an active record, I mean *melting down*! I've never seen anything like it. I'm going to add the record to our after-6pm playlist.'

That was all I needed to hear. We were off to the races. But still, no one else wanted to give this record a try. They were all too afraid of possible tune-out. I called everyone and told them I'd put my entire reputation on the line for 'Man In The Box.'

'I'm not asking you to add the record to your playlist, just do me a favor and play it once, during an evening shift, then call me in the morning.'

I begged, I borrowed, I called in every favor I had and offered favors for the future . . . just for one spin. And every single time someone played the record, the result was the same.

'Holy shit, Rap, what is this thing? I don't get it, but the request phones are lighting up like I've never seen before.'

'It's a phenomenon,' I would answer. 'You don't have to understand it, you just have to play it.'

As hard as I tried to spread the word, I only got one station a week to add the record—only one. But little by little, we were up to ten stations, then fifteen, then twenty. In those days, that was enough to build some kind of momentum. If we stopped at fifty stations, it would have been seen as a successful breakthrough. But I couldn't stop. I was on a mission.

A typical week might start with no advance adds and no advance upward rotations. Both are needed to keep songs and albums moving up the charts. I would get on the phone to all the local guys and the indies and declare, 'We are breaking this band! It's not gonna die this week! Get out there and find me some adds and upward moves!'

I remember one week when a good buddy of mine, Brian Krysz, who programmed WSHE-FM in Miami, dropped the record. I couldn't understand it, because once 'Man In The Box' was being played, it showed no burn factor, and listeners never got tired of hearing it.

I discovered this late on a Tuesday afternoon, but I couldn't get hold of Brian, so I called his wife, Sheila, in a panic.

'Sheila, jeez, I hate to bother you, but I'm in the middle of breaking a band called Alice In Chains and Brian has dropped the record! Can you please, please find him and have him call me?'

I was friends with both Sheila and Brian (you gotta love a guy who named his children Met and Jet), but I was taking advantage just a bit here. Surprisingly, though, Sheila took my side.

'He did what? Again?'

Brian clearly had an MO. But I wasn't surprised. He loved turning his listeners on to new music, but in trying to give so many new bands their shot on the airwaves, he was forced to constantly juggle to make way for the next new thing.

Five minutes later, Brian called me back. I breathed a big sigh of relief.

'Bri, what the hell? I'm right in the middle of breaking Alice In Chains, and you drop the record?'

'Sorry, man, I was just making room for something else.'

'But Brian, it's *me*,' I said, hoping that counted for something. 'Come on, man, if you drop it, the record's gonna go backward on the charts. I can't have that.'

'All right, Rapper, I'm putting it back in now.'

Whew! It felt like I'd dodged a big bullet to the heart. Truth is, though, Brian Krysz was always there when it mattered.

That's how it went throughout the entire campaign—one station, one or two upward moves a week. But slow and steady wins the race. Once 'Man In The Box' was added to any playlist, it stayed there for weeks on end, and the requests were never-ending.

Dave Brown called again.

'Rap, I can't get rid of this record. I've been playing it for two months and it has absolutely no burn factor!'

We were finally beginning to make some steady progress. The band and their manager, Susan Silver, were supportive of anything I needed, especially when it came to making the band available for fan meet-and-greets. The band loved the story of Adam first hearing their music and waking me up to how good it was. He became their mascot. Backstage, I would find Jerry running around with Adam on his shoulders and the rest of the band giving him high-fives.

My depression was lifting, and I was feeling my oats again. A friend who knew I was looking for a sports car called to tell me about a 1973 Porsche 914 for sale. It was a beautiful bright red model with a black interior, but when I tried sitting in it, the cockpit felt cramped. Then I pulled the lever below the seat, and lo and behold, there was room for it to go back a bit. *CLICK.* Perfect!

OMG, I thought. *I think this is my car.* I ran home to tell Sharon.

'Listen, I have been depressed as hell, I thought my career was over. Now we have a good chance to break one of the biggest rock bands of all time. If I can get that done, I'd love to buy this car and name it Alice. I wish I could tell you it's an investment, but it's only a two-seater—a total toy.'

Sharon understood. She has stood by my side during my down times and has always been there to help put me back together. When the tough times come, that's when you know if your marriage is strong.

'I get it,' she said. 'Go break the band and buy the car.'

Two months passed, and we finally reached 'Breaker' in *R&R*, which meant your record had proven itself to be a bona fide hit. Now we had to convince the holdouts at rock radio that the jury was in. They didn't have to understand it, but they did now have to come to the party.

Finally, we had every station except one—the all-important WNEW-FM in New York. I paid a visit to another good buddy, program director Dave Logan, and told him the story of how the record had been proven beyond the shadow of a doubt. The band was breaking, doing sell-out club business, and we had now sold a quarter of a million records, meaning we were halfway to gold. Then I performed a half-hour magic show, just for him. He was impressed, but still no add.

One week went by, then another, until finally he called me.

'I just added "Man In The Box." Sorry, it took me a second to get the trick.'

I could feel his smile over the phone. Thanks, Dave. I bought the 914. The band loved the story and the license plate, 'Alice 18' (18 means life in Judaism).

Not too long after, we celebrated a gold record—five hundred thousand copies of *Facelift* sold. The band came to visit Columbia headquarters, which was now at 550 Madison Avenue in what used to be the AT&T building. I took them upstairs to show them the large, impressive conference room, which featured a massive oval table that I believe appeared in one of the *Wall Street* movies. It was stunningly beautiful. On the edge of the table, in front of each chair, were bronze plaques with names of the former execs who sat there. The blinds, lights, and video screen all worked electronically.

Cantrell immediately jumped on the table, while Layne reclined in one of the chairs and put his feet up. Sean had a field day with the buttons on the lectern, pushing all of them at once. The large blinds that covered the big windows overlooking the West Side were going up and down like horses on a carousel, as was the video screen behind us. Every light in the room (and there were lots of them) was continually blinking on and off. The whole effect reminded me of a Pink Floyd stage production.

'We'll show them who's in charge around here now!' Layne said.

We all fell backward in laughter. Adam and his friend Evan had come along for the ride to hang out with the guys. They just stared in amazement.

• ● •

One of Alice's greatest attributes is their authenticity. When it looked like a new band and a new sound was on the rise, *Rolling Stone* magazine sent a photographer to Seattle for a photo shoot. She met the band at one of their houses. They were dressed in their usual garb—shorts, flannel shirts, thick leather work boots.

'Okay,' the photographer announced. 'It's time for the shoot. Go change.'

'Into what?' they asked quizzically.

'You know, something black and mysterious. And put on some of that large silver jewelry, like ankhs—I want you to look like The Cult.'

'Sorry, this is us. This is how we are.'

After a few more controlling words from the photographer, they threw her out. You gotta love those guys.

Eventually, there appeared a candid picture of the band standing by a chain-link fence dressed in their usual garb. It looked weird at the time. Who wears work boots with shorts? The rest is history. As Seattle bands continued to wear loose-fitting thrift-store clothing, an entire fashion movement began. More importantly, this new sound became so popular that with Alice, Pearl Jam, Nirvana, and others, it required its own format—alternative rock radio.

'Can't you guys write *one* happy song?' I once asked the guys. 'Or at least an *even* kind of song?'

'Sorry, Rap, just dark and darker,' was the reply, followed by some good-natured laughter.

• ● •

After three long months of 'Man In The Box' commanding heavy rotation at the FM format, the record finally began to fade. It was time to release a second single. The story of how the song finally broke, after initially facing such adversity, was so dramatic and compelling that everyone in the entire singles meeting was sad to see it go. Most of all, Donnie.

'Donnie, don't think of "Man In The Box" as dying,' I told him. 'Just think of it riding off into the sunset like in a great cowboy movie.'

He liked that. Everyone did.

I wanted 'Sea Of Sorrow' to be the next single. It was easier on the ears and had some great melodic hooks. Establishing 'Man In The Box' had been the toughest challenge of my career. Now, I thought, *Let's go for one that will slide more easily onto the airwaves.* Donnie, who always preaches to go with songs that sell albums, even if they're harder to establish, also voted for 'Sea Of Sorrow.' The relentless grinding battle for 'Man In The Box' had worn out even him. The choice seemed to make sense. But Adam Rappaport disagreed. Nearing his tenth birthday, he decided to rebel.

We were backstage after one of Alice's shows in New York, waiting for the band to towel down so we could say hi. When I explained the decision regarding the second single to Adam, he became animated.

'That's a mistake, Dad. "Sea Of Sorrow" isn't the real Alice In Chains. You want "Bleed The Freak," that's the *real* Alice In Chains.'

I was beginning to impart my reasoning when Adam spotted Donnie across the room. Right in the middle of my sentence, he bolted for Donnie.

'No! No! NO!' I called out, arms crisscrossed in the *stop-immediately* position. But he was long gone. I ran after him and got close enough to hear his little voice tirade.

'Donnie, Donnie! You're making a big mistake!'

He repeated what he'd told me word for word.

'Don't put out "Sea Of Sorrow," you want to put out "Bleed The Freak." That's the *real* Alice In Chains sound!'

It was funny at first, seeing little Adam squeaking out his passion to Donnie, who towered over him. But I arrived at the scene too late. Donnie did not look pleased at being lectured by a nine-year-old on what singles to release. I grabbed Adam and gave Donnie a look, as if to say, *Hey, he's just a kid.* Donnie looked back at me with hard eyes. Oops.

But wouldn't you know it, Adam was right. 'Sea Of Sorrow' fared okay on rock radio but failed to move the needle any further. That being said, we were in great shape. Between having two tracks on the radio and the band on tour, by the new year we had a platinum album. More importantly, Alice

In Chains had helped change the face of rock. The posers would quickly disintegrate. We were headed for a new future of meaningful rock music. The genre was saved.

Close to twenty years later, long after I'd left Columbia, I went to see the band play in New York with their new lead singer, William DuVall. They were awesome, and I hoped the band and their manager, Susan Silver, would remember me. Backstage, it was like no time had passed. I was greeted with hugs and salutations, and I thanked them for their kind remembrance.

'Are you kidding, Rap?' Susan replied. 'You have an automatic backstage pass to this band for the rest of your life.'

It meant so much. And I still have the car.

• ● •

After Alice In Chains, I felt complete. A calm spread over me. I felt I had accomplished everything I was supposed to in the world of promotion. I'd been promoting rock music for well over twenty years, and now I finally felt I was done. I confided this to Donnie, but I told him I had a lot of creative marketing ideas that could help expose and establish our music beyond what I'd been able to accomplish as a promotion man. Then Donnie did what probably no other record company president would consider.

'Well,' he said, 'if you really believe you can get these things done, let's come up with a title for you, I'll give you a budget of $300,000 and a year to see what you can do.'

Don Ienner had vision, and I am very thankful that he saw mine. I became the VP of Broadcasting and Event Marketing and thus began a whole new career at Columbia Records. Event marketing meant garnering the attention of thousands of people at a time. I had a big imagination, and Donnie had given me the money to unleash it.

I hired a young visionary, Josh Rosenthal, from the alternative music promotion department, and a wonderful gal named Rasa Alksninis, who was very tuned into the new music scene in the Village at the time. Together with my close friend, producer/engineer Mitch Maketansky, we created our own radio series, *The Columbia Records Radio Hour*, which aired live every month or so on Sunday mornings across a hundred radio stations, coast to coast, from Sony Music Studios. The show featured our great roster of established and up-and-coming singer/songwriters performing for an intimate audience of about three hundred people. The live aspect made the show incredibly exciting, and the series became so popular that we eventually added other labels' artists along with our own to bring even more gravitas to each event.

Our secret sauce was coupling like-minded artists on the same show who would perform solo but also do some songs together. You can hear one-of-a-kind performances and combinations like Shawn Colvin with Mary Chapin Carpenter, Rosanne Cash with David Byrne, Bruce Cockburn with Lou Reed, Youssou N'Dour and Jackson Browne, Boz Scaggs with Booker T & The MG's, plus The Jayhawks, Leonard Cohen, James Taylor, Little Feat, The Dave Matthews Band, and more. Both volumes of our five-star-rated collection *The Best Of The Columbia Records Radio Hour* are still available and can also be found on streaming services. Indeed, I just heard Jeff Buckley's entire performance on YouTube, listed as *Jeff Buckley Live At Columbia Records Radio Hour, New York, NY, June 4, 1995.*

We also developed virtual radio promotion tours for our bands by using satellites to broadcast interviews and live performances from Sony Studios. What used to take a week of a band flying from city to city with acoustic instruments to play live on the air now turned into a band setting up their full gear in our studios, making camp, and reaching a dozen or more stations across the country in a day. It worked like a charm for both new artists and established superstars. A band like Aerosmith could set up in the studio with their own engineer and sound just like they do in concert. The guys would call morning shows across the country, do a brief interview, play a couple of requested hits, and finish by debuting a new song live over the air. Some artists did two full days of this. Steve Perry broke the record while promoting his first solo album when he did three days' worth, reaching over thirty key markets. It was easy and relaxed—we even had a proper lunch break built into the schedule. We nicknamed the idea ColumbiaCast.

I remember one very special day when I was at Sony Studios producing a live radio show from the big soundstage featuring Rob Halford's band at the time, Fight. There were four hundred fans in the audience, cheering them on. On that same day, the staff at the studio were also mixing one of the *Columbia Records Radio Hour* best-of albums; in another room, they were setting up for a ColumbiaCast; and in a fourth room, the Automatic Productions people were working on stop-motion graphics for the opening titles of the TV show I was producing, A&E's *Live By Request*. I took a moment just to take it all in.

I co-developed the Emmy Award-winning *Live By Request* with my old friend Tony Bennett, his manager son Danny, and Mitch Maketansky, along with Andy Kadison, Jodi Hurwitz, and the rest of Sony Music Studios Automatic Productions team. The show played like a big, warm smile. Fans could call in, talk to their favorite artist, request their favorite song, and watch them perform it in an intimate setting. We produced more than forty live, two-hour prime-time specials with some of the world's top artists, including David Bowie, James Taylor, Neil Diamond, Elton John, Don Henley, Willie Nelson, Elvis Costello, The Bee Gees, Earth Wind & Fire, and more.

The series began, of course, with Tony. In the years leading up to that program, he and I formed a great relationship. He was an extraordinary person. Every time we worked together, he wanted to know about *my* life and what *I* was doing. He was that way with everyone. Once, when I told him I had become a competitive épée fencer, he very animatedly told me that he had recently gotten into Japanese stick fighting.

'You know, Paul, if my schedule wasn't one of constant travel, you and I would become good friends. We could become fencing partners.' He meant it.

For the opening of that first *Live By Request*, I suggested that Tony arrive at Sony Music Studios in a black stretch limousine and have a camera outside follow him into the studio.

'Nah,' he replied, shaking his head. 'I'm not that guy.'

'Okay, it is New York,' I said. 'How's about one of those Central Park horses and carriages?'

'Nope, I'm gonna pull up in a yellow.'

'A yellow taxi?'

'Yep, that's me.'

The next day, when I called my father—a huge Tony Bennett fan—to see how he'd enjoyed the show, he bellowed in his loud Brooklyn voice that his favorite part was seeing Tony arrive at a big fancy TV show in a yellow cab.

'That's why I love him so much,' Dad told me. 'He's one of us—he's an everyman.'

Another passion of Tony's was drawing and painting. He was an excellent watercolorist. After *Live By Request* got going, we did an encore performance with him. During rehearsal, he called me and the director, Larry Jordan, over for a chat.

'I just really want to thank you guys for all you've done to make this show a success,' he said. Then he pulled out two framed, Tony Bennett original paintings and gave us one each. We were speechless. But that's just who Tony was.

Tony was a consummate professional with an incredible work ethic, and I was always having to catch up with him.

'Hey, Tones, we need to do this, this, and this.'

'Yeah, Paul, I already did that on the flight. What's next?'

He was always early for rehearsals. I wanted so much to have some of the rock bands I dealt with go on the road with Tony for a week to see how a real professional works. Total focus, *no* attitude.

PREPARE TO LAUNCH

'WHAT IS *THAT*?!'

The TV news anchorman's eyes are bugging out. Their traffic helicopter's camera swings up from the usual views of crowded freeways, revealing an unidentified craft flying side-by-side not more than thirty yards away. On his monitor and for all the world to see is a giant flying machine—an airship painted and decorated in a way that looks fantastical, reminiscent of the flying machine in the movie *Master Of The World*, which sprung from the imagination of Jules Verne in his *Robur The Conqueror*.

'The traffic is not the big story today,' the reporter blurts out. '*This is!*'

The airship is huge and painted in stunning colors. In the middle are two giant orange faces with large, menacing eyes staring at each other. They look like giant eel heads or some kind of ocean creatures. The orange images are brilliantly contrasted against a bright chartreuse background that also has a mouth, and when that image comes into focus it shares the eyes of the orange creatures, creating a 3-D effect revealing a third face staring eerily straight at you. Multicolored flames stream out of the rear of the large eel heads.

The nose of the airship has yet another face that appears to be a prehistoric yellow bird with a large beak and a long red tongue shooting out its mouth, while attached to the back of the craft are four giant rocket-ship-style fins in orange, chartreuse, yellow, and blue. The tip of the tail, painted in concentric rings, looks like a bee stinger. The whole thing looks positively psychedelic, almost like a living creature itself. The only clue to what this creature might be is written on the underside in white letters against a dark blue background. Two words: Pink Floyd.

The camera pulls back to reveal a pink gondola with two yellow, turbo-propelled airplane engines, one on each side. It's then that you realize that what you're looking at is, in fact, a giant blimp. But it appears to have arrived from another world.

The usual traffic report has just exploded into a breaking news story. 'What is that?!' the announcer asks. 'And where is it going?'

'We don't know,' the excited helicopter reporter replies, 'but we're going to follow it until it lands and report back!'

The airship finally sets down in a field not too far from the local airport. By now, many other people are following it. Other television stations with their cameras, newspaper reporters, and curious members of the general public, including a lot of Pink Floyd fans.

The psychedelic flying machine is finally tethered by ground crew members to a large red-and-white stanchion that looks like a candy cane. The engines are shut down, and two pilots wearing black uniforms emerge from the gondola. They are rushed by the crowd, all taking pictures and buzzing with a million questions. But the pilots are mute. They do not speak but just hand everyone a five-by-seven-inch notecard that reads:

YOU HAVE SPOTTED THE PINK FLOYD AIRSHIP

DO NOT BE ALARMED

PINK FLOYD HAVE SENT THEIR AIRSHIP TO NORTH AMERICA

TO DELIVER A MESSAGE

THE PINK FLOYD AIRSHIP IS HEADED TOWARDS A DESTINATION

WHERE ALL WILL BE EXPLAINED UPON ARRIVAL

PINK FLOYD WILL COMMUNICATE

The episode made it into the next morning's newspapers, and it did so in every city the airship visited along its mysterious journey, from its birthing place in North Carolina all the way to Los Angeles, piquing the interests of thousands along the way. And this inaugural voyage, with the silent pilots handing out the cards, was just the beginning. A teaser campaign alerting Pink Floyd fans and other curious folks across the country that something big was about to happen.

• ● •

Of all the bands I worked with, the one I became closest with was Pink Floyd. I'd spend over twenty-five years getting to know them and the extended Pink Floyd family of managers, producers, engineers, graphic designers, roadies, and assistants. Over time, I began to feel like a family member myself. I even got to play on the Pink Floyd cricket team in a match against the EMI Records guys. As Roger Waters began coaching me on how to play the 'long on' field position, I was expecting a long, drawn-out explanation. Instead, he held up the dark red, tightly stitched cricket ball in his hand, looked me in the eye, and simply said, 'Rap, when someone hits this ball, you run like fuck, and go get it!' Of course, there's a bit more to it, but that was a start. When it was my turn to bat, no matter how many times I reminded myself to run with it in my hands, like any kid who grew up playing baseball I dropped the damn thing and ran halfway across the pitch before I realized I had to go back and get it. Even so, I managed to score a few runs for the team.

In 2019, I went to see Nick's Saucer Full Of Secrets solo concert at the Beacon Theater in New York, featuring the early music of Pink Floyd. The show was phenomenal, but I was most touched by our meeting after the show. When I congratulated him on Pink Floyd's long and storied history, he looked up at me and said, 'Rap, you realize you are a big part of our history.' I'd always been proud of what I was able to accomplish for the band, but to hear that firsthand from Nick knocked me off my feet.

We'd had an excellent run in 1987 with *A Momentary Lapse Of Reason*, the band's first album after Roger left, and based on that success, I knew Pink Floyd had another great album and tour in them. In 1994, that next album and tour were at hand. Now, the job was to propel them and their music to a new level of excitement and bring it to the attention of new fans. In my new marketing position, I was prepared to lead the charge.

This time around, I wanted to create anticipation like people hadn't known since The Beatles. When they came to America, everyone, and their grandmother knew about it. I wanted to try to create a similar excitement for Pink Floyd's new album and tour, which would prove to be their ultimate spectacular. I wanted entire cities to focus on this event. Even if you weren't quite sure who Pink Floyd were, you were going to find out.

When planning a promotion or marketing event, I always tried to take a page from the artists I was working with and create an experience that felt like a natural extension of their music. As well as selling albums and CDs, I always wanted to put a smile on fans' faces as part of that process. I wanted them to feel part of the tribe.

One of the highlights of any Pink Floyd concert production was their inflatables, especially the legendary pig, which had floated over many stadiums during past tours. On a winter's afternoon in January of '94, I was looking out across the Hudson River from the window of our relatively new, twenty-sixth-floor offices on Madison Avenue when the Budweiser blimp floated by. It was huge, majestic, and painted from stem to stern in that well-known red-and-white logo. It was floating effortlessly about a thousand feet above the river.

That's it! I thought. *Talk about inflatables, this is the biggest inflatable in the world!*

I ran out of my office to ask Rasa to find out how much it would cost to rent a blimp the size of Budweiser's, or even larger. I then called Steve O'Rourke to tell him about my idea, and he said that he'd been thinking of something similar—a hot air balloon. Having ridden in one, I told him a blimp would be better because we could control where it went—a hot air balloon only goes where the wind takes it.

Rasa found Airship International, an aircraft company run by a very interesting fellow named Lou Pearlman. Lou would go on to create both The Backstreet Boys and *NSYNC, but that's another book in itself. Right now, he specialized in giant airships, and he was very interested in having his company associated with Pink Floyd. He told me that to rent and custom paint the biggest airship in the world for three months would cost one million dollars. That's before you got to the hidden costs, which included a special paint that had to be imported from France and a sizable ground crew to follow the airship along the different routes it took and be available for each landing. That's a lot of hotel rooms, food, equipment repair, and more.

I was able to negotiate Lou down to three quarters of a million dollars because he so wanted to be involved with something so cool. But in any case, even though Don Ienner liked my marketing events and was willing to back me with the money I needed for them, there was money and then there was ... *money*. With the label already set to spend at least two million dollars on promotion and marketing for the band, adding another three quarters of a million bucks to an already bursting budget would be a tough sell. Donnie would see me walking toward him in the hallway and yell, 'I don't want an airship! I don't need an airship!' and then run the other way.

One day, I cornered Donnie and tried to explain.

'Listen, it will be the biggest billboard in history, and the beauty of it is, it floats from city to city. It will be written about in all the local newspapers and will get tons of TV coverage as well. And just to make sure that people look up and see it, I will invite local rock radio stations to do their morning shows live from the airship. Just imagine: *Hi, this is Lin Brehmer from WXRT in Chicago. We're broadcasting live from the Pink Floyd Airship this morning. We'll be flying by the Sears Tower at around 9:30, so give us a wave as we pass by!* We'll create contests for the fans at the greatest record stores in the country: *Win a trip on the Pink Floyd airship!*

Donnie was getting warmer on the idea, but in the end, I had to call in O'Rourke for backup.

'Steve,' I told him, 'he likes it, but I can't close him by myself.'

Steve talked to the band and Michael Cohl, the national promoter for the tour. Then he called Donnie and told him that the band really wanted the airship. Not only did they think it was very Pink Floydian, but they wanted to log time flying the airship themselves. Cohl said that if we brought the airship to Canada, where he was based, and he could use it to help sell concert tickets, he'd chip in $250,000. O'Rourke told Donnie the band would pay the same, leaving Columbia to pay the last $250,000. Donnie agreed.

The next thing I knew, I was talking with my old buddy Storm Thorgerson, Pink Floyd's longstanding graphic designer. Storm had co-founded the graphic design company Hipgnosis with his partner Aubrey 'Po' Powell, creating renowned album covers for Led Zeppelin, Black Sabbath, Genesis, Peter Gabriel, and many more, not to mention the most iconic cover of all, Pink Floyd's *The Dark Side Of The Moon*.

Storm's method was to stage real events and photograph them. 'I like photography because it is a reality medium,' he said, 'unlike drawing, which is unreal. I like to mess with reality . . . to bend reality. Some of my works beg the question of, is it real or not?' For instance, the image on Led Zeppelin's *Houses Of The Holy* was not painted or done on a computer. Those are real children dressed in costumes climbing up an outcrop of rocks somewhere in Northern Ireland. The beds you see on Pink Floyd's *A Momentary Lapse Of Reason* cover are not just three or four beds with the rest filled in by CGI. Those are seven hundred beds on a beach! And, if you notice, the sand is wet. That's because it rained during their first attempt at the shot the day before, and they had to take all the beds off the beach and then bring them back again the next day. One of Storm's most endearing qualities was that if he ran over budget, he would spend his own money to get the shot right. He was an artist, a perfectionist, and that's why he was in such high demand.

I called Storm to tell him about the airship.

'Rap, I do album covers, videos, posters, art lithographs,' he replied. 'I don't do blimps.'

'Well, my friend, you're gonna do this one.'

But Storm was reticent. I had to get him to see that it was possible.

'What's the worst that can happen, Stormy? You'll fuck it up, and then we'll just paint it all over again.'

Storm had a good laugh and then began to get excited by the challenge. As with all of his work, he attacked this project with very deep thought. His artwork always reflected what the music was about. The first thing he always did was to go to the recording studio and listen to the music that was being made. He wanted his album covers to make people stop and contemplate. He wanted you to visually experience what you would soon be hearing.

Because Floyd's new album was largely about communication, Storm chose to decorate the airship with faces, arranged as if they were talking to one another. But his real genius was his understanding of how the ship would be viewed. Some people might see it from the side, but many others would see it from the bottom, looking up. Storm had to create a 360-degree look so that no matter where you were when you viewed the thing, you would see enough of the incredible imagery and know that it had been created by Pink Floyd.

The press conference to announce the new album and tour was scheduled for the beginning of January 1994. The airship had been built and painted in North Carolina. I went down there to supervise. Being a bit of a painter myself came in handy, and I was able to help bring Storm's vision to life.

The biggest issue with the ship was that it had to fly across the country in time to make the press conference. Airships only travel at about thirty-five miles per hour and are reliant on good weather. No one had ever successfully flown an airship across the country during the winter. The last person to try was Howard Hughes, and he'd crashed in Texas during an ice storm. Talk about anxiety. But somehow our guys made it. They were even a few days ahead of schedule.

The public and news media in other cities had seen the airship as it crossed the country, and some had gotten those mysterious cards from the pilots. But no one in Los Angeles knew it existed. We invited press, radio, local television news, MTV, and other assorted media to have lunch and 'high tea' with us at a place called the Pink Café in the park outside the Rose Bowl, where the band were scheduled to play two nights in April. It was a mysterious invite in that there was no such thing as a Pink Café, or any café, in that park, just a beautiful serene setting nestled in a valley between two very large hills. The news folks had an inkling of what might be announced, but they had no idea what was about to unfold.

We built the café as an outdoor popup restaurant with tables and chairs, white tablecloths, and a large buffet table featuring finger sandwiches, scones, jam, fresh cream and strawberries, and two giant silver samovars brimming with hot English tea. There was a proper entrance and a beautiful sign on top that read, 'Welcome to the Pink Café.'

Everyone came and had a great time. They were all sitting and chatting away when all of a sudden they heard the sound of engines like those you might hear from a small aircraft. They looked up to see what appeared to be a psychedelic flying machine coming over one of the hills. As it got closer, the crowd started to get excited as they tried to make out what it was. Things got intense when the gigantic craft headed straight toward them. Before you knew it, the two-hundred-foot Pink Floyd airship was hovering not more than thirty feet directly over our heads. The sound of the engines was deafening, and wind was blowing off the large turbo fans. Being directly beneath it was a bit scary. The scene was reminiscent of the movie *Close Encounters Of The Third Kind*, when the giant mothership suddenly appears out of the night sky, hovering over all the spectators. I swear, some of our guests with big imaginations thought they might be sucked up by this alien-looking craft and be carried away.

After making its striking entrance, the airship moved about twenty yards laterally and landed. After it was tethered, the door of the pink gondola opened, and a small set of stairs popped out. Then, one at a time, a dozen waiters and waitresses dressed in black and white came down the stairs carrying large silver serving trays covered with silver domes like you'd see in a fine dining restaurant. They made their way over to our tables and laid the trays right in the middle of each one. When the word was given, the waiters lifted the domes simultaneously. Under each were stacks of dark blue folders filled with information about the new album and tour. The whole experience was surreal. Radio and television reporters rushed from their tables to their vans to report back to their stations.

After much buzzing among the astonished crowd, Steve O'Rourke and Michael Cohl stood at a lectern and fielded questions. I thought for sure that one of the band members would be there too, but there was no sign of them. I asked Steve about that afterward.

'They're still mixing the record,' he whispered.

'Mixing the record?!' I was panicked. 'Steve, this album has to be manufactured and shipped in three weeks!'

'I know.'

It was always like that with the Floyd. They adhered to Peter Gabriel's notorious declaration, 'A deadline is a point you pass on the way to completion.' Easy for the artist to say, not so easy for the record company. You would hear nothing at all about a new project, then they would announce one seemingly out of nowhere, and absolute pandemonium would ensue. Everything had to be done all at once, and at light speed. Despite our pleading, it was always the same.

As well as coming up with the airship idea, I was asked by Donnie to product manage the entire project. It turned out that by the time 1994 rolled around, I was the only one left at the label who the band felt they could trust. To help me out, Donnie also assigned a very talented marketing manager named James Roy Diener who was well versed in all the intricate details it takes to put out an album. (James later went on to help create Maroon 5, among other achievements.)

Though the album release deadline was getting close, the guys hadn't come up with a title yet. The name *Pow Wow* was bandied about for a while, but because the band were sensitive about not upsetting any Indigenous peoples, O'Rourke asked me to get hold of the major American Indian Chiefs and ask their permission to use the expression. When you work with Pink Floyd, you often find yourself in the strangest of situations. I had just been supervising the painting of a giant airship in a remote part of North Carolina, and now I had to get hold of American Indian Chiefs. Google didn't exist yet, and the internet was in its infancy. How the hell was I going to find these people? And, if I did, which chiefs would speak for the majority of the American Indian population? After doing some research (remember that?), I found the phone numbers for the two largest Indian tribes in America, the Navajo and Cherokee Nations. The first told me that the words 'pow wow' were white man's words, so they didn't care. The Cherokee Chief said that they were huge Pink Floyd fans and 'would be honored' if the band named their album that.

Time was getting short now. The salesmen needed a title in order to solicit the album in time for it to be sold into stores to make the release date that coincided with the tour's debut performance at Joe Robbie Stadium in Miami. I was calling Steve every day until we were just one week away, but to no avail. By that Thursday morning, my nerves were shattered. I couldn't wait any longer. So, I called David Gilmour at home.

'Hi, David. Listen, I would never call you at home unless it was really important. I know the record company gives you all sorts of deadlines with built-in time cushions, but no joke, we are really up against now. If I don't have an album title by tomorrow afternoon, we're going to miss the release date by at least a week, and that means that you will be playing two sold-out shows at Joe Robbie Stadium in front of 160,000 people with no records in the stores. I don't want to think about how many sales we'll lose.'

'Ha, ha,' he replied. 'Don't worry, Rapper, I've had the title for two weeks now. I'm just pulling O'Rourke's chain.'

'Well, can you please let go of that chain now, and tell him the title right away so he can call me and tell *me* the title?'

Three hours later, I got a call from Steve.

'Hi, Rap,' he began, playing up the drama. 'I want you to know that *I'm* your hero. I just disturbed David Gilmour, in his bath, to get you the title of the album.'

'Really. What is it?'

'*The Division Bell.*'

'The what?'

'*The Division Bell.*'

I had no idea what that meant. I knew a lot of things that other people didn't know, like how to do fancy card sleights or how to block an oncoming épée attack, but not being that well-read in general, I thought I was about to get skewered for not knowing a term that the rest of the world was familiar with.

'Okay, Steve, you can laugh at me if you want, but I don't know what that is.'

'You *don't know* what the division bell is?'

'No, I'm sorry.'

I cringed. My body winced. Here it comes. I'm about to be made to feel foolish.

'Rap, the division bell is the bell that rings in between the Houses of Parliament, signaling the members to come together to take a vote.'

I let out a long breath. *Nobody* in this country would know what the fuck the division bell was, nor what it meant. Thank God—my worldly knowledge was not in question.

'Look, Steve, I hate to break it to you, but nobody in America will know what the fuck that means. But that's okay, it's a great title, considering the theme of the album, and we can easily educate people.'

Steve was quite shocked that no one knew what the division bell was. But we were both relieved that we finally had a title, and a cool one at that, even though it had come down to the very last day.

· ● ·

The Pink Floyd airship proved to be one of the greatest marketing events of all time, exceeding even my wildest expectations. We decorated the inside of the ship with Pink Floyd posters, and every passenger who won a trip via their local record store was given a Sony Walkman upon entering. The winners sat down, buckled themselves in, put on their headphones, and hit play. *The Division Bell* boomed into their heads while the airship took off and soared for an hour as they enjoyed a low-altitude tour of their home city.

The airship held two pilots and ten passengers. Because it flew at only thirty-five miles per hour, it was quite easy to steer, so aside from the band taking turns flying it, the pilots also let friends and family members take a few minutes at the wheel. Our younger son Sam, who was nine years old at the time, even took a turn in the co-pilot's seat as the ship flew around Manhattan.

'Hey, Sam, you see the Statue Of Liberty over there to your right?'

'Yeah, Dad!'

'Don't hit it.'

It turned out the airship was also the biggest toy I ever had. Just like my model airplanes and rockets, but this one was life-size! One of the intriguing things about an airship is if you cut the engines, it will hang in mid-air, suspended just like Superman. While we were still in Hollywood after the press conference, I had the pilot 'park' the giant ship right beside the Capitol Records Tower, the famous circular building that looks like a stack of 45s.

John Fagot was Capitol's head of promotion at the time and had his office there. We parked right outside his window, and I called him on my cell phone.

'Hi, John, I've got a surprise for you, open your blinds.'

Everyone in that building keeps their blinds shut at certain hours of the day to keep the hot sun from blazing through the large windows. John opened the blinds to the sight of a huge psychedelic blimp almost as big as the Capitol building itself right outside his window and fell out of his seat.

'HOLY SHIT! Rap are you in that thing?'

The most fun I ever had with it was at the band's tour debut at Joe Robbie Stadium. The *Divisional Bell* production was so big and spectacular, with Floyd's one-of-a-kind lighting and stage effects now being performed on massive stadium stages, that the band needed two versions of the stage set—it took days to erect and assemble, so they'd play one show while the other set was being built in the next city. They wanted the airship to be a part of the opening show, immediately after the encore, and I was put in charge of making it happen.

Marc Brickman was once again the lighting designer for the tour, having been with the band since the tour for *The Wall* in 1980. He also did the production design alongside Mark Fisher.

'I need the airship to be seen magically hovering over the stage as the smoke clears from all the pyro,' Marc told me. 'But you can't have it arrive too soon, or the pyro could blow it out of the sky.'

In other words, make the airship appear magically without blowing it up and killing the crew and the band. Uh-huh. Got it.

Some of the airship pilots were real daredevils, and only one of them volunteered for this mission. Because blimps move so slowly, desperate measures had to be taken to achieve the effect. After the show started, the airship flew from a nearby airfield and parked itself on the side of the stadium, hovering about thirty feet off the ground. It would be well hidden from the audience by the large stadium walls until it was needed. I was given a walkie-talkie labeled *Floyd 1*; the co-pilot held *Floyd 2*.

I had a production headset that enabled me to listen to all of Marc's cues to the lighting and effects crews. When the encore song—once again 'Run Like Hell'—ended and Marc called for the pyro, I was to give the airship the go-signal to appear just as the smoke cleared. It would have been easy if Joe Robbie had walls that surrounded the entire stadium—then we could have just floated the thing straight up from behind the stage—but in those days there was a big opening at the end of the stadium behind the stage, so the airship would have to come from the left side, up and over the stadium walls, then shoot to the middle—and quick!

Brickman cued the pyro.

'Floyd 1 to Floyd 2, prepare to launch,' I yelled into my walkie-talkie. 'Now! Go, Go, Go, GO!'

Then I saw something I'd never seen before, and I realized why only one of the pilots had volunteered for the job. The only way to achieve the speed needed to get the airship behind the stage at the right moment was to shoot it vertically straight up into the air, gun the engines at full force, and then do a nose dive, pulling out at the last second to level the ship. The momentum of the nose dive would slip the airship into position at the appropriate time, just missing any active pyro. But it was a dangerous maneuver. Gunning an airship so big, straight up in almost a vertical position, was no simple matter. If the angle was too steep, it could nose backward, and then, well . . . forget about killing the crew, we'd be killing the fans.

There was a kid standing next to me watching all of this. When the airship shot straight up out of nowhere, climbing for the heavens, he looked at me and offered, 'Wow, I hope they're not eating their lunch.' My nerves were on fire, and the levity was much needed.

As the smoke cleared, high above the stage, there it was, the Pink Floyd airship in all its glory. Brickman hit it with two huge powerful spotlights, and the crowd went nuts.

• ● •

One of the most difficult things about being a product manager is that you find yourself right in the middle of the band's desires and what the record company needs to do to make everything affordable. When it comes to Pink Floyd, with so many different creative components to factor in, you are pushed to the limit. This was a challenge for me because I was such a big fan of the band, I had a big imagination myself, and I was friends with these guys. But I also had to try to be a good soldier for the label, so I had to pick my battles.

I flew over to London to hear some of the rough mixes of *The Division*

Bell album so that I could report back to Donnie and have my first meeting with David Gilmour and Storm Thorgerson about the album cover and packaging ideas. Bob Ezrin was producing the album, and he and David played me some parts of it to give me an overall feel. What I heard was very exciting and harkened back to the Pink Floyd albums of old, but it was still in bits and pieces, so it was left to my imagination to figure out what the finished product would sound like.

I called Donnie.

'Rap, how is it? Is it great? Will it sell four million albums?!'

'Hell, Donnie, I don't know. If all the bits and pieces are put together right, it could be one of their best yet. But I only heard bits and pieces.'

'I just want to know if it will sell four million albums. *Tell me* it will sell four million albums!'

There was no other answer he was going to accept. I threw caution to the wind, looked to the heavens for an answer, and when none came, I just mouthed the words he wanted to hear.

'Yes, Donnie, it will sell at least four million albums.'

I love Donnie, but the problem with working for him is that if that album only sold 3,999,000 copies, I'd never hear the end of it.

After the listening session, we all went up the hill for a nice lunch.

'So, Rap,' Storm began, 'you know those little plastic nibs that hold the album booklets in CD packages? We find them quite cumbersome, troublesome, and frankly a great pain in the arse for our fans—or any music fans, for that matter. So, we don't want those on our CD package. Also, since this album is all about communication, we want the title to be embossed in braille on the CD spine of the jewel case. We want those with impaired sight to still feel a part of the total Pink Floyd experience.'

I knew that custom jewel cases were not going to fly for us in the States, because way too many CDs were going to be manufactured there. The cost of creating custom molds for jewel cases would be astronomical. I figured if I was to survive and do my job the best I could for both parties, I had to nip some things in the bud and not just be the messenger boy bringing back a list of all the band's demands for Donnie to have to deal with.

'Storm,' I began, 'I know that during this project and campaign, you and I are going to have some pretty incredible ideas. *Hello*—we're already building a $750,000 airship! You and I are going to have to fight for everything we want. So, we have to prioritize what's most important. Think about this. Even if we are successful in talking the record company into creating and building customized CD jewel-case molds just for this album, do you know how many CDs we're going to be manufacturing in just a very short period of time? If we project four million for the year, what if one or two of those molds crack during manufacturing? Can you imagine how many sales we'll lose while we're waiting for new molds to be built?'

Gilmour looked over, and I could see he immediately agreed with my logic. In the end, I believe EMI in Europe was able to accommodate a run of those custom jewel cases, but they didn't press nearly the number of CDs that we did in the States.

I dodged a bullet on that one, but next came the request for the extra color. If you add a fifth color to the typical four-color printing process, it can look amazing, but it can also be cost-prohibitive—so much so that the label never permitted it.

The sky on *The Division Bell* cover is one of the most striking blues you'll ever see. Storm felt he might have to add an extra fifth color of blue to create the true Pink Floyd mesmerizing experience. I knew the label would fight that, but I was prepared to take Storm's side for this one if need be. Whenever I told Storm there might be a battle over budget, he'd give me his favorite line.

'But Rap, *we're Pink Floyd.*'

That line could get you a lot from any record label, but not everything.

I got home from my trip to London to find a hysterically funny phone message from him. It was a serious message, but with it came Storm's wacky sense of humor and his wonderful English accent. I believe he may have been a bit in his cups, which even made him sound funnier.

'Hi, Paul, Storm here. I want to make it perfectly clear that you nor Sony have absolutely no right to use any of *my* artwork on this project unless I approve it. I believe the cover will need a fifth color, but perhaps it won't—but I think it will, but . . . maybe it won't. At any rate, if you print it four-color and it looks like shite, we won't pass it—if it doesn't look like shite, then we will pass it. Any attempt by you or your peers to have the manager, Steve O'Rourke, intercede will only result in him yelling at me, and the situation will remain the same! But who knows? Maybe it will look great. Cross your fingers, hasta la vista, and keep taking tablets! Bye!'

Fortunately, the exceptionally talented head of our art department, Artie Yeranian, figured out how to make the album cover pop to everyone's satisfaction using the four-color process. Storm was mightily impressed.

I'm always amazed when I think back at just how wacky things could get. I mean, we're talking a multi-million-dollar business here, but art ruled for the most part, and the characters in charge could travel on roads well beyond eccentric. Sometimes they were just out of their fucking minds. As funny and as out-there as he could be, I would place Storm mostly in the eccentric category. He had clear creative visions, and he fought very hard for them to come to fruition. I remember once being in Steve's office and hearing his end of a very heated conversation.

'No, Storm, NO! A million pounds—that's it, that's all!'

Where Pink Floyd was concerned, Storm was in charge of all things visual. He was working on movies for the live show, the album cover, booklet inserts, posters, and single cover art. And now David Gilmour wanted to press at least ten thousand blue vinyl LPs and create blue-colored cassettes as well. Storm called to explain given all that needed to be done and how we should try to accomplish it.

'Rap, I'm extremely busy, you see, so why don't I send you the album cover art, have your guys make their recommendations, then you pop over on the Concorde, show it to David, then he'll make his changes, then you fly back on the Concorde, continue to work on it, then pop back over to us on the Concorde...' and so on and so on.

'Stormy, I love you, I really do, but this isn't 1975, and we don't have endless buckets of money for me to keep flying back and forth on Concorde.'

Out came his favorite line.

'But Rap, *we're Pink Floyd.*'

By now time, I had my favorite reply ready.

'I *know*, and I'm your *biggest fan*! But this just isn't gonna happen.'

I told Storm that as Pink Floyd's chief art director, he must come to the

States to oversee everything, or at least bring an assistant with him who could stay on after he completed the broad brushstrokes. He confided in me a fear of travel and that he might get lost. Kennedy International is a very large airport, and he was afraid he wouldn't be able to find his driver. I assured him that there would be no way that he was going to miss him.

Rasa made up a special sign for Storm. When he arrived, as he walked past all the drivers holding their little black-and-white signs containing passengers' names, Storm looked up to see one driver with a giant three-by-four-foot poster with *STORM!* painted in bright blue with a big yellow lightning bolt blasting through the middle. Not only did Storm see his sign, but everyone in the whole fucking airport saw it.

'Ha, ha,' he laughed dryly on the phone to me while driving into Manhattan. But I knew he loved it.

Upon his arrival at my office, I showed Storm at least thirty different colors of vinyl that were readily available. Of course, none of them would do, and he insisted on creating his own special version of Pink Floyd Blue. Just as I had respectfully requested, he enlisted his assistant, Peter Curzon, to stay in the States to oversee everything after he left to resume his duties back in the UK.

Anyone who has seen a copy of the collector's vinyl edition of *The Division Bell* will know that all of that meticulous fussiness was well worth it. I've never seen a prettier blue in all my life. But the funniest part of the story is that when the band first asked for colored vinyl, 1 I told them that while it certainly would look pretty, it wouldn't sound very good. I suggested they use black virgin vinyl, since Pink Floyd had always been concerned with achieving state-of-the-art fidelity. I even called their head recording engineer, Andy Jackson, and had a word with him about it, wanting to be absolutely sure this was what they wanted.

'Andy, you know this colored vinyl is going to sound like shit, right? What you really want is black virgin vinyl—it's the very best quality.'

But Andy reiterated David's desire to create a fun collector's item, so we set about creating large chunks of distinctive, unique 'Pink Floyd Blue' vinyl using Storm and Peter's formula. The vinyl sat in a pile at our pressing plant in Atlanta, waiting to be made into records. The Columbia Records sales staff pre-sold the coming blue vinyl collector's piece in less than a *Dark Side Of The Moon* heartbeat.

As noted already, Pink Floyd is like a giant family, with all sorts of people working on different parts of the project at once—the album, the stage show, effects, sound, movies, and so on. Sometimes that makes communication cumbersome, and one hand may not always know what the other is doing.

About three weeks after all of this went down, I got a call from Steve O'Rourke.

'What's all this I'm hearing about colored vinyl, Rap? We don't want colored vinyl—it will sound like shit! We want black virgin vinyl. Don't you know black virgin vinyl is the highest quality vinyl?'

My brain exploded.

'Yes, Steve, of course I know that. And that is why I asked everyone on your team, including Andy Jackson, if they were absolutely sure they wanted blue vinyl instead of black virgin vinyl. Now that we have already pre-sold the colored vinyl to our accounts, and we actually have a very large pile of blue vinyl now sitting on the floor of the pressing plant, where do you suggest I put this blue vinyl?! *Because I know where I'd like to put it!*'

I'm usually a very mild-mannered person, but this one sent me over the edge. Thankfully, I detected a silent chuckle over the phone. My consternation was not lost on Steve, and he quickly acquiesced.

'Well, Rap, I guess we'll be having blue-colored vinyl,' he laughed.

EPILOGUE
THIRTY-THREE
AND A THIRD

WHEN I LOOK BACK, it's hard to believe everything that happened in my career. But it did, and I am forever thankful for it. Was it all just fun and games? No, it wasn't, and I had some tough times along the way. But I've chosen not to dwell on those, because my main mission here is to try and bring to life the very large, colorful, and magnificently unbelievable world that the music business was for at least a couple of decades.

I do believe a good life is like a good stew. It needs some spicy and salty elements to create a well-rounded, fulfilling experience. And even though I had some down times, I learned from them, and I wouldn't change them.

There would be more adventures to follow after the Pink Floyd airship, and there was even one last meaningful moment waiting for me when I finally left Columbia in March 2003. Generous early retirement packages were offered to those of us with enough years of service. As I walked out of 550 Madison for the last time that day, I calculated I had worked for Columbia Records for exactly thirty-three and one third years—having made most of my living promoting and marketing 33 1/3 LPs.

Wow, I thought, looking up at the heavens. *No one else is gonna care about this, but thanks. Thanks a lot!*

SPECIAL THANKS

To my wife, Sharon, for her never-ending patience during the long journey of ideas, reads, re-reads, re-re-reads, this is the last re-re-re-read I promise (you get the idea).

Daniel Paisner, journalist, author, and A-lister ghostwriter who believed I had a story to tell, pushed me to tell it, and looked over my shoulder to make sure my work was good.

Clinton Heylin, writer/historian, world's authority on Bob Dylan (*The Double Life Of Bob Dylan* volumes 1 and 2, a must read) for being a great friend and explaining the ropes of writing and publishing, and scaring the shit out of me in the process.

Renowned singer-songwriter Willie Nile, who was so moved by the stories at the funeral of our friend legendary record man Rocky Del Balzo that he convinced me to write this book.

Harold Bronson, Mogan David & His Winos bandmate and Rhino Records co-founder, who insisted that with hard work I need not rely on a ghostwriter.

Judy Libow, Atlantic Records Rock promotion legend, whose *Classics Du Jour* gave me the opportunity to write a blog for ten years, which enabled me to find my writer's voice. And Brianne Farquhar, who enhanced my posts and made me look like a rock star.

The Big Three:

Rick Williams, super-talented rock radio programmer and musicologist who helped fact check my manuscript.

Bob Willcox, Columbia colleague marketing maven, my first 'slash and burn' editor. If you wish you could have read about my romantic, whirlwind, drug-induced, five-day sex marathon with a renowned LA Rock DJ, blame Bob, who ditched the entire chapter. 'Rap, nobody cares.'

My soul brother Jim McKeon, who has helped me through this entire process in so many ways I've stopped counting. This book has gone from good to great because of Mac.

My friend Fran Lebowitz, for her time, expertise, belief in this book, and guiding me on how to professionally approach agents and publishers.

Stacey Glick, who showed me there are still people in this world that have a heart big enough to help someone on their journey, regardless of any remuneration they might receive.

Photographers Henry Diltz, Lester Cohen, and Jimmy Ienner Jr, who were gracious enough to let me use their photos gratis. They don't make many guys like this anymore.

Mark Seliger, for a portrait photo that's so good, when I look at it, I want my own autograph!

Perry Margouleff, world renowned guitar collector, analog record producer extraordinaire, Les Paul expert, songwriter, vintage car aficionado, and appreciator of all things fine art (have I left anything out?), who has become one of my best friends in life, helping me keep my focus.

George Gilbert, wiz record-biz attorney and brother in all things music and story.

Gary Baker, my attorney, who fought for all my contracts at Columbia Records. He could get so intense on my behalf that the label told me they got the message and could I please ask him to back off just a tad. Gary even beat the Bank Of New York for Sharon and me. He's that good.

Columbia Records colleagues and special mates Michael Pillot and Mark Spector, two extraordinary record men, for their constant encouragement and support.

Mitch Maketansky, best friend, producer/engineer, and guitar buddy, who I've shared so many wonderful adventures with. Together, we actually made Lou Reed smile!

To my very hardworking assistants at Columbia, Gail 'Brueser' Bruesewitz, Robin Solomon-Schlager, Cathy Ann Thiele, Rasa Alksninis Mokhoff, Lisa Maketansky, and Tom Radd, who always elevated our work and helped me become the best I could be.

Jawbone Press—Tom Seabrook and Nigel Osborne. These are the cool kids of publishing. A special tip of the hat to Tom, who edits like Roy Thomas Baker produces records—exquisitely. And to Paul Palmer-Edwards for the cover. Artful quality, super to work with—in short, the dream team. Go to the Jawbone site, check out their titles, you will want some!

For their help on this journey:

George Athan, Sam Bellamy, Danny Bennett, George Chaltas, Steven Clean, Jim 'Rocky' Del Balzo, Rick Dobbis, Mark Fischer, Gregg Gavitt, Bob Geldof, Holly Gleason, Herbie Herbert, Nick Mason, Pat 'Bubba' Morrow, Jim Ladd, Jon Landau, Paul Loasby, Drew Macko, Mary Beth Medley, Claire Mercuri, Richard Neer, Alan Oreman, Steve O'Rourke, Peter Jay Philbin, Redbeard, Larry Reymann, Keith Richards, Felissa Rose, Jane Rose, C.K. Bower Rider, Josh Rosenthal, Steve Schenck, John Scher, Garilynn Alpern Stanfield, Danny 'Cisco' Zelisko.

And to all of you in the rock radio and record community who brought your own magic into my life and filled me with these wonderful tales to tell forever.

ALSO AVAILABLE FROM JAWBONE PRESS

Riot On Sunset Strip: Rock'n'roll's Last Stand In Hollywood Domenic Priore

Million Dollar Bash: Bob Dylan, The Band, And The Basement Tapes Sid Griffin

Bowie In Berlin: A New Career In A New Town Thomas Jerome Seabrook

Hot Burritos: The True Story Of The Flying Burrito Brothers John Einarson with Chris Hillman

To Live Is To Die: The Life And Death Of Metallica's Cliff Burton Joel McIver

Jack Bruce Composing Himself: The Authorised Biography Harry Shapiro

Return Of The King: Elvis Presley's Great Comeback Gillian G. Gaar

Seasons They Change: The Story Of Acid And Psychedelic Folk Jeanette Leech

A Wizard, A True Star: Todd Rundgren In The Studio Paul Myers

The Resurrection Of Johnny Cash: Hurt, Redemption, And American Recordings Graeme Thomson

Entertain Us: The Rise Of Nirvana Gillian G. Gaar

Read & Burn: A Book About Wire Wilson Neate

Big Star: The Story Of Rock's Forgotten Band Rob Jovanovic

Recombo DNA: The Story Of Devo, or How The 60s Became The 80s Kevin C. Smith

Neil Sedaka, Rock'n'roll Survivor: The Inside Story Of His Incredible Comeback Rich Podolsky

Touched By Grace: My Time With Jeff Buckley Gary Lucas

A Sense Of Wonder: Van Morrison's Ireland David Burke

Bathed In Lightning: John McLaughlin, The 60s And The Emerald Beyond Colin Harper

What's Exactly The Matter With Me? Memoirs Of A Life In Music P.F. Sloan and S.E. Feinberg

Who Killed Mister Moonlight? Bauhaus, Black Magick, And Benediction David J. Haskins

Lee, Myself & I: Inside The Very Special World Of Lee Hazlewood Wyndham Wallace

Seeing The Real You At Last: Life And Love On The Road With Bob Dylan Britta Lee Shain

Long Promised Road: Carl Wilson, Soul Of The Beach Boys Kent Crowley

Throwing Frisbees At The Sun: A Book About Beck Rob Jovanovic

Confessions Of A Heretic: The Sacred & The Profane, Behemoth & Beyond Adam Nergal Darski with Mark Eglinton

The Monkees, Head, And The 60s Peter Mills

Complicated Game: Inside The Songs Of XTC Andy Partridge and Todd Bernhardt

Perfect Day: An Intimate Portrait Of Life With Lou Reed Bettye Kronstad

Adventures Of A Waterboy Mike Scott

Becoming Elektra: The Incredible True Story Of Jac Holzman's Visionary Record Label Mick Houghton

I Scare Myself: A Memoir Dan Hicks

Shredders! The Oral History Of Speed Guitar (And More) Greg Prato

Fearless: The Making Of Post-Rock Jeanette Leech

Tragedy: The Ballad Of The Bee Gees Jeff Apter

Shadows Across The Moon: Outlaws, Freaks, Shamans And The Making Of Ibiza Clubland Helen Donlon

Staying Alive: The Disco Inferno Of The Bee Gees Simon Spence

The Yacht Rock Book: The Oral History Of The Soft, Smooth Sounds Of The 70s And 80s Greg Prato

Earthbound: David Bowie and The Man Who Fell To Earth Susan Compo

What's Big And Purple And Lives In The Ocean? The Moby Grape Story Cam Cobb

Swans: Sacrifice And Transcendence: The Oral History Nick Soulsby

Small Victories: The True Story Of Faith No More Adrian Harte

AC/DC 1973–1980: The Bon Scott Years Jeff Apter

King's X: The Oral History Greg Prato

Keep Music Evil: The Brian Jonestown Massacre Story Jesse Valencia

Lunch With The Wild Frontiers: A History Of Britpop And Excess In 13½ Chapters Phill Savidge

More Life With Deth David Ellefson with Thom Hazaert

Wilcopedia: A Comprehensive Guide To The Music Of America's Best Band Daniel Cook Johnson

Take It Off: KISS Truly Unmasked Greg Prato

I Am Morbid: Ten Lessons Learned From Extreme Metal, Outlaw Country, And The Power Of Self-Determination David Vincent with Joel McIver

Lydia Lunch: The War Is Never Over: A Companion To The Film By Beth B. Nick Soulsby

Zeppelin Over Dayton: Guided By Voices Album By Album Jeff Gomez

What Makes The Monkey Dance: The Life And Music Of Chuck Prophet And Green On Red Stevie Simkin

So Much For The 30 Year Plan: Therapy? The Authorised Biography Simon Young

She Bop: The Definitive History Of Women In Popular Music Lucy O'Brien

Relax Baby Be Cool: The Artistry And Audacity Of Serge Gainsbourg Jeremy Allen

Seeing Sideways: A Memoir Of Music And Motherhood Kristin Hersh

Two Steps Forward, One Step Back: My Life In The Music Business Miles A. Copeland III

It Ain't Retro: Daptone Records & The 21st-Century Soul Revolution Jessica Lipsky

Renegade Snares: The Resistance & Resilience Of Drum & Bass Ben Murphy and Carl Loben

Southern Man: Music And Mayhem In The American South Alan Walden with S.E. Feinberg

Frank & Co: Conversations With Frank Zappa 1977–1993 Co de Kloet

All I Ever Wanted: A Rock 'n' Roll Memoir Kathy Valentine

Here They Come With Their Make-Up On: Suede, Coming Up … And More Adventures Beyond The Wild Frontiers Jane Savidge

My Bloody Roots: From Sepultua To Soulfly And Beyond: The Autobiography Max Cavalera with Joel McIver

This Band Has No Past: How Cheap Trick Became Cheap Trick Brian J. Kramp

Gary Moore: The Official Biography Harry Shapiro

Holy Ghost: The Life & Death Of Free Jazz Pioneer Albert Ayler Richard Koloda

Conform To Deform: The Weird & Wonderful World Of Some Bizzare Wesley Doyle

Happy Forever: My Musical Adventures With The Turtles, Frank Zappa, T. Rex, Flo & Eddie, And More Mark Volman with John Cody

Johnny Thunders: In Cold Blood—The Official Biography, Revised & Updated Edition Nina Antonia

Absolute Beginner: Memoirs Of The World's Best Least-Known Guitarist Kevin Armstrong

Turn It Up! My Time Making Hit Records In The Glory Days Of Rock Music Tom Werman

Revolutionary Spirit: A Post-Punk Exorcism Paul Simpson

Don't Dream It's Over: The Remarkable Life Of Neil Finn Jeff Apter

Chopping Wood: Thoughts & Stories Of A Legendary American Folksinger Pete Seeger with David Bernz

Through The Crack In The Wall: The Secret History Of Josef K Johnnie Johnstone

Forever Changes: The Authorized Biography Of Arthur Lee & Love John Einarson

I Wouldn't Say It If It Wasn't True: A Memoir Of Life, Music, And The Dream Syndicate Steve Wynn

Jazz Revolutionary: The Life & Music Of Eric Dolphy Jonathon Grasse

Down On The Corner: Adventures In Busking & Street Music Cary Baker